Fifty Jewish Women
Who Changed the World

Fifty Jewish Women Who Changed the World

DEBORAH G. FELDER AND DIANA ROSEN

CITADEL PRESS
KENSINGTON PUBLISHING CORP.
www.kensingtonbooks.com

CITADEL PRESS BOOKS are published by

Kensington Publishing Corp.
850 Third Avenue
New York, NY 10022

First printing: July 2003
First paperback printing: February 2005

10 9 8 7 6 5 4 3 2 1

Printed in the United States of America

Library of Congress Control Number: 2002113400

ISBN 0-8065-2656-4

For my grandmother, Frances Daransoff Felder.
                                    —D.G.F.

For all those women who helped me change my world.
                                    —D.R.

If I am not for myself, who will be for me?
And if I am only for myself, what am I?

—Hillel

CONTENTS

INTRODUCTION

This book represents the confluence of two major areas of study—women's history and Jewish history. The two have not always belonged to each other. In *Why History Matters,* the historian Gerda Lerner, an Austrian Jew who immigrated to America after escaping the Nazi terror and went on to become a pioneer and leading scholar in women's history, recalls her childhood experience learning Jewish history: "Had I been a boy and studied Talmud, I would have learned Jewish history in a positive way. I would have learned about the existence of wise rabbis and great leaders; I would have studied that mysterious mental construct which held the community together for all these persecuted millennia. I was a girl, and the lifeline of Jewish learning—Talmud, Mishna, Midrash—was out of my reach. All I got was indoctrination in gender restrictions and a thorough exposure to the great silences—the denial of the past, the suppressed voices, the absence of heroines."

The presence of women in Jewish history, it seemed, was either nonexistent, limited to a few biblical figures, or only understood in the context of domesticity. Yet, any understanding of Jewish—and world—history is incomplete without an awareness of the invaluable contributions of women. It would be this awareness in the midst of the women's movement of the 1960s and 1970s that would lead scholars like Professor Lerner to form an academic canon focusing on women's history. From this area of study grew a greater recognition of the ways in which women of all ethnic groups have profoundly influenced past and present history and culture.

In *Fifty Jewish Women Who Changed the World* we present the fifty Jewish women we feel deserve special recognition for their achievements. Many of the women featured in the book are so famous that they stand out as obvious choices for inclusion; other women, while equally significant, may be discovered by readers for the first time. We also have included an Honorable Mentions list of fifty additional women for readers to peruse and consider.

It was admittedly a difficult task to choose only fifty women from past and current history's extensive pool of extraordinary women. Our criteria were based on who we felt have had the greatest historical and cultural impact, and whose lives and work reflect a diversity of achievement and experience. A Jewish identity has been central to the lives of many of the women profiled in the book; for others, it was and is a less critical presence.

The preponderance of American women on our list reflects, to a great extent, the immigrant experience in the United States and underscores what has always been a challenging issue for immigrants and minorities: the difficulty of assimilation. The majority of the American women in the book either came to the United States from countries in Eastern and Western Europe or were the daughters or granddaughters of immigrants. Those who came to America during the great waves of immigration that began in the late nineteenth century and lasted until the early twentieth century did so to escape the pogroms in their native countries and to create better lives for themselves and their children. The women who emigrated in the 1930s and early 1940s escaped the Nazi persecution that would result in the Holocaust. The Israeli Prime Minister Golda Meir was a triple immigrant: she was born in the Ukraine, came to the United States with her family, and then immigrated to Eretz Israel. It is also interesting to note the number of women on the Honorable Mentions list who were born elsewhere.

The women we have chosen represent a variety of areas of accomplishment. In the field of art there is the innovative sculptor Louise Nevelson and the multitalented Judy Chicago, whose monumental work, *The Dinner Party,* commemorates celebrated women through the ages. Sarah Bernhardt, Barbra Streisand, Beverly Sills, the dancer and choreographer Anna Sokolow, and the incomparable comic actress, Molly Picon, who kept alive the vibrant language of Yiddish and the brillance of Yiddish theater, represent the performing arts. Poets and authors include Emma Lazarus, Edna Ferber, Gertrude Stein, Dorothy Parker, Betty Friedan, Grace Paley, Susan Sontag, Barbara Tuchman, and Cynthia Ozick. There is influential labor leader Rose Schneiderman, radical socialist Rosa Luxemburg, social reformers Rebecca Gratz and Lillian D. Wald, and everyone's favorite anarchist and free-speech advocate, Emma Goldman, as well as Hannah Greenebaum Solomon, founder of the National Council of Jewish Women, Henrietta Szold, founder of Hadassah and a pioneer in the creation of a Jewish homeland in the country then known as Palestine, and Sally Priesand, the first officially ordained woman rabbi. In the world of business there is Dorothy Schiff, the former publisher of the *New York Post,* and Estée Lauder, the founder of a highly profitable cosmetics empire. Fashion has not been forgotten: the influential designer Pauline Trigère is profiled here.

The women featured in the book range in time period from biblical women, whose timeless stories have always been important sources of inspiration, faith, and cultural memory, to twentieth—and twenty-first—century women such as Anne Frank, psychologists Melanie Klein and Anna Freud, political philosopher Hannah Arendt, Nobel scientist Rosalyn Yalow, mathematician Emmy Nöether, and Supreme Court Justice Ruth Bader Ginsburg, all of whom have influenced the world through their talent, courage, innovative discoveries, capacity for leadership, and intellectual brilliance.

All of these women have incredible stories to tell and much to teach us about women's history, world history, Jewish culture, and the often complicated issue of Jewish identity. We hope our choices will provoke lively debate and lead to positive discourse on the indisputable contributions of Jewish women in every sphere of achievement.

We would like to thank those who have been so helpful in the preparation of this book, especially the librarians and academics whose knowledge and guidance was invaluable to us. We are also greatly indebted to our ever-patient and supportive editors, Margaret Wolf and Francine Hornberger. And last, but certainly not least, we acknowledge with gratitude the excellent sources that are available on women's biography and history, on Jewish history, and on Jewish women. Every work written on these subjects is significant, for as Gerda Lerner has correctly stated, "The past becomes part of our present and thereby part of our future."

Fifty Jewish Women
Who Changed the World

Sarah, Rebekah, Rachel, and Leah: The Four Hebrew Matriarchs

Your wife will be a fruitful vine within your house;
your children will be olive shoots around your table.

The Lord bless you from Zion.
May you see the good of Jerusalem all the days of your life.
May you see your children's children.
Peace be upon Israel!

—From Psalm 128, "A Song of Ascents"

THE MIDDLE PORTION of the Book of Genesis is a collection of tales about the biblical patriarchs and matriarchs. These are stories based on legends, but that does not diminish the historical significance of the characters nor lessen the tales' resonance as sources of inspiration, faith, and cultural memory. The goal of the biblical authors who transcribed the patriarchal stories was to bolster their faith, to explain their connection to the Lord, and to delineate the Almighty's historical purpose. In the twelfth chapter of Genesis this purpose becomes clear in the covenant the Lord makes with Abraham, the chosen ancestor of the House of Israel: the Lord will give Abraham and his offspring the land of Canaan, will "make of him a great nation," and through his relationship with God he will be the means by which he and other human families will receive the Almighty's blessing.

Although the patriarchs—Abraham, Isaac, and Jacob—are traditionally considered the central characters in these sagas, the matriarchs receive attention as equally important figures in the fulfillment of the Lord's covenant; it is these "Mothers of Israel" who ensure that the Lord's promises are passed on to the rightful heirs.

The first Hebrew matriarch is Sarah, originally called Sarai (in Hebrew, "princess"), the daughter of Terah and the wife of Abraham. After she is introduced, we are told right away that "Sarai was barren; she had no child" (Genesis 11:30), a situation that will later prove to be a serious obstacle to the execution of the Lord's covenant. Abraham and Sarah migrate from Ur, Abraham's native city in upper Mesopotamia, to Haran, also in Mesopotamia. It is in Haran that Abraham is instructed by the Lord to "Go from your country and your kindred and your father's house to the land that I will show you" (Genesis 12:1). The obedient Abraham journeys to Canaan with Sarah and a group of people that includes Abraham's nephew Lot.

Not long after they settle there, a severe famine strikes, forcing Abraham and Sarah to seek refuge in fertile Egypt. Anticipating that Pharaoh will kill him and take Sarah as a concubine because she is so beautiful, Abraham tells his wife to pretend that she is his sister, "so that it may go well with me because of you, and that my life may be spared on your account" (Genesis 12:13). Sarah's response to this request is unrecorded: she either did not have any say in the matter or, as a dutiful and loving wife, she agreed to the plan. The Bible only tells us that she "was taken into Pharaoh's house" as a concubine. Abraham's plan works to his self-interest; he lives and prospers in Egypt, "for her sake." He might have stayed there if, according to the Bible, the Lord had not intervened.

After the Almighty "afflicted Pharaoh and his house with great plagues because of Sarai" (Genesis 12:17), Pharaoh discovers Abraham's deceit and orders him and his wife to leave Egypt with "all that he had," indicating that Abraham will leave the country a rich man. How Pharaoh discovers that Sarah is Abraham's wife is unclear. According to Flavius Josephus, a first-century A.D. Jewish historian and soldier, who authored *Jewish Antiquities,* a history of the Jews from the creation to the war with Rome, it is the courageous Sarah who reveals the truth because of her fidelity to Abraham, the effect of which would secure her escape from Pharaoh's harem. It is similarly unclear what kind of "great plagues" were visited upon Egypt; without denying the possibility of divine intervention, it is also possible that the Nile flooded Abraham's pastures, locusts destroyed his crops, or that thieving nomads raided his granaries, thus prompting Abraham and Sarah to decide that it would be wise to tell the truth and take their remaining riches back to Canaan.

Once back in Canaan, Abraham and Sarah settle in the hill country. The Lord repeatedly assures Abraham that he will found "a great nation," and in an additional promise that will hold great significance for the future of the region, informs him "To your descendents I give this land, from the river of Egypt to the great river, the river Euphrates" (Genesis 15:18). However, the covenant is in jeopardy because the now-elderly Sarah is barren. The Lord rejects Abraham's decision to name an heir from among one of his slaves, and it is Sarah who suggests a likely solution that involves a practice common at the time: Sarah offers one of her handmaids as her husband's concubine, telling him, "it may be that I shall obtain children by her" (Genesis 16:2). Sarah chooses her Egyptian slave girl, Hagar, who conceives a child.

The story then takes an interesting dramatic turn. Sarah becomes jealous of Hagar and fumes to her husband, "May the wrong done to me be on you! I gave my slave girl to your embrace, and when she saw that she had conceived, she looked on me with contempt. May the Lord judge between you and me!" (Genesis 16:5). As Savina J. Teubal observes in *Ancient Sisterhood: The Lost Traditions of Hagar and Sarah,* "Although Abraham's infraction is not clearly defined, the text seems to indicate that Abraham's behavior generated doubt regarding Sarah's claim to Hagar's child. Sarah's severe reproach must have stemmed from the terms of an accord or contract that Abraham had breached. Abraham's offense, deserving of malediction, was his intent to override the authority of the matriarch by instigating the rebellion of Hagar, thus attempting to deprive Sarah of her legal right to an heir." Abraham defers to Sarah's authority over her slave, replying, "Do to her what you please." Sarah mistreats the pregnant Hagar, who runs away into the wilderness. There, the Lord orders her to return to Sarah and "submit to her," and promises Hagar that her unborn child will be a son and have many offspring. Hagar returns and gives birth to Ishmael ("God hears").

The Lord promises another son and heir to the incredulous Abraham, now ninety-nine, and ninety-year-old Sarah. This will be a child that Sarah will conceive and bear. Since "it had ceased to be with Sarah in the manner of women," Sarah laughs at the absurd disproportion between the divine promise and human possibility, and asks, "After I have grown old, and my husband is old, shall I have pleasure? Shall I indeed bear a child now that I am old?" (Genesis 18:11–13). Repeating a theme common in the Old Testament, the Lord articulates the need for Sarah to have faith in divine power and favor by asking, "Is anything too wonderful for the Lord?" (Genesis 18:14). Sarah conceives and after bearing a son, says, "God has brought laughter for me; everyone who hears will laugh at me" (Genesis 21:6); Abraham and Sarah's son is fittingly named Isaac ("he laughs").

The relationship between Sarah and Hagar becomes strained once again when Sarah sees Ishmael and Isaac playing together. Sarah refuses to accept Ishmael as the equal of Isaac, and tells Abraham, "the son of this slave woman shall not inherit along with my son Isaac" (Genesis 21:10), and insists on the banishment of Hagar and the boy. After obtaining the Lord's approval, Abraham casts Hagar and Ishmael out into the wilderness with only a small ration of bread and water. With the Lord's help, Hagar and Ishmael survive; Ishmael will become the reputed ancestor of the Arab people.

The story of Sarah and Hagar can be seen as one of separation, stressing individualism over collective enterprise. As Savina Taubel observes, "What began as a cooperative effort between Hagar, Abraham, and Sarah, for the benefit of the community, ended with each party concerned solely with his or her own future." The Lord becomes a separate guiding presence for each character, making it possible for them to explain their circumstances and justify their choices and behavior (a concept that will be repeated in the biblical narratives that follow). Thus imbued with a sense of individual empowerment, Sarah, the matriarch, defines her preeminence in the community (and by extension, the superiority of the matriarchs who follow her) and secures the inheritance—and the continuing promise of the Lord's covenant—for Isaac, her one descendent.

After Sarah dies at the ripe old age of 127, Abraham buries her in a cave at Machpelah in Hebron, on land he purchases from the Hittites. (The cave will later be the tomb of Abraham, Isaac, Rebekah, Jacob, and Leah). The patriarch decides to find a wife for his son, but he is unwilling to choose a woman from among the Canaanites, a fertility-worshipping culture, whose influence he perceives as corrupt. He sends his oldest and most trusted servant to his homeland in upper Mesopotamia to find a likely candidate with the caveat that the woman chosen by the servant must agree to come back to Canaan to live.

The servant sets off with ten camels and "choice gifts" for the prospective bride and, while stopped at a well one evening, sees the daughters of the townspeople coming to draw water. He prays to the Lord to "grant me success today," and "Before he had finished speaking, there was Rebekah," described in the narrative as "very fair to look upon, a virgin, whom no man had known." Rebekah willingly draws water for the servant and his camels, offers him the hospitality of her family's house, and reveals that she is the daughter of Abraham's nephew, all of which the servant treats as a sign from the Lord that she is the right wife for Isaac. After an elaborate negotiation with Rebekah's older brother, Laban, a deal is made, and Rebekah readily agrees to return to Canaan to marry Isaac. When she arrives in Canaan, "Isaac brought her into his mother Sarah's tent.

He took Rebekah, and she became his wife; and he loved her" (Genesis 24:67).

After a period of barrenness Rebekah conceives twins. It is a difficult pregnancy, prompting her to complain, "If it is to be this way, why do I live?" The Lord responds, "Two nations are in your womb, and two peoples born of you shall be divided; the one shall be stronger than the other, the elder shall serve the younger" (Genesis 25:22–23). The birth is described: "The first came out red, all his body like a hairy mantle; so they named him Esau. Afterward his brother came out, with his hand gripping Esau's heel; so he was named Jacob" (Genesis 25:24–26).

The common themes of sibling rivalry and maternal favoritism are played out in the story of the slow-witted, easily deceived Esau, and Jacob, the quiet but clever trickster: "Esau was a skillful hunter, a man of the field, while Jacob was a quiet man, living in tents. Isaac loved Esau, because he was fond of game; but Rebekah loved Jacob" (Genesis 25:27–28). Esau sells his birthright—the rights of the eldest son, including leadership of the family and a double share of the inheritance—to his brother in return for a bowl of stew Jacob is cooking, but it is Rebekah who is instrumental in achieving the blessing ordained by the Lord in Genesis 25.

Isaac, old and losing his sight, fears that death is near and asks Esau to hunt and prepare some game for him, after which, as the first-born son, Esau will receive his father's blessing. Rebekah listens to Isaac's conversation with her elder son, and tells Jacob how he can trick his father into bestowing his blessing upon him instead. The deathbed blessing, considered by ancient peoples to be an important gift to the recipient, will make Jacob his brother's lord and provide him with servants, grain, and wine. Rebekah cooks Isaac's favorite meal, covers Jacob with a kidskin, so that he will be as hairy as his brother, and sends him to his father with the "savory food, and the bread that she had prepared." The ruse is successful, and when Rebekah learns that Esau has vowed to kill his brother for supplanting him, she tells Jacob, "Now therefore, my son, obey my voice; flee at once to my brother Laban in Haran, and stay with him a while, until your brother's fury turns away" (Genesis 27: 43–44). To expedite his departure and to justify his absence to Isaac, Rebekah expresses her fear that, like his brother, Jacob will marry a Canaanite woman. Her assumption that Isaac will share this fear is correct: Isaac instructs Jacob to go to "your mother's father; and take as wife from there one of the daughters of Laban, your mother's brother" (Genesis 26:2).

Once Jacob departs, Rebekah's role in the narrative is finished; she is not mentioned again and her death is not recorded. Through a combination of maternal self-interest and attention to divine imperative, she has fulfilled the Lord's prophecy concerning the ascendancy of her beloved younger son and provided a context for the events that will transform Jacob, the supplanter, into the embodiment of Israel in the expansion of the Lord's covenant with Abraham. That expansion will be realized in the sons borne to Jacob by Leah and Rachel, who, as Ruth 4:11 asserts, "together built up the house of Israel." With Rachel and Leah's servants, Bilhah and Zilpah, considered "secondary wives," Jacob's progeny will number twelve sons, who will produce the twelve tribes of Israel.

The story of Rachel, Leah, and Jacob contains echoes of the earlier Abraham-Sarah-Hagar triangle and recalls the sibling rivalry between Jacob and Esau. The theme of deception that figures so prominently in the second patriarchal story is also present in the narrative. Upon his arrival in Haran, Jacob sees Laban's daughter, Rachel, a shepherdess, approaching the well, a scene that recalls to Jacob the meeting of his mother and father. Jacob waters her flock, and then "kissed Rachel, and wept aloud" (Genesis 29:11). One Midrashic interpretation of the scene between Jacob and Rachel reads, "From the moment he saw her at the well, his soul was bound to hers. . . ."

Laban has an elder daughter, Leah, and the narrative compares the sisters: "Leah's eyes were lovely, and Rachel was graceful and beautiful" (Genesis 29:17). Jacob loves Rachel, but because of his hasty retreat from Canaan, he has not brought any gifts with which to woo her. In the absence of a bride-price, he agrees to work for his uncle for seven years to win Rachel; the years "seemed to him but a few days because of the love he had for her" (Genesis 29:20).

According to the custom of his country, Laban must marry off the elder daughter first, a fact which he has concealed from his nephew, and which harkens back to Rebekah and Jacob's treatment of Esau. On the morning of the wedding, Laban has Leah dress as the bride and heavily veils her to conceal her identity. Jacob marries Leah and only discovers the switch the following morning. Upset at the ruse, Jacob confronts his uncle, who agrees to give him Rachel in return for another seven years of labor. Genesis 29:30 records, "So Jacob went in to Rachel also, and he loved Rachel more than Leah."

After Leah, the unloved wife, conceives first and bears four sons in succession, the envious Rachel gives her maid, Bilhah, to Jacob, so that "I, too, may have children through her." Not to be outdone, Leah, who has stopped conceiving for the time being, presents Jacob with *her* maid, Zilpah. Each maid produces two sons; each sister proclaims the births proof of her supremacy as Jacob's wife. In Genesis 30, Rachel begs her sister to give her some of the mandrake root Leah's son has picked (mandrakes were thought to contain aphrodisiac properties that stimulated conception). Leah replies, "Is it a small matter that you have taken away my husband? Would you take away my son's mandrakes also?" (Genesis 30:15). Rachel strikes a bargain with her: she will allow her sister to replace her in the marriage bed that evening in exchange for the mandrake root. The evening apparently turns into years, since Leah conceives three more times, producing two sons and a daughter.

Finally the Lord "remembered Rachel" and "heeded her and opened her womb;" she bears a son, Joseph, whose story bridges the era of the patriarchs in Canaan and the Hebrews in Egypt, and is the last in the Genesis narrative. Later, when Jacob takes his family back to Canaan, Rachel bears a second son and dies in childbirth. Jacob, now called Israel, buries her in present-day Bethlehem, although another tradition locates her grave in an area north of Jerusalem. There is no mention of Leah other than as a passive character after Chapter 31, and no record of her death.

Midrashic sources and biblical scholars have attempted to compare Rachel and Leah, and to define their relationship. In some interpretations, Leah is pious, dutiful, and long-suffering; in others, she is a hypocrite and a deceiver, an outsider who is full of resentment toward her younger and more beautiful sister. Rachel has been praised as noble and selfless for remaining silent during the bridal substitution of her sister for herself; her behavior shows an understanding of the shame her sister would feel if the deception were to be revealed. In the Genesis narrative she appears more capable of positive action and wifely loyalty than her sister.

In Chapter 31, it is Rachel who, as she prepares to leave Haran for Canaan with Jacob, Leah, and their children, defies her father by stealing his household gods, small carved wooden or stone statues, the possession of which would ensure Jacob's leadership of the family and legitimize his claim on any property won from Laban. She hides them in a camel's saddle and when the enraged Laban catches up to the party and begins to search her tent for the idols, she sits on the saddle and expresses her regret that she cannot rise to greet him because she is menstruating and is therefore considered "unclean." Rachel's theft of the idols eventually leads to a treaty between Jacob and Laban, who have been antagonistic toward each other almost from the start.

Like the stories of the two previous matriarchs, the tale of Rachel and Leah is essentially a human drama of family relationships together with a divine component that serves to remind the reader of the family's ultimate destiny: to realize the Lord's covenant with Abraham that will result in the nation of Israel.

In *Judaism and the New Woman*, Sally J. Priesand, the first woman to become a rabbi, describes the four matriarchs: "They are portrayed as overprotective mothers concerned with the preservation of a people. As instruments through which that people would survive, they did anything and everything that was required of them— even if that sometimes meant acting in ways unworthy of praise. . . . The matriarchs were guilty of jealousy, favoritism, and robbery, but they acted to protect Israel. They perceived the dangers that threatened Israel's destiny and pushed their sometimes blind husbands into action." Sarah, Rebekah, Rachel, and Leah are honored and respected by Jewish tradition as steadfast and decisive wives and mothers whose devotion to their children and their families symbolizes the promise of Israel and the cohesion and continuation of a culture.

Deborah

The inhabitants of the villages ceased, they ceased in Israel, until that I Deborah arose, that I arose a mother in Israel.

They chose new gods; then was war in the gates: was there a shield or spear seen among forty thousand in Israel?

Awake, awake, Deborah: awake, awake, utter a song: arise Barak, and lead thy captivity captive, thou son of Abinoam.
—Judges 5:7–8, 12 "Song of Deborah,"
from the *King James Bible*

A PROPHET, POET, warrior, and the only woman judge featured in the Bible, Deborah stands out as a unique figure in Jewish history and lore. There are several heroines named in biblical scripture, as well as three other women prophets, but none of them possesses Deborah's authority, influence, or diversity of talents. In her role as a judge and a military leader she was on a par with men, an unusual situation in what was a patriarchal society. She has been compared to Joan of Arc and was the only judge already serving in a position of leadership when, according to scripture, she was commissioned by God to deliver the Israelites from their enemy, the Canaanites. As a prophet, she correctly predicted the death of Sisera, the captain of the Canaanite army: "for the Lord shall sell Sisera into the hand of a woman" (Judges 4:9).

Deborah appears in chapters four and five of the book of Judges, which is the seventh book of the Old Testament. The era of the judges spans the years from c.1200–1020 B.C., from the death of Joshua and the Israelite settlement of Canaan to the time of the prophet Samuel and the beginning of the monarchy. The Deborah story may have been written around 750 B.C. The book of Judges is a series of tales chronicling the exploits of various Hebrew tribal chieftains, called judges, throughout the years. The tribes battle one another and fall into apostasy when good leaders die. The uncompromising influence and power of the Lord is considered instrumental in determining military and moral victory or defeat, and by the fourth book, when "the children of Israel again did evil in the sight of the Lord" by abandoning the all-important first commandment and worshiping the Canaanite gods, Baal, Astarte, and Asherah, "the Lord sold them into the hand of Jabin king of Canaan that reigned in Hazor: the captain of whose host was Sisera, which dwelt in Harosheth of the Gentiles." (Judges 4:2). The twenty-year enslavement of the Israelites was due as much to a lack of leadership and tribal unity as it was to religious apostasy; it would take Deborah's spiritual faith and bold military vision and leadership to defeat the Canaanites and their "nine hundred chariots of iron" (Judges 4:13).

Deborah, whose name in Hebrew can mean "a bee," "she rules," or "one who is eloquent in speech," is introduced in Judges as the wife of Lapidoth, an obscure man who is never mentioned again. As a judge, she played an important role in government. She provided legal counsel and settled disputes, and according to some sources, was a keeper of the tabernacle lamps. Her house was on the road between Ramah and Beth-el in the hill country of Emphraim, known for its olive and palm trees. There, she gave her counsel while sitting under the leaves of a date palm.

Much of what Deborah undoubtedly heard from the people was a willingness to revolt against the oppression they were experiencing under the yoke of Jabin, and at some point, it is not clear when, she decided it was time to act. She summoned Barak, an Israelite general from the Naphtali tribe, from his home in Kedesh, and convinced him to ready ten thousand men from the Naphtali and Zebulun tribes for war. Her part in the incursion was to lead a force from Kedesh with the intention of provoking the Canaanite army into battle. She told Barak, "I will draw unto thee to the river Kishon, Sisera, the captain of Jabin's army, with his chariots and his multitude; and I will deliver him into thine hand" (Judges 4:7). Barak's response illustrates both his faith in Deborah's vision of victory, carrying with it, as it does, the Lord's approval and perceived help, and his need for her presence as co-commander: "If thou wilt go with me, then I will go: but if thou wilt not go with me, then I will not go" (Judges 4:8). Deborah agreed, made her prophecy concerning the fate of Sisera, and the plan was put into execution. The Canaanite troops were "discomfited" until all had fallen "upon the edge of the sword, and there was not a man left" (Judges 4:16).

What followed was the fulfillment of Deborah's prophecy. Sisera fled on foot to the tent of Jael, the wife of a Kenite named Heber. Since Jabin and the Kenites, an Israelite tribe, were at peace, Sisera expected to find refuge there. Jael agreed to shelter him ("Turn in, my lord, turn in to me; fear not"), hid him under a "mantle," brought him a drink of milk, and covered him up again. Then, in a deliciously violent passage, the Bible reports that Jael "took a nail of the tent, and took a hammer in her hand, and went softly unto him, and smote the nail into his temples, and fastened it into the ground: for he was fast asleep and weary. So he died" (Judges 4:21). Soon afterwards, Barak, in pursuit of Sisera, arrived, and Jael invited him in to see the body of the dead Canaanite captain.

Jael's motive for killing Sisera is open to speculation. It could be that Jael opposed the Kenites' alliance with the Canaanites, or that she killed Sisera as an act of atonement for her own or her tribe's apostasy. Tradition obliges us to accept the fact of Deborah's powers as a prophet, but it is interesting to contemplate other possibilities:

that she, herself, expected to kill Sisera in battle, or that she planned the killing with Jael and was fortunate that the plan succeeded. In any event, the "children of Israel prospered and prevailed against Jabin the king of Canaan, until they had destroyed Jabin king of Canaan" (Judges 4:24).

The next chapter of Judges is an epic poem, the "Song of Deborah," a thirty-one-verse celebration of the Israelites' great conquest, composed and sung by Deborah and Barak, transcribed by one of the Bible's many presumed authors, and passed down as an oral retelling, part of an identifiable body of biblical tradition.

One of the earliest martial prose poems in history, the "Song of Deborah" is probably the oldest extant example of Hebrew literature. Because it is virtually the only sizable document that exists prior to the time of David, it is of great historical value. It is primarily a battle ode composed, writes Harry M. Buck in *People of the Lord,* "in the flush of victory with all the exuberance of a primitive army that has just inflicted defeat on its enemies. The poetic form, with its episodic character and dissonant movement, suits it for the reminiscence of a great battle and marks it as an ode to be sung, perhaps at cult festivals or by wandering minstrels." It is a lively reenactment of the events chronicled in the previous chapter, with added material, including the information that the victory over Sisera was due to a sudden downpour that made it impossible for the Canaanite chariots to maneuver. Principal credit is given to Deborah for providing sufficient unity for the raid and special care taken to praise the all-powerful Lord "for the avenging of Israel, when the people willingly offered themselves." Jael is singled out as "blessed above women," and is described as having not just hammered a nail into Sisera's head but afterwards "she smote off his head, when she had pierced and stricken through his temples" (Judges 5:26). Deborah and Barak end their song with a prayerful coda: "So let all thine enemies perish, O Lord: but let them that love him be as the sun when he goeth forth in his might" (Judges 5:31). It is noted in the last line of Judges 5:31 that "the land had rest forty years." This statement does not seem to belong to the odic style of the "Song of Deborah," and was almost certainly added afterward by the biblical author who transcribed the poem.

The importance of the Israelites' triumph over the Canaanites was

as much symbolic as it was necessary for the development and survival of a unified nation characterized by religious faith, law, and
liturgy. "It is unlikely," observes Buck, "that the Hebrews made any
important territorial gains, but the telling and retelling of the story
had much to do with the future of Israel." Deborah's part in the
Jews' righteous victory, together with her celebratory song, provided
much inspiration for later generations of Israelites and solidified her
status as one of the greatest heroines in history.

Ruth and Naomi

Only eighty-five verses tell Ruth and Naomi's story. To talk of it takes much longer. Not that the greatest stories are the shortest—not at all. But a short story has a stalk—or shoot—through which its life rushes, and out of which the flowery head erupts. The Book of Ruth—wherein goodness grows out of goodness, and the extraordinary is found here, and here, and here—is sown in desertion, bereavement, barrenness, death, loss, displacement, destitution. What can sprout from such ash? Then Ruth sees into the nature of Covenant, and the life of the story streams in. Out of this stalk mercy and redemption unfold. . . .

—Cynthia Ozick, "Ruth," in Judith A. Kates and
Gail Twersky Reimer, *Reading Ruth:*
Contemporary Women Reclaim a Sacred Story

ONE OF THE most popular biblical stories, the story of Ruth and her mother-in-law, Naomi, is revered as an innocent and entertaining pastoral tale of loyalty, love, and spiritual redemption. The Book of Ruth is set in the period of the Judges, although the bloody tribal warfare that is a feature of the Book of Judges is not reflected here. The Septuagint, the Greek version of the Old Testament, places the book between Judges and Samuel I. The Hebrew Bible places Ruth among its third section, called "Writings," or *Kethuvim*. It was probably composed between 450 and 300 B.C.; dates both before and after the sixth-century Babylonian Exile have been suggested. The first five verses of Ruth take place in Moab, a nation that occupied the territory east of the Dead Sea and south of the river Arnon. The Moabites were considered by the Israelites to be related to them through Lot, the nephew of Abraham, but differences in religion and culture, together with conflicting claims to the same territory, had resulted in enmity between the two nations.

The Book of Ruth begins in a time of famine, when Naomi (meaning "pleasant" in Hebrew) emigrates from Bethlehem to Moab with her husband, Elimelech, and their two sons. Sometime after Naomi's husband dies, her sons marry Moabite women, Ruth ("friend") and Orpah ("back"). Ten years later, when her sons die, the bereaved Naomi learns that the famine in Israel has ceased and she decides to return to Bethlehem. Her daughters-in-law offer to accompany her, but Naomi turns them away, feeling that without her sons (to be their husbands), she is of no use to them. Orpah remains in Moab, but Ruth clings to Naomi and asserts her loyalty and fealty to her mother-in-law in one of the most famous and endearing biblical stanzas:

Do not press me to leave you
or to turn back from following you!
Where you go, I will go;
where you lodge, I will lodge;
your people shall be my people,
and your God my God.
Where you die, I will die—

there will I be buried.
May the Lord do thus and so to me,
and more as well,
if even death parts me from you!
(Ruth 1:16–17)

Naomi sees that Ruth is determined to go with her, and "said no more to her." The two women proceed on to Bethlehem, where the barley harvest is beginning. There, the women of the town greet Naomi by asking, "Is this Naomi?" Naomi's response emphasizes her grief and lack of spiritual faith:

Call me no longer Naomi,
call me Mara,
for the Almighty has dealt very bitterly with me.
I went away full,
but the Lord has brought me home again empty;
why then call me Naomi
when the Lord has dealt harshly with me,
and the Almighty has brought calamity upon me?
(Ruth 1:20–21)

In Bethlehem, Ruth becomes a Jewish convert, and the two women live modestly on whatever Ruth gathers from the unharvested grain left in the fields for the poor, in accordance with Hebrew law. While gleaning in the fields of the wealthy Boaz, Ruth attracts his attention and wins his favor. Boaz praises her for her attentiveness to her mother-in-law and for leaving her native land to come "to a people that you did not know before." He blesses her by saying, "May the Lord reward you for your deeds, and may you have a full reward from the Lord, the God of Israel, under whose wings you have come for refuge!" (Ruth 2:11–12). Boaz shares his meal with Ruth and gives instructions to ensure that she gathers enough grain. When Naomi sees how much wheat her daughter-in-law has gleaned and discovers where it has been gathered, she takes a step toward regaining her faith by recognizing Boaz's benevolence toward Ruth as a blessing from the Lord, "whose kindness has not forsaken the living or the dead!" She reveals that Boaz is a kinsman and in order to obtain "some security" for Ruth, so that "it may go well with you," urges her to choose Boaz as her husband by pressing the levirate marriage claim upon him. (According to Deuteronomy, the brother-in-law of a childless widow was obligated to marry her and rear a child in the name of his dead brother; extending this claim to a mere kinsman shows the fluidity of Jewish law even as it affirms the practice of levirate marriage, and, most important, serves the ends of the story.)

Naomi advises Ruth on how to press her claim: "Now wash and anoint yourself, and put on your best clothes and go down to the threshing floor; but do not make yourself known to the man until he has finished eating and drinking. When he lies down, observe the place where he lies; then, go, uncover his feet and lie down; and he will tell you what to do" (Ruth 3:3–4). Ruth dutifully follows Naomi's instructions. When the startled Boaz awakes to find her lying at his feet, Ruth tells him to spread his cloak over her to show that he, as next-of-kin, will accept her as his wife. (Sexual overtones are present in this passage: *feet* in Hebrew can be a euphemism for "genitals"; the spreading of the cloak suggests the possibility of consummation.) Boaz is very willing, but he informs her that there is an even closer male relative, whose claim must be respected. Boaz meets the unnamed kinsman at the city gate, where business and legal matters are transacted, before ten elders of the city (leading male citizens who interpreted traditional Israelite law and settled disputes; it is possible that the reference in the Book of Ruth is the source of the Jewish practice of requiring a *minyan,* that is, ten men, to conduct worship services). Boaz tells the man that Naomi is selling Elimelech's land and offers it to the kinsman with the stipulation that he also marry Ruth "the Moabite, the widow of the dead man, to maintain the dead man's name on his inheritance" (Ruth 4:5). The kinsman refuses, knowing that to accept Ruth would damage his own inheritance, since a son she might bear would be considered the heir of her deceased husband. Ruth and Boaz are now free to marry.

Naomi's situation then reaches a happy conclusion. After Ruth gives birth to a son, the townswomen approach Naomi to assure her that, with the child's birth, goodness has grown out of goodness and blossomed: "Blessed be the Lord, who has not left you this day without next-of-kin; and may his name be renowned in Israel! He shall be to you a restorer of life and a nourisher of your old age; for your daughter-in-law who loves you, who is more to you than seven sons, has borne him." Thus restored to faith, Naomi becomes the baby's nurse. The women give the child a name, saying, "A son has been born to Naomi" (Ruth 4:14–17). The child, Obed, will be the father of Jesse, and the grandfather of King David. This genealogical information gives the story importance in Christian as well as Jewish tradition, because, according to the New Testament, David is included among the ancestors of Jesus.

There are moral and spiritual lessons that can be understood and appreciated in a deeper reading of Ruth and Naomi's story. The attachment of Ruth and Naomi underscores the fidelity and loyalty that bind a family together. The mercy and redemption Ruth and Naomi receive after having suffered great tribulation emphasize the affirmation of the Covenant, which is realized through faithful commitment to the God of Israel. Finally, despite her status as a foreigner, Ruth, the Moabite and proselyte, is accepted by Boaz and goes on to become the ancestor of two great kings and a prophet of great influence, a result that illustrates the wisdom and necessity of religious and cultural tolerance.

Mary, or Miriam of Nazareth

Quis non potest contristari? *Who could not share her great sorrow?*
—Jacopone (Benedetti) Da Toda, thirteenth-century
Italian mystic and poet

THE STORY OF Miriam of Nazareth—the woman known as Mary, mother of Jesus—has gained the status of cult or legend through the efforts of thousands of poets and artists, and the passion of millions of fervent believers.

Can a factual biographical essay on the life of Mary be done? To ask that, one must also ponder whether the Gospels are truth or corruptions of oral history. Many scholars aver that these stories could not possibly have been written at the time of the events depicted, that they—and the story of Mary—are the culmination of centuries of the fabrication upon fabrication or storytelling that has taken on a life of its own. One cannot deny, however, that her admirers are legion, loving her for being what many believe to be the human side of Jesus.

In the Gospel according to Luke, one can find only a few paragraphs about Mary, but they have been enough to build the legendary story of Mary into a kind of transcendent truth. What we do know is that she was a "Jewish maid of Galilee" who lived during the mostly peaceful reign of Herod Antipas, some 170 years after the time the Maccabees rose up against the Syrians and about seventy years before the destruction of the second temple in Jerusalem.

She was probably born about 22 B.C.E. to Anne and Joachim, who lived in a small village on the southernmost side of the mountains of Galilee. She became betrothed to the carpenter Joseph sometime between 7 and 4 B.C.E.

Joseph and Mary, with Mary now pregnant, traveled to take part in the census (a form of taxation) as ordered by Caesar Augustus. Because Joseph was from the House of David, they traveled from Galilee to Nazareth to Judea to the city of David—Bethlehem—and it was there that Mary gave birth to a boy child whom they named Yeshua, Jesus. As is the custom in Judaism, he was circumcised and welcomed into the House of David.

When Jesus was about twelve, the story goes, he and his parents traveled with many of their community to Jerusalem, for their annual pilgrimage to celebrate Passover. In all the excitement of leaving Jerusalem, it was a while before Joseph and Mary discovered that their eldest son was not with them. They quickly returned to the temple to find Jesus and the rabbis in an animated discussion. When Jesus was older, he preached what he had learned that day in the temple, making him an enemy to the Romans who killed him because they thought he posed a threat. And so, Mary the mother mourned, as the mothers of all the slain children mourn.

Over the centuries, from Gnostics through twentieth-century pontiffs, leaders of the Church have switched the focus off and on Mary. She has been the Second Eve or the Mother of God. She has been venerated like a saint and called the Blessed Virgin.

According to Catholicism, Mary gave birth to Jesus although she was a virgin, and had no other children. Other Christian sects dispute her virginity, citing the original Greek word to describe her, *parthenos,* as meaning not virginal but "unmarried young maiden," thus pointing to a corruption of thought based on a corrupt reading of the word.

The study of Mary, known as Mariology, has ardent supporters around the world who, at different times throughout history, have depicted Mary as an image of the divine or, at other times, observed her as a mortal being infused with inordinate grace. In any case, the New Testament offers nothing in the way of genuine substantiation for her becoming the icon she is to many.

One of the interesting aspects for Jews is the attitude toward Judaism that appears in the "histories" of Mark, Matthew and Luke, in which Jesus is generally recognized as Jewish and preaches as a Jew to fellow Jews. In John, however, Jesus is depicted as being opposed to the Jews and the Jews are opposed to him. He has ceased to be Jewish.

As Christianity separated itself from Judaism and the veneration of Mary as the Mother of God *(theotokos)* became rooted in the anti-Jewish theology of the early Church, Jesus was no longer thought of as Jewish, and therefore, his mother, Mary, also was no longer associated as "the Jewish maiden of Galilee."

Does any of this matter to those who believe in the magic of Mary? Probably not. Her most magnetic appeal remains that of Mother or Mother Goddess, the source from which all life comes, independent of her theological role as the mother of Jesus and, certainly, independent of her own Jewish heritage.

Williston Walker, in *A History of the Christian Church* writes, "There seems little doubt that the cult of the Virgin originally attracted and replaced the devotion that had been offered to the 'mother goddesses' of Egypt, Syria, and Asia Minor; at the same time, however, it was her [Mary's] role as the chosen vehicle of the Incarnation which set her, in Christian eyes, above martyr or apostle as the noblest and holiest of human persons."

For artists, poets, composers, and architects, Mary is the woman of all women. She inspires, humbles, makes awestruck. She is full of sweetness and innocence. In scenes of the baby Jesus with his mother, we view the ecstatic joy of motherhood, and in pietàs, we are touched by the inconsolable grief of child loss, the sorrow that has no comfort.

Mary lived in the desert, and if the originating Gospel stories are to be believed, she was of modest dress, with few possessions. Yet that original "reality" is never shown. Instead, artists have added the rapture of color, the luxuriant folds of velvet clothing, and elaborate jewelry and crowns, with the most telling accessory, the glow of piety and genuine love in her face, frequently painted in what Goethe described as a "subdued state of light."

Mary, as mother of all mothers, has been the imaginative subject of nearly every great sculptor, painter, and craftsman in tapestry, glass, and book illustration. She is in the work of Rembrandt and Rubens, Salvador Dali and Gerard David, and her hair color, dress, appearance, age—everything—are the result of the artists' visions, not her reality. Botticelli's annunciation is all elegance and delicacy; Paul Gauguin brings a haunting green to the Calvary; and Hans Memling's *Adoration of the Angels* shows a red-haired Mary with elaborate braids and a porcupine crown. Stephan Luchner's *Presentation of Jesus in the Temple* is rich and lush with solid circles of gold behind mother and child to set them apart from the gathering. In El Greco's *Mater Dolorosa,* the simply dressed Madonna casts a halo that gives a golden aura to the soft green head covering.

But, can artists—mortals that they are—really imagine what a god (or goddess) looks like? Were the earliest painters of Mary following the direction of the Church to deify her or make her the image of a universal mother to match its claims to be the universal church? Did they intend to wipe out the references to her Jewish heritage?

The answers to these questions belong to biblical scholars. What is unquestionable is that Mary remains a provocative figure, one that writers still attempt to explain, one that artists still attempt to create images of in every medium, and an icon that architects will continue to design settings for, to glorify the real, or implied, spiritual power attributed to her.

Mary is an archetypical mother figure, venerated, adored, and admired. After two millennia, the most common image of her echoes kindness and goodness. She is, above all, the paragon of grace, the source of unconditional love, and the essence of the human over the divine.

Doña Gracia Nasi

(1510?–1569)

The Inquisition, which would spread throughout the Catholic world, was just beginning its terror, torture and burning. [Doña Gracia Nasi] would become the self-appointed protector and political liaison for its chief targets: the conversos. These were the Spanish and Portuguese Jews, who, like her own family, had been forcibly converted to Catholicism in the decades prior to her birth in 1510. These converts were being subjected to ethnic cleansing by Inquisition officials who were making wholesale arrests on the spurious charge that they had relapsed into Jewish practice, whether true or not . . .

Ultimately the conversos, and most of the openly-professing Jews of the Eastern Mediterranean would view Doña Gracia as their unquestioned leader. She would be revered as much for her wisdom and compassion as her capacity to stand up to tyranny; not to mention her willingness to give

up her fortune to ensure the survival of this "remnant" of Israel, as her
people were called in those days.
                    —Andrée Aelion Brooks, *The Woman Who Defied Kings:*
                    The Life and Times of Doña Gracia Nasi—
                    A Jewish Leader During the Renaissance

WHEN CALLED UPON to name influential women of the Renaissance, most people would be likely to mention women such as Lucrezia Borgia, Catherine de Medici, or Diane de Poitiers. The name of Doña Gracia Nasi would not immediately spring to mind. Yet in world history—and especially in the history of the Sephardim—Doña Gracia stands out as a figure of great courage, fortitude, and ingenuity during an era in which rabid persecution of the Jews existed in tandem with the humanistic perspective that had given rise to a new flourishing of the arts and sciences. During her lifetime she was compared to the biblical heroine, Deborah; similarly, Doña Gracia's success in saving a large number of Jews from the fires of the Inquisition would help to ensure a future for what then comprised a major segment of world Jewry.

The story of Doña Gracia Nasi can be said to have begun in 1478, when Ferdinand and Isabella of Spain, with the reluctant approval of Pope Sixtus IV, established the Inquisition to discover and punish converted Jews who were either suspected of apostasy or of insincerity toward their adopted religion. In 1492, after fourteen years of terror, torture, and murder, the surviving Spanish Jews were expelled from the country. During this diaspora, the exiles migrated to countries throughout the Mediterranean and western Europe, including the Italian city-states, the Netherlands, and Portugal. The Inquisition would become institutionalized in these countries and city-states, to be revived periodically as a way for the state to practice ethnic cleansing, seize the assets of wealthy *conversos,* openly practicing as well as nonpracticing Jews, and to persecute adherents of the new religion of Protestantism.

In 1497, as a precondition of his marriage to the daughter of Ferdinand and Isabella, Manuel I ordered all Portuguese Jews to convert to Christianity or leave the country. The converts, among them Doña Gracia's parents, were known by gentiles by the interchangeable terms, *conversos* or "New Christians," or by the more pejorative term, *marranos* (pigs). The *conversos* called themselves by the Hebrew term for converts: *anusim.* They pursued a variety of occupations in every class of life and practiced Judaism in secret.

Doña Gracia Nasi, born Beatrice de Luna in Lisbon, was the oldest child of Alvara and Phillipa de Luna, who had come to Portugal from the Spanish province of Aragon during the expulsion. Her father was a trader in silver and other commodities, and Beatrice and her sisters and brother grew up in privileged upper-class circumstances with connections at the royal court. At home, Beatrice was called Gracia, the Iberian form of the Hebrew name, Hannah. Much later, after she had left Portugal, renounced her Christian conversion, and began to practice Judaism openly, she would take the last name of her son-in-law, Don Joseph Nasi. In the Jewish communities of pre-expulsion Spain, the word *nasi* was a title given to leading Jewish citizens.

Nothing is known about Doña Gracia's childhood; but given her family's status, she undoubtedly had a *conversa* wet nurse, and as a child would have been well tutored in a variety of subjects, including reading, writing, languages, music, poetry, the classics, history, politics, and even mathematics. Like other *converso* families, the de Lunas lived both as Catholics and as Jews, observing Jewish dietary and Sabbath customs insofar as it was possible for them to do in secret. But as Andrée Aelion Brooks observes, "Leading a double life, religiously speaking, was not easy. It led to terrible feelings of guilt and confused identity. . . . What made matters worse was that religion was not separated from the core of a person's existence and identity. It was a fundamental way of interpreting the world before the advent of scientific explanations. Besides, many brooded over the fact that following the 'wrong' faith could condemn their souls to hell."

In addition, the *conversos,* like the Eastern European Jews of the late nineteenth century, were subject to sporadic acts of persecution. One example is the Lisbon Massacre of 1506, during which some two thousand *conversos* were murdered by a crowd of men, women, and even children in the belief that the Jews and their "Jewish blood" were responsible for a recent outbreak of the Black Death. "No amount of wealth, connections or repeated reciting of Catholic devotions would make them feel safe again," writes Brooks. "No amount of baptismal water tossed over them would wash away centuries of hatred. The idea of being vulnerable because of Jewish blood, and not because of Jewish practice, became a new and unsettling concept."

In 1528, the eighteen-year-old Gracia was wed to her uncle, Francisco Mendes, a wealthy and prominent merchant from an illustrious Jewish courtier family in Aragon. His family, whose Jewish name was Benveniste, had arrived in Lisbon in 1492, when Francisco was about ten years old. Unlike his wife, who was baptized as a baby but had received a rudimentary Jewish education, Francisco had studied Hebrew and was well versed in Jewish tradition and ritual by the time he was forced to convert at the age of fifteen. Gracia and Francisco had only one surviving child, a daughter named Ana.

Francisco and his brother, Diogo, would expand their mercantile activities into a profitable banking syndicate, with headquarters in Lisbon and Antwerp. Among their clients were the Holy Roman Emperor, Charles V, and the Portuguese king, João III, both of whom needed a constant flow of cash to maintain their royal courts. Between 1531 and 1535 the Mendes brothers tried unsuccessfully to use their great wealth to stave off the establishment of the Inquisition in Portugal by bribing those in power, including the pope. When Francisco Mendes died in 1535, Doña Gracia, as his widow, retained sole ownership of his fortune. The Portuguese king, eager to seize the Mendes family's assets and fearful that Doña Gracia would move to Antwerp, beyond the reach of the Inquisition, demanded that her daughter Ana Mendes be turned over to the court as a hostage, to be married off to a nobleman or kept as the king's mistress. "With the child at the royal palace," writes Brooks, "the mother would not be inclined to move too far away. And then, once the Inquisition was established, it might be possible to confiscate the mother's inheritance, too."

In 1537, after negotiating a series of payoffs, obtaining a guarantee of safe conduct by the English, and informing the court of her intention to take a short "business related" trip to Antwerp, Doña Gracia, her daughter, and several members of her household left Portugal for Belgium. There she successfully ran the family business with her brother-in-law, and on Diogo's death in 1542 inherited the entire Mendes banking and trading empire. Now the administrator of one of the largest fortunes and one of the greatest businesses in

Europe, "La Señora," as Doña Gracia was called, used her political contacts and financial resources to help Jews in Portugal and Spain escape the Inquisition, most of them through a network that quietly moved hundreds of Jews on spice ships to Antwerp, and from there to an eventual destination in the Ottoman Empire, a Muslim area outside the control of the Inquisition.

In 1545, Doña Gracia and her family were again forced to flee the Inquisition in Antwerp. They went to Venice, where, through a series of intricate business maneuvers, Doña Gracia had been able to transfer much of her fortune. In Venice, during a revival of the Inquisition in 1547, Doña Gracia's greedy sister, Brianda, denounced her as a heretic and a "secret Jew" in the hope of securing the family fortune for herself and her daughter. Doña Gracia immediately fled with her daughter to Ferrara, taking her assets with her. There, from 1549 to 1552, she was allowed to practice Judaism openly and gained renown as a patron of printing and literature. The *Ferrara Bible,* printed two years after she left the city for Constantinople, would be dedicated to her "because," reads the inscription, "your greatness deserves it and because your own birth and love of your land imposes this well-deserved obligation."

After transferring her assets to Constantinople, Doña Gracia arrived in the city in 1553. There she assembled a consortium of Jews and Muslims to trade in such commodities as wheat, pepper, and raw wool for the production of European textiles. She soon gained political and economic influence at the Ottoman court, which enabled her to convince the sultan, Suleiman the Magnificent, to intervene with Pope Paul IV on behalf of Jews persecuted by the Inquisition in Ancona, Italy. In retaliation for the burning of twenty-three Ancona Jews, she helped to organize a boycott of Ancona's Mediterranean trade, an act that resulted in the freeing of the city's Jews, many of whom made their way to lands in the Ottoman Empire.

In 1560, Doña Gracia and her nephew, Don Joseph Nasi, secured from Suleiman a long-term lease on the former Jewish town of Tiberias. They had the walls of the ruined town rebuilt, erected a yeshiva, which attracted numerous scholars, housed and fed newly arrived Jewish refugees, and financed the establishment of agriculture, fishing, and silk farming. During the 1560s Doña Gracia administered her settlement with the same acumen and sense of purpose that had characterized her earlier business and humanitarian activities. She faced a number of difficulties, however, including an unwillingness on the part of the Turks to actively support the security of the new colony, a lack of new immigrants over the years, and the distancing of her politically motivated nephew from the project. The settlement would decline after Doña Gracia's death and collapse by 1575.

The circumstances of Doña Gracia's death in 1569 and her place of burial are not known, which seems odd, given the reverence and love accorded her during her lifetime. However, it is highly possible that lost records account for this lack of knowledge. Predictably, her surviving siblings squabbled over the terms of their inheritance. Moses di Trani, one of the rabbis called in to render a legal opinion, chose the occasion to eulogize this remarkable woman: "Many women have done mighty deeds," he wrote, "but Gracia has surpassed them all."

Rebecca Gratz

(1781–1869)

All accounts agree in praise of this unusual woman. Beautiful in face . . .
noble of soul and pure of heart, she is not unworthy of having applied to
her the exquisite words used of a rare woman by George Eliot, that "were
all virtue and religion dead, she'd make them newly, being what she was."
        —Rabbi David Philipson, from the introduction to
        Letters of Rebecca Gratz

IN AN ERA of the "gentlewoman" who pursued the Victorian idea of
romance, and devoted herself to her husband and children, Rebecca
Gratz was an anomaly. She was a woman who remained unmarried
by choice, yet made such an impact on children's welfare that some

of the organizations that she began still survive more than a century after her death.

Rebecca Gratz was born the seventh of twelve children to Miriam Simon, whose father was a prominent Jewish merchant of Lancaster, Pennsylvania, and Michael Gratz, a descendent in a long line of rabbis. He and his brother Barnard were orphaned at an early age in their native Silesia (now Germany). They immigrated to Philadelphia, then the nation's capital and perhaps the city of the most diverse ethnic and religious makeup.

Michael and Miriam Gratz were so socially prominent, wealthy, and attractive that three of the nation's leading portrait artists painted their family: Thomas Sully, Edward Malbone, and Gilbert Stuart.

The Gratzes were active members of one of Philadelphia's oldest synagogues, Mikveh Israel. They amassed a considerable personal library, and their eldest daughter, Richea (Mrs. Solomon Hays), was the first woman to attend college in America. The family also founded Gratz College, outside of Philadelphia in Melrose Park, the oldest independent, nondenominationally affiliated college of Jewish studies in the Western Hemisphere.

As a teenager, Rebecca, beautiful and well schooled, was part of the growing social and literary elite of Philadelphia, and she corresponded with a number of the great personalities of her day: Maria Edgeworth, a British educator and novelist; Catherine Sedgwick, an American author; Fanny Kemble, a British actress; Grace Aguilar, the Jewish-British theologian; and many others. She counted among her acquaintances Washington Irving, to whom the story is attributed that Rebecca was the model for Sir Walter Scott's 1820 novel, *Ivanhoe*. In the book, a "Hebrew maiden" named Rebecca, refuses to marry out of her faith. Yet no correspondence of Rebecca's to or from Scott is known, nor has any letter been found between Scott and Irving to bear out this charming albeit untrue story. It is true, however, that Rebecca read the book and enjoyed it. She wrote one friend, "Have you received *Ivanhoe*? When you read it tell me what you think of my namesake Rebecca."

In 1829, she wrote to her childhood friend, Maria Fenno Hoffman, "I felt a little extra pleasure from Rebecca's being a Hebrew maiden. It is worthy of Scott in a period when persecution has recommenced in Europe to hold up a picture of the superstition and cruelty in which it originated."

Rebecca Gratz was a prolific correspondent her entire life and a patron of the arts. She read essays, poetry (which she also wrote), and the popular fiction of the day. She was also concerned enough about the portrayal of Jews in books that she would write authors of any errors.

She led a busy social life with friends, and enjoyed these experiences until, at the age of nineteen, she was chosen by her other family members to be the caretaker for her father, now crippled by a severe stroke. At first unhappy by her role as family nurse, she eventually came to embrace it, and attended to the births of her twenty-seven nieces and nephews. She also cared for other relatives who became ill at one time or another.

Marriage was certainly a choice, especially after her mother's death in 1808 and her father's in 1811, and her family could have matched her with any of a number of suitable gentlemen. But she was unenthusiastic. She wrote, "There appears no condition in human life more afflictive and destructive to happiness & morals than . . . an ill-advised marriage." Only nine of her siblings reached adulthood, and only five of those ever married, the men married non-Jews and the women, Jews. Rebecca lived with her brothers Hyman, Joseph, and Jacob, along with sister Sarah, who died in 1817.

Rebecca and her sisters, and twenty other women, both Jewish and gentile, founded the Female Association for the Relief of Women and Children in Reduced Circumstances to help women from formerly affluent families who had suffered a reversal of fortune. She became treasurer, in part, because the rules of membership directed that the treasurer "must be chosen from the unmarried ladies" of the organization, to enable them to control the finances of the group. Civil laws of the 1800s gave husbands control of their wives' funds and any that she handled for another purpose or person. (According to Jewish law, women could own property and enter business contracts on their own as unmarried or married women, but secular (civil) law in the 1800s did not recognize women's equality.)

In 1815, Rebecca helped to organize the Philadelphia Orphan Society, a private, nonsectarian group that both sheltered and educated poor orphaned children until they found adoptive homes. She served as board secretary for more than forty years.

The early 1800s were a time of Christian proselytizing, and Rebecca became aware of the Christian Sunday School movement. In response to what she believed was a need to strengthen Jewish education among children, and women, she started a small religious school for her siblings and their children in 1818, thus developing the prototype for the Hebrew Sunday School, which she organized twenty years later. Gratz understood that Jews would remain a minority; however, with her school, she not only created a way for Jewish children to learn about their religious heritage, but also established it in a way that blended into the American way of life.

In 1819, she helped to establish the Female Hebrew Benevolent Society to "create a Jewish presence in the benevolent community." The organization provided food, clothing, fuel, and other necessities for the impoverished Jews of Philadelphia and sought to "protect the poor without encouraging pauperism." The organization was the first Jewish women's organization in North America that was not affiliated with a synagogue, and as such, did not require its clients to belong to a congregation nor to attend any religious services. It was solely dedicated to solving the immediate needs of the individual. Here again, Gratz served as secretary for forty years, proving her mission that Jews could take care of themselves and that by doing such, the stature of Jewish women in the community would be elevated.

In 1823, her sister Rachel died in childbirth, leaving behind six children and a distraught husband, Solomon Moses. Rebecca immediately took the children into her own home and continued to be involved even after Moses remarried.

Concerned with the "mental impoverishment of those who are rising to take their places among the thousands of Israel scattered throughout the families of the earth," Gratz sought help for the future of Philadelphia's 750 Jews. In 1835, she developed a solution: a Jewish education program. The Female Hebrew Benevolent Society resolved that a Sunday school be established, and appointed teachers among the young women of the congregation. It opened in April of 1838, with sixty students and Gratz as school superintendent. She served the school for twenty-five years, personally grading homework, developing curriculum material, and teaching in English, not Hebrew. The school was coeducational, met weekly, and was free to all.

Most important, it was the first Jewish institution to give women a public role in the education of Jewish children. Serving as a model, the school's framework was duplicated in other communities from Charleston to Savannah to Baltimore. The Hebrew Sunday School provided Jewish girls with a religious education for the first time, and encouraged many of its female graduates to return as instructors for younger girls. It was always offered to anyone who wanted to "hear the word of God, to learn His commandments, and receive instruction in the religions of Israel."

Gratz and her teachers had to develop their curricula themselves. Among those who helped Gratz were Sim'ha Peixotto who wrote *Elementary Introduction to the Scriptures* and her sister, Rachel Peixotto Pyke, who wrote a companion book, *Scriptural Questions*. Ellen Phillips and Louisa Hart also helped Gratz develop her school.

The school changed its name in 1858 to the Hebrew Sunday School Society, which combined its religious studies with vocational training, and the original Rebecca Gratz Sewing School opened in April of 1876 with eight teachers and fifty-three students. The Louisa Hart Sewing School opened in 1880, and by 1912 total enrollment for the Society was four thousand students meeting in several branches established throughout Philadelphia.

The 1850s were also a time of other new beginnings for Gratz. Aware that some poor Jewish children were sent to live in non-Jewish orphanages, Gratz thought that that would undermine their ability to obtain a Jewish education. She lobbied the Benevolent Society to establish a Jewish orphanage, and in 1855 the Jewish Foster Home became the first Jewish orphanage in the country, housing Jewish children from both the U.S. and Canada who had become bereft because of poverty or the loss of one or both of their parents. This was a time of large families and women died more frequently in childbirth, leaving some husbands unable to cope without the assistance of neighbors, other family members, or older children to tend the youngest ones.

In 1855, at the age of seventy-four, Gratz became secretary for the Jewish Foster Home, a job she performed in addition to serving on the boards of the Society and the Philadelphia Orphan Asylum and performing her duties as Sunday School superintendent.

Gratz used her considerable skill as a correspondent to counsel her nieces and nephews against slavery and sectionalism, and continued to champion the causes of the organizations she founded until well into her eighties.

In 1869, at the age of eighty-eight, Rebecca Gratz died. She is buried in the cemetery of Mikveh Israel in Philadelphia. The Jewish Foster Home eventually merged with other institutions to become the Philadelphia Association for Jewish Children; the Benevolent Society and Hebrew Sunday School contributed to the community of Philadelphia for 150 years, finally merging with the Talmud Torah Schools of Philadelphia in 1986. Under its new arrangement, coeducational teaching of Jewish studies, first begun by Rebecca Gratz almost two centuries ago, remains a vital link to the future of Jewish education for youth and women.

Sarah Bernhardt

(1844–1923)

There she is, the incarnation of wild emotion which we share with all live things, but which is gathered in us in all complexity and inscrutable fury. She represents the primeval passions of woman, and she is fascinating to an extraordinary degree. I could love such a woman myself, love her to madness; all for the pure wild passion of it. Take care about going to see Bernhardt. Unless you are very sound, do not go. When I think of her now I can still feel the weight hanging in my chest as it hung there for days after I saw her. Her winsome, sweet playful ways; her sad, plaintive little murmurs; her terrible panther cries; and then the awful inarticulate sounds, the little sobs that fairly sear one, and the despair and death; it is too much in one evening.

—D. H. Lawrence, quoted in Arthur Gold and Robert Fizdale,
The Divine Sarah

DURING WORLD WAR II, when the Germans occupied Paris, one of the many vindictive and destructive acts committed by the Nazis was the desecration of a statue erected to memorialize France's greatest actress, Sarah Bernhardt. It was the last of the anti-Semitic attacks Bernhardt had faced throughout her career—when she appeared in Russia and Canada, she was pelted with stones and had anti-Semitic insults hurled at her; journalists and reviewers of her performances took delight in attacking her "vile Jewish habits" and persistently alluded to her "Hebrew blood." Despite such viciousness, Bernhardt triumphed, undimmed, as one of the world's greatest stage stars.

Sarah Bernhardt was the first theatrical superstar, an actress of such renown that she became a cultural icon, as notorious for her off-stage love affairs, unpredictable behavior, and outrageous eccentricities as she was for the intensity and passion of her acting. Bernhardt set the standard against which all the great actresses who followed her came to be measured, defining for all time the essence of the tempestuous, temperamental diva: self-absorbed, self-promoting, and completely captivating. Few actors before or since have created such an indelible legend or provided such a template for dramatic acting.

Sarah Bernhardt's reputation as a great romantic tragedienne had its roots in a background as colorful and dramatic as any of the heroines—or heroes—she played. Born Rosine Bernard in Paris, Bernhardt was the daughter of Youle Bernard, a Dutch-born, Jewish seamstress and courtesan. At the time, many Parisian brothels offered to their clients Jewish and black girls to cater to the exotic tastes of their customers, and Youle Bernard capitalized on her good looks and charm to attract to her salon such luminaries as Alexandre Dumas, père, and the opera composer Gioacchino Rossini. Her daughter, Sarah, was born October 23, 1844. The identity of Sarah's father is uncertain and her birth certificate disappeared, along with many others when the Hôtel de Ville, the Paris city hall, was destroyed by fire during the uprising associated with the Paris Commune of 1871. Candidates for paternity have included a highborn naval officer surnamed Morel and law student Edouard Bernhardt. Sarah would eventually take Bernhardt's surname.

Sarah Bernhardt was educated in convent and boarding schools well apart from her mother's fashionable Paris salon. She was sensitive, high-strung, and given to dramatic outbursts, and her childhood was marked by rebelliousness and bitter loneliness. Although she had been suspended three times from convent school for unruly behavior, she decided to become a nun as an alternative to following in her mother's footsteps. She was persuaded, however, to try a career as an actress instead, when her mother's current lover, the Duc de Morny, secured a place for her in the prestigious conservatoire of the Comédie Française.

Bernhardt's stage debut in 1862 was not encouraging. The most powerful theater critic in Paris noted that she "is a tall attractive young woman with a slender waist and most pleasing face. . . . She carries herself well and pronounces her words with perfect clarity. That is all that can be said for the moment." After critics panned her next two performances, the seventeen-year-old Bernhardt tried to poison herself by drinking liquid rouge. A violent quarrel with a respected actress in the company caused her dismissal, and she was forced to take small parts in lesser Paris theaters. As a contract player for the Odéon Theatre she played roles in works by George Sand, Shakespeare, Molière, and Racine. Her first notable success came in 1869, when she played a male page in *Le Passant,* which was given a command performance before Napoleon III and the Empress Eugénie in the Tuilleries.

During the Franco-Prussian War (1870–1871), Bernhardt refused to abandon besieged Paris and opened a hospital in the Odéon. Following the armistice, she triumphed in an 1872 revival of Victor Hugo's *Ruy Blas,* directed by the author. Her success earned her a return to the Comédie Française, where she attained full stature as an actress with her superb portrayals in Racine's *Phèdre* and in Hugo's *Hernani.* Called the actress with "the golden voice," Bernhardt was praised for the poetic intensity of her dramatic interpretations and her passionate identification with the characters she played. English critic Lytton Strachey once wrote, "To hear the words of Phèdre spoken from the mouth of Bernhardt . . . is to come close to immortality, to plunge shuddering through infinite abysses, and to look, if only for a moment, upon eternal light."

Throughout her career, Bernhardt acted with such intensity that she frequently fainted at the end of a performance, leaving her audience breathless. Mark Twain once observed that "There are five kinds of actresses: bad actresses, fair actresses, good actresses, great actresses—and then there is Sarah Bernhardt." In 1885, a young Sigmund Freud saw Bernhardt act, and he recorded his reaction:

> I can't say anything about the piece itself. . . . But how that Sarah plays! After the first words of her lovely, vibrant voice I felt I had known her for years. Nothing she could have said would have surprised me; I believed at once everything she said. . . . I have never seen a more comical figure than Sarah in the second act, here she appears in a simple dress, and yet one soon stops laughing, for every inch of that little figure lives and bewitches. Then her flattering and imploring and embracing; it is incredible what postures she can assume and how every limb and joint acts with her. A curious being: I can imagine that she needn't be any different in life than on the stage.

Freud would keep a photograph of the actress prominently displayed in his office for years.

Off stage, Bernhardt generated both adoration and controversy. She traveled with, and sometimes slept in, a coffin lined with letters from her lovers (said to exceed a thousand). Her entourage often included a menagerie of exotic pets. From 1874 to 1896 her sculptures were exhibited at the Salon, where, according to biographers Arthur Gold and Robert Fizdale, "they fetched prices high enough to exasperate professional artists and irritate her fellow actors." In 1877 she toured Paris in a hot-air balloon outfitted especially for her and used the experience as the basis for a novel, *In the Clouds*. Hailed as a national treasure, Bernhardt, like the *Mona Lisa*, became a must-see for tourists in Paris. Men fought duels over her; priests railed against her, and it is said that at least one woman killed herself after failing to get a ticket to a Bernhardt performance.

In 1880 Bernhardt embarked on tours of England and America, a move that established her worldwide reputation and made her, in effect, the first international theatrical superstar. She traveled throughout the United States in a private train, the Bernhardt Special, and was continually greeted by crowds eager for a look at her and hopeful of securing an autograph. During her American tour, Bernhardt premiered her most famous role, Marguerite, in *La Dame aux Camélias*. One critic wrote that "Only a beautiful, worldly woman, born and bred in Paris, only a master at transforming prose into poetry could combine restraint, feverish gaiety, and a tragic yearning for love with the infinite cynicism and careless insolence that was the product of a courtesan's life." Bernhardt returned home, however, to a hostile reception. The French felt that she was squandering her great talent abroad and shunned her. She won them back when she unexpectedly appeared on the stage of the Paris Opéra during a benefit performance commemorating the tenth anniversary of the departure of Prussian troops from France, and gave an emotionally powerful spoken rendition of "La Marseillaise."

A French patriot and a supporter of humanitarian causes, Bernhardt stood against the establishment in the 1897 conviction of the Jewish captain Alfred Dreyfus, sentenced to life imprisonment on Devil's Island for treason. What became known as *L'Affaire Dreyfus* split the country between anti-Dreyfusards, who accused all Jews of being traitors to France, and those who were convinced that Dreyfus was a victim of deep-seated anti-Semitic prejudice and military corruption, and had been framed. When the writer Emile Zola published *J'Accuse,* his famous indictment of the Dreyfus affair and of the French establishment, a threatening crowd marched on the author's home shouting, "Death to Zola!" only to be stopped in their tracks when a second-floor window flew open and Bernhardt appeared. She had come to pay her respects and congratulate Zola on his courageous article. The crowd dispersed at the sight of the famous actress, and the next day a newspaper headline read "Bernhardt at Zola's. The Great Actress Is With the Jews Against the Army."

Bernhardt managed several theaters in Paris before leasing the Théâtre des Nations, renaming it the Théâtre Sarah Bernhardt. Here, she revised some of her former successes and created a sensation when, in 1899, she appeared in the title role of *Hamlet.* In 1901 she played Napoleon's son in *L'Aiglon,* which was written for her by Edmond Rostand. Although a knee injury sustained in 1905 led to the amputation of her right leg in 1915, Bernhardt continued to act on stage and in films, becoming one of the first stars of the fledgling medium. When she died in Paris, between six hundred thousand and a million fans lined the streets of her funeral procession. One fan, to soothe the mourners' collective grief at her passing, allegedly declared, "Immortals do not die."

More a comet than a star, Sarah Bernhardt dominated the world stage for over sixty years. The last great actress of the nineteenth century, she became the first great actress of the twentieth century, and few performers before or since have moved audiences as Bernhardt did, or succeeded in such a wide variety of roles. For an actress who never performed any of her parts in anything but French, she moved audiences around the world regardless of their abilities to comprehend her spoken language. For many who saw her on stage and in her few film appearances she was simply, as Oscar Wilde called her, "the Divine Sarah."

Emma Lazarus

(1849–1887)

Not like the brazen giant of Greek fame,
With conquering limbs astride from land to land;
Here at our sea-washed, sunset gates shall stand
A mighty woman with a torch, whose flame
Is the imprisoned lightening, and her name
Mother of Exiles. From her beacon-hand
Glows world-wide welcome; her mild eyes command
The air-bridged harbor that twin cities frame.
"Keep, ancient lands, your storied pomp!" cries she
With silent lips. "Give me your tired, your poor,
Your huddled masses yearning to breathe free,
The wretched refuse of your teeming shore.
Send these, the homeless, tempest-tost to me,
I lift my lamp beside the golden door!"

—Emma Lazarus, "The New Colossus"

IN 1883 NEW YORK politician and fundraiser William Maxwell Evert asked several eminent authors, including Mark Twain, Walt Whitman, and the poet and essayist, Emma Lazarus, to compose original works for a literary auction held to raise money for the pedestal on which the Statue of Liberty would stand. Lazarus, who worked from inspiration and did not feel able to create good poetry on demand, refused to comply with Evert's request until another fundraiser, Constance Cary Harrison, suggested that she consider what the statue would mean to the thousands of immigrants who would see it as they sailed into New York harbor to seek a life of freedom and opportunity in the United States.

Lazarus had recently published articles condemning the persecution of Jews in Russia, and was working to help Jewish immigrants through the auspices of the Hebrew Emigrant Aid Society. She found Harrison's suggestion to be the source of the inspiration she needed. She agreed to submit a poem, and the result was "The New Colossus," the sonnet quoted above, which is engraved upon the pedestal of the Statue of Liberty. It is the work for which she is best known and honored, and its significance cannot be underestimated. However, Emma Lazarus also deserves recognition as one of the most popular authors of her day and for being the first important American writer to create works with an authentic Jewish voice.

Emma Lazarus was born in New York City, the daughter of Moses Lazarus, a prosperous sugar refiner, and Esther Nathan Lazarus. She was the fourth daughter in a family of six girls and a boy. Both parents were descended from distinguished Sephardic families, who had arrived in the New World in the seventeenth century (one of Emma Lazarus's cousins was Supreme Court Justice Benjamin Nathan Cardozo). Emma grew up in New York and Newport, Rhode Island, in an environment of wealth and culture. Educated by private tutors, Emma studied mythology, music, American poetry, European literature, and German, French, and Italian. In the biographical memoir that prefaces Lazarus's collected poems, her sister, Josephine, describes Emma's nature: "She was a born singer; poetry was her natural language, and to write was less effort than to speak, for she was a shy, sensitive child, with strange reserves and reticences, not easily putting herself *en rapport* with those around her. Books were her world from her earliest years; in them she literally lost and found herself."

Lazarus began writing and translating poetry early, and at seventeen her father had her poetry collection, *Poems and Translations: Written Between the Ages of Fourteen and Sixteen,* printed "for private circulation." The following year, the collection was published commercially. Soon afterward, Emma Lazarus met Ralph Waldo Emerson at a social gathering and was drawn to what she described as his "wisdom and goodness." Emerson became Lazarus's mentor; when she published her second, critically acclaimed volume, *Admetus and Other Poems* (1871), she dedicated the title poem to him. Lazarus and Emerson corresponded until Emerson's death in 1882, although their relationship became temporarily strained when Emerson failed to include her poetry in his 1874 anthology, *Parnassus.* The same year Lazarus published her only novel, *Alide: An Episode of Goethe's Life,* which was based on Goethe's autobiographical writings and which was also well received.

During the 1870s she contributed poetry to magazines such as the *Critic,* the *Century,* and *Lippincott's;* and in 1878, she published her only other work of fiction, a story titled "The Eleventh Hour," in *Scribner's* magazine. In 1876 she privately published *The Spagoletto,* a verse drama set in Renaissance Italy, which concerns a nobleman who commits suicide after his beloved daughter takes a lover. Lazarus herself was very attached to her father and became even more emotionally dependent upon him after the death of her mother in 1874; it has been suggested by her biographer, Heinrich Jacob, that *The Spagoletto* reflects some of her conflicted emotions regarding their relationship.

Although Lazarus's uncle was a rabbi and the family belonged to the Congregation Shearith Israel, the oldest synagogue in New York, Emma Lazarus, according to her sister, Josephine, received no "positive or effective religious training" at home and only attended services during her childhood. Drawn to the sort of transcendental love of nature that characterized the works of Emerson, Thoreau, and Whitman, Lazarus, in an 1877 letter, wrote that while her "interest and sympathies" were with the Jews, "my religious convictions (if such they can be called) and the circumstances of my life have led me somewhat apart from our people."

The earliest expression of Jewish consciousness in Lazarus's writing appears in *Admetus and Other Poems,* which includes the poem "In the Jewish Synagogue in Newport." As critic Edward Wagenknecht observes, "In her late essay on Longfellow, she objects to his poem, 'The Jewish Cemetery at Newport,' because, though tenderly sympathetic, it sees no future for the Jewish people as a people, but her own earliest poem on a Jewish subject, 'In the Jewish Synagogue in Newport,' expressed precisely the same point of view." However, Lazarus did study, in German, the Hebrew poetry of Medieval Spain and published several English translations in the *Jewish Messenger.* In 1881 she published a highly respected translation of Heinrich Heine's poems and ballads, some of which were on Jewish themes. Fascinated by Heine, who had been born a Jew but baptized and educated as a Catholic, Lazarus would later publish an essay on him in which she explored his "fatal and irreconcilable dualism" and expressed admiration for his ability to understand this aspect of his nature.

Lazarus's attitude toward Judaism and Jews changed dramatically in 1881–1882, after the assassination of Czar Alexander II of Russia resulted in a series of pogroms against Russian Jews and generated a wave of immigration to the United States. In addition to her work with the Hebrew Emigrant Aid Society, which included meeting Eastern European immigrants on Ward's Island, she helped to establish the Hebrew Technical Institute, as well as agricultural communities for newly arrived Jewish immigrants.

Lazarus's writing also reflected her new sense of commitment and identity. Her poem, "The Banner of the Jew," which appeared in the June 3, 1882, edition of the *Critic,* was an invocation to oppressed Jews worldwide to "Recall today / The glorious Maccabean rage" and to "Strike! for the brave revere the brave!" The same year, her blank-verse play, *The Dance to Death,* was first published in the *American Hebrew* weekly magazine. The play celebrates the heroism and faith of fourteenth-century German Jews who were wrongly accused of causing the Black Death and murdered. Lazarus dedicated *The Dance to Death* to George Eliot, who had explored Jewish cultural identity in her novel, *Daniel Deronda.* Lazarus wrote that Eliot, "did most among the artists of our day toward elevating and ennobling the spirit of Jewish nationality." Later that year, *The Dance to Death,* together with Lazarus's translations of several ancient Hebrew poems, were reissued in an inexpensive book titled *Songs of a Semite: The Dance to Death and Other Poems,* which proved to be a popular success.

Lazarus also published a number of essays on the subject of Judaism, Jews, and anti-Semitism. In 1882 she wrote a strong rebuttal to a *Century* article rationalizing the Russian pogroms in which she defended Jews and Judaism and sharply criticized Christianity for tolerating and enabling the centuries-long persecution of the Jews. She became a regular contributor to the *American Hebrew,* for which she wrote such pieces as "Judaism: the Connecting Link Between Science and Religion" (1882), "An Epistle to the Hebrews" (1882–1883), "Cruel Bigotry" (1883), and "The Last National Revolt of the Jews." In "An Epistle to the Hebrews," a series of fifteen open letters that appeared between November 1882 and February 1883, Lazarus anticipated the modern Zionist movement by a decade by advocating a Jewish homeland in what was then Palestine. The highly assimilated Lazarus family did not welcome the new emphasis on Jewish themes and issues in Emma's work. Her youngest sister, Annie, a Catholic convert, characterized much of her writing as "sectarian propaganda" rather than literature.

In the summer of 1883 Lazarus visited England and France, where she met Jewish leaders and such personages as Robert Browning, Thomas Huxley, and William Morris, whose socialism she defended in an essay titled "A Day in Surrey with William Morris."

After Moses Lazarus's fatal illness and death in 1885, Emma was plunged into a deep depression, and, according to her sister, Josephine, "she decided to go abroad again as the best means of regaining composure and strength." By the time she returned to New York in 1887 she was seriously ill with cancer. She died on November 19, and was buried in the family plot at Beth Olom Fields Cemetery in Brooklyn. One of her last published works was the prose poem, "By the Waters of Babylon," which traces Jewish exiles through history and ends with an appeal for acceptance of Eastern European Jewish immigrants—the new exiles. After her death, the *American Hebrew* published the "Emma Lazarus Memorial Number," and in 1888, her sisters Annie and Mary published *The Poems of Emma Lazarus, I and II.* Volume I contains Josephine Lazarus's biographical account, which also appeared in the *Century.*

Emma Lazarus is read today primarily by scholars interested in her life as a Jewish-American woman writer of the Victorian age. As Francine Klagsbrun observes in *Emma Lazarus in Her World,* Lazarus's work "reflects the discomfort of a woman who was not totally at home in the Christian world she inhabited but had not quite found her footing in the Jewish one either. It has the feel of outsideness, of a writer who held herself too much apart, too much above the people she sought to defend and counsel." The tension of living in two worlds would be reflected later in the works of more widely read authors such as Henry Roth, Saul Bellow, and Philip Roth. Lazarus's fame chiefly rests on "The New Colossus," in which she acknowledges yet another diaspora, while at the same time holding out an invitation born of hope that the New World will offer Jewish immigrants sanctuary from the deeply anti-Semitic Old World they had left behind.

Hannah Greenebaum Solomon

(1858–1942)

Who is this new woman? . . . She is the woman who dares to go into the world and do what her convictions demand.
— Hannah Greenebaum Solomon, founder of the
National Council of Jewish Women

HANNAH GREENEBAUM SOLOMON lived a life that was touched with great irony. She grew up in a kosher home with parents who founded Chicago's first Reform temple. She became one of the most outstanding civic leaders of her time when a woman's place was in the home. And, she was a mother, married to a man who not only accepted her activities outside the home, but also was her greatest champion.

Hannah was born seven years before the Civil War, in 1858, the fourth of ten children to Sarah (Spiegel) and Michael Greenebaum. Her father was a prosperous hardware store owner and her mother kept house, one that always welcomed friends, family, and guests. Sarah helped begin Chicago's first Jewish Ladies Sewing Society, which provided clothing for the poor, usually handmade by its members. Michael championed the rights of slaves, and founded the Zion Literary Society.

Michael Greenbaum had immigrated to the United States in 1847 at age twenty with every intention of returning to his native Germany. Soon realizing what opportunities were here, he stayed, bringing over his siblings as he could.

During the great Chicago fire of 1871, when Hannah was just thirteen, the Jewish community was nearly destroyed, yet ironically the Greenebaum home stood untouched. Her father was a volunteer fireman. Her parents sheltered families who had lost their homes for days on end until permanent homes were made available.

Although they hired a Shabbos goy (a.k.a. shamas) to light fires and do other tasks avoided on the Sabbath, Greenebaum thought that the Jewish Sabbath should be consecrated on Sunday, his idea of blending in with his newly adopted community versus honoring the tradition of his Jewish ancestors. His campaign failed, and his daughter Hannah, in perhaps her only unpopular gesture, picked up the campaign later on.

Like the young women of her day, Hannah learned piano (with Carl Wolfsohn), studied Hebrew and German at her temple school, went to public grade school, and attended West Division High School, then Chicago's only public high school. She was twenty-one when she married clothing merchant Henry Solomon, easily settling into a life of wife, mother of three children, and community volunteer.

Hannah and her sister Henrietta (Mrs. Henry) Frank became the first Jewish members of the Chicago Women's Club in 1876. The group was founded in 1875 as a literary group, although it also made practical contributions to the community. Henrietta presided over the group from 1884 to 1885.

She saw no contradictions in her roles as volunteer and activist with her position of wife and mother; Solomon compartmentalized her work, believing her activities for children and women were a natural extension of her religious obligations to contribute to her community. Her involvement in both secular and Jewish life honed her organizational skills, and her fellow volunteers named her chair of the Jewish Women's Committee.

The committee met in 1890 in anticipation of the 1893 World's Columbian Exposition in Chicago. The four-day Congress of Jewish Women was scheduled to meet in the ubiquitous Woman's Building, but the congress leaders, including Solomon, would have no part of that. They were not there to fetch coffee, but to discuss ideas and make plans for the future. Instead, they convened at the World Parliament of Religions at the Exposition. It was the first nonsocial gathering of female Jews in American Jewish history.

The event drew important leaders from all over the country, and set the tone for what American Jewish women could do. Orator and Sunday school administrator Ray Frank Littman, the first woman since Deborah to deliver a sermon from a pulpit during the Days of Awe, offered the opening prayer.

Henrietta Szold addressed the World Parliament of Religions twice during the Exposition. She was then editorial secretary of the Jewish Publication Society of America, and a pioneer in the concept of night school for teaching English as a second language to immigrants. (It was years before she began another famous Jewish women's group, Hadassah.)

At Solomon's urging, the congress became a permanent organization, and she was unanimously elected president of the group, thereafter known as the National Council of Jewish Women (NCJW). The goals of the original ninety-three members were religious, philanthropic, and educational. Solomon and others believed that educating women about Judaism was critical, and they designed "study circles," which informed women of both the tenets and the practice of their religion. They felt it was the responsibility of women to teach their children about Judaism.

Solomon warned the members of this club that some would be criticized for neglecting their husbands or children. As evidence of her own "radical" behavior, she spoke publicly, becoming the first woman to speak from several synagogue bimas around the country.

She also assisted the Chicago Woman's Club, which helped to develop the framework for the Cook County juvenile court in 1899. Solomon helped found the Bureau of Personal Service to serve the

Jewish immigrants in Chicago's seventh ward. (She chaired the City Ward Leaders' Committee.)

The year 1899 marked a personal tragedy, when her son Herbert died. This event gave greater weight to her work with the Bureau, which provided family counseling; supervised loan programs; improved housing conditions; and served as a conduit that linked immigrants to the proper social service agencies. It later became part of the Associated Jewish Charities coordinating Jewish philanthropies, with Solomon as the only woman sitting on its executive board.

Within her social services network, she was deeply involved in the pioneer settlement house movement working with Jane Addams of Hull House, the Maxwell Street Settlement, and the Chicago Civic Federation.

The Chicago NCJW created a Sabbath school for girls, eventually adopted by Temple Sinai's education program. All of these activities, philanthropy, education, and social service, were considered by Solomon to be part of her religious duties.

In other secular activities, Solomon worked with the Illinois Industrial School for Girls, Illinois Federation of Women's Clubs, and was charged by the Women's City Club to investigate the city's waste disposal system, part of the complex set of problems plaguing the city at a time of increasing immigration to already over-crowded areas. Interestingly, Solomon always dressed the part of the well-heeled matron—handkerchief cotton and parasol in summer, sturdier wool in winter—and was never seen without her hair and clothing impeccably done.

She strongly supported women's suffrage, although the NCJW had no formal position, and she was a delegate to the 1904 International Council for Women conference in Berlin, where she represented The Council of Women of the United States along with Susan B. Anthony and May Wright Sewall.

As a Reform Jew, Solomon supported a movement to change the Saturday Sabbath to Sunday, as her father had attempted earlier. She was challenged by the membership and during the debate said her now-famous line, "I do consecrate the Sabbath. I consecrate every day in the week." Not dissuaded, the membership attempted to oust her from the presidency, but she remained in office until 1905.

Her husband Henry died in 1913, leaving their remaining children, Helen and Frank, to manage the family business, and Solomon unencumbered to pursue the volunteer activities that kept her going from dawn to night, activities viewed with surprising humor by her family.

In 1920, in *American Hebrew,* she wrote that ". . . the last thirty years have been devoted to proof of our boast that woman's sphere is the whole wide world, without limit . . ."

By 1925, the NCJW had more than 50,000 members, and its New York chapter played a vital role in aiding new arrivals at Ellis Island, particularly women. The organization was the first Jewish women's group to establish Sabbath schools in communities without synagogues; provided advocates for children in court proceedings; sponsored adult study circles to promote learning and leadership; and offered vocational training for girls and women.

Through her continued involvement in her community, public schools incorporated a penny lunch program, the first probation officers for juvenile delinquents were attached to the courts, and she helped coordinate war efforts for World War I through the Women's Division of the Illinois State Council of Defense. She helped crystallize the issues of the day, from public health insurance and low-cost housing to eradicating slums and improving child labor laws. Ironically, these issues remain unresolved, and are the crux of the work being performed by today's NCJW.

Solomon collected her articles and speeches into *A Sheaf of Leaves,* which was published in 1911, and wrote her autobiography, *Fabric of My Life,* which was published posthumously in 1946. Hannah Greenebaum Solomon died during the middle of World War II, in 1942, at age eighty-five in Chicago. Her funeral was conducted at her childhood synagogue, Temple Sinai, and she is buried in Graceland Cemetery.

Solomon's legacy is being carried out daily by the dedicated members of the National Council of Jewish Women. Constantly updating its programs to meet the demands of the day, it developed the Ship-A-Box program of toys and educational materials for the youngest survivors of the Holocaust and to subsequent generations of Israeli children. The program lasted for fifty years. The council also funds training of teachers at Hebrew University in Israel, trains social workers and educators for work with Holocaust survivors, and organized the first nationwide "golden age" programs for recreation and friendship among senior citizens.

The NCJW served as an accredited nongovernmental observer to the United Nations; helped organize the first White House Conference on Aging; launched the Senior Service Corps, adapted by the U.S. government for its Retired Senior Volunteer Program (RSVP); and published the first nationwide surveys of day care facilities and studies for foster children.

Henrietta Szold

(1860–1945)

Save the Child! . . . The women of the world cannot but recognize that the cause of the Jewish child is their cause . . . [women] are the natural protectors of childhood . . . the guardians of the generations . . .
— Henrietta Szold, in remarks to the membership of
Hadassah about Youth Aliyah, 1942

AMERICAN-BORN HENRIETTA Szold was a superbly organized, scholarly woman, a pacifist, teacher, writer, and world-renowned leader, who would have given up everything for a child of her own. Yet, in the deepest sense, she gave the gift of life to more than two hundred thousand children through her efforts with Youth Aliyah.

Because of her dedication and personal attention, these children won the blessings of safety from the nightmare of the Holocaust, and from hunger and the abandonment of war. Because of her leadership with Hadassah and its many long-range programs, she helped to establish a social welfare and medical infrastructure in Palestine, fulfilling her personal vision for Zionism.

In Henrietta's day, Israel was still called Palestine, and she envisioned a country where both Jews and Arabs could live together in peace as the cousins she believed them to be. She was one of the progressive-thinking intellectuals from the early 1900s to 1930s, who included philosopher Martin Buber, Rabbi Judah Magnes of Temple Emmanu-El, Justice Louis Brandeis, and others who championed Zionism.

As part of the Brith Shalom and Ibud groups of European, British, and American intellectuals, she believed that Palestine could be a binational, Arab-Jewish state. Even when walking the streets of Jerusalem, stoned by young Arab boys, she held onto this belief. "There is nothing but Zionism . . . to save us," she told the Zionist Organization of America (ZOA).

Born in Baltimore in 1860, she was the eldest child of Rabbi Benjamin and Sophie (Schaar) Szold, Hungarian Jews who had emigrated in 1859 so that Rabbi Szold could lead Congregation Ohem Shalom (lover of peace). He had studied in Vienna and participated in the failed democratic revolution of 1848. As a teacher, he met his future wife, Sophie, when he tutored her in her family home. The couple had four other daughters.

Conservative Jews, the lively Szolds spoke German at home (not Hungarian), and her father taught Henrietta Hebrew and French. While barely a teenager, she herself taught Hebrew, Jewish history, and the Bible at her father's synagogue. She was the valedictorian of her Western Female High School in 1877 and her high marks remain uncontested. She taught at Western for a while, and then taught for fifteen years at Miss Adams' English and French School for Girls. Her subjects included languages (English, German, French, and Latin), mathematics, history, physiology, and botany, which was fostered by her personal passion for flowers, and nurtured by her mother's gardening and membership in the Baltimore Botany Club.

She read Charles Dickens and George Eliot and was a lifelong member of the International Longfellow Society from 1916 on—part of her enjoyment and appreciation of the literary culture of her time, particularly novels and poetry.

Rabbi Szold was a leader in the Baltimore Association for the Education and Moral Improvement of the Colored People in an era in which public sales of slaves were as common in Baltimore as they were in Atlanta. As a testament of his support for that association, he walked behind its membership in Abraham Lincoln's funeral cortege.

His influence for community involvement had a great impact, and Henrietta found it natural to convince the Isaac Baer Levinsohn Literary Society (of Hebrew linguists known as Hebraists) to start an adult night school so that the flood of immigrating Russian Jews could be taught English, American history, and the skills and cultural information necessary for a smooth adjustment to their new country. It was one of the first such programs in the country.

Henrietta hired the teachers, developed the curriculum, and raised the funds to provide supplies and books. It began with thirty pupils in November 1889, and within a decade, served five thousand people, necessitating the city to officially take over and manage the program. Although it served Christians and Jews, Henrietta was deeply affected to hear stories of anti-Semitism experienced by many of these immigrants. These fueled her feelings of Zionism and she joined one of the first Zionist groups in the country, Hebras Zion (Zionist Association of Baltimore). She continued her work with Russian immigrants from 1889 to 1893 when she left to join the Jewish Publication Society as its executive secretary. (The JPS, founded in 1888, is the oldest American publisher of Jewish literature.)

When her father died in 1902, Henrietta and her mother moved to New York City, where she intended to edit his many papers. She was admitted to the Jewish Theological Seminary on the condition that she would "not pursue rabbinical studies," but instead would pursue studies related only to her editing work. The seminary, and the intellectual climate of New York, were ripe to nurture her growing interest in Zionism, and she participated in a number of "study circles," salons of culture and intellectual debate that were popular at the turn of the century. In 1907, one of these was the Hadassah study circle, which would have a pivotal role in her life in just a few years.

She wrote a regular column for the *Jewish Messenger* of New York City, called "Baltimore Letter," using the pseudonym, Shulamith. It was in these columns that she sharpened her analysis of current events and Jewish-American culture. The *London Jewish Chronicle* referred to her as a "leading Jewish essayist in America."

Her major contributions to the JPS were her incisive editing skills, which she applied to the *American Jewish Year Book* with Cyrus Adler. Because of her fluency in Hebrew, German, and English, she was called upon to translate a number of works from 1900 to 1907, including the two-volume *Ethics of Judaism* by Moritz Lazarus, *History of the Jews* by Heinrich Graetz, *The Renascence of Hebrew Literature* by Nahum Slouschz, and *Jewish History: An Essay in the Philosophy of History* by Simon Dubnow. The Schiff Library of Jewish Classics began during her time at JPS, and its Bible translation project evolved into the publication of the Jewish *Revised Standard Version*.

While working on another book, *The Legends of the Jews* written by seminary professor Louis Ginsburg, Henrietta experienced her first love. At age forty-nine, she had no intimate knowledge of male-female relationships. She had been her father's confidante and heir apparent to his scholarship, and had, literally, worked continuously as a teacher and writer for more than thirty years without pause. Although three of her surviving sisters were married, she apparently had not considered that path herself although she obviously had met and enjoyed many of the best minds of the time at study circles, at JPS, and through her family.

Her feelings for Ginsburg were expressed but not reciprocated. He left to visit Berlin, and he married an eighteen-year-old woman he met there after knowing her a brief time. Ginsburg was more than ten years younger than Henrietta (some say fifteen), and he most likely viewed their association more as a fruitful working collaboration than a romantic relationship. Letters to her revealed his insensitivity to the depth of her feelings, and the experience left her devastated. Although she received several marriage proposals later in life, she never recovered from this rejection. Years later, when his wife died, Ginsburg married one of Henrietta's cousins.

Like so many people bereaved in such a manner, she decided to take a trip. With her mother as a companion, she visited Palestine where she saw beauty and history—and the crushing catastrophes of disease and inadequate medical facilities. Trachoma (chronic contagious conjunctivitis) was blinding children at a dreadful rate, and Szold believed that improved standards of sanitation and providing medical care could prevent the disease from spreading.

She returned to America in 1910, to lay the groundwork for an organization that would meet the needs of all the people of Palestine. On February 24, 1912, thirty-eight women of the Hadassah study circle met at Temple Emmanu-El and pledged to dedicate themselves to the cause of Zionism with the newly named Hadassah Chapter of the National Daughters of Zion. The seven signers of the original invitation for membership included Szold, Mathilde Schechter, Emma Leon Gottheil, Rosalie Solomon Phillips, Sophia Berger, Lotta Levensohn, and Gloria Goldsmith, all accomplished, educated, and socially prominent American-born women in New York City.

In 1913, they sent their benefactors, Nathan Straus and his wife, along with nurses Rose Kaplan and Rachel (Rae) Landy, to Jerusalem to establish the Hadassah's nurses settlement, a program based on the settlement houses of Jane Addams and Lillian D. Wald.

At their first convention in June 19, 1914, the group renamed itself Hadassah and renewed their pledge to establish Jewish institutions and enterprises in Palestine, and to foster Zionist ideals in America. Henrietta Szold was elected its first president, and she began its powerful campaign to live up to its motto of Aruchat Bat Amik, "healing the daughter of my people" (after Jeremiah 8:19–23: "Is the Lord not in Zion? . . . is there no physician there? When then is not the health of the daughter of my people recovered?").

Also in 1914, Louis D. Brandeis (then Supreme Court Justice) appointed Szold to direct the American Zionist Medical Unit for Palestine, and in 1918 with funding of $250,000 she arranged for forty-four doctors, nurses, and administrators to go to Palestine.

Justice Brandeis, along with Judge Julian W. Mack and other Zionist leaders, recognized Szold's gift of leadership and arranged a life stipend for her after her mother died in 1916. This enabled her to meet her day-to-day needs and fully dedicate herself to the task ahead. She resigned from the JPS, and Zionism became her vocation for the rest of her life.

The American Zionists blended into the Zionist Organization of

America and Szold chaired the committee for educational work. Returning to Palestine in February 1920, she wore many hats: director of the medical unit, director of the nurses' training school, and director of health work in Jewish schools. In 1934, just fourteen years after the establishment of Hadassah, a key part of their mission was realized: the building of the Rothschild-Hadassah University Hospital on Mount Scopus.

After almost four years she returned to the U.S. and continued her work with Hadassah and the World Zionist Organization. She returned to Palestine as minister of health and education and was elected to the National Council of Jews in Palestine in 1930. She was then seventy years old.

The honors and recognition were beginning, and Szold was presented with the honorary Doctor of Hebrew Letters from the Jewish Institute of Religion, the first woman to receive such an honor.

Again, she planned to return to the U.S., but the rumors of Nazi cruelties were proven an all-too-vivid reality. Recha Freier of Berlin developed a plan for teenagers fifteen to seventeen years old to live on communal settlements in Palestine, thus escaping almost certain death. Under the name Youth Aliyah, Szold put her magical organizational touch to the task and in 1934, she stood on the pier at Haifa and greeted the first group of boys. By 1939, after personally greeting as many caravans as possible, Szold had arranged for Youth Aliyah to bring sixty-two hundred refugee children to Palestine.

Szold went to Germany herself in 1937 to further coordinate the work of Youth Aliyah, but she encountered resistance from the British government in getting permission to bring more children to Palestine. Although exceptionally tolerant, she was not naive. She believed that the Balfour Declaration, which established the possibility of Israel, was betrayed by the government of Great Britain and that it deliberately tried to disrupt efforts for peace between Arab and Jew. Still, she clung to her belief in the "strength of the remnant of Israel even if the remnant is small."

Working with her associate, a German émigré named Hans Beyth, she helped children from Poland and all over Eastern Europe achieve freedom through Youth Aliyah in 1943 and 1944. Beyth was later killed by Arab fighting in the area while on his way to conduct Youth Aliyah business.

On her eightieth birthday, addressing a group of children, she advised them to "live wisely and energetically" to "accomplish noble acts and think great thoughts." No better epitaph could be written for this woman. The mother of the Jewish settlement in Palestine devoted her life to children, to attempting mutual understanding and peace between Arabs and Jews, and to championing the cause of Zionism.

In 1944, she developed pneumonia and nearly bedridden, she died on February 13, 1945, at Hadassah Hebrew University Hospital. She was buried in the Jewish Cemetery on the Mount of Olives while a boy from Youth Aliyah recited Kaddish for this "Mother of Youth Aliyah," just as she had recited it for both her parents.

Thousands mourned her death, but her legacy lives on. Her scholarship, her writing, her zeal for Zionism could not have foretold how much of a part she would play in giving health, life, and education to hundreds of thousands of people in a land now called Israel. Her innate genius to lead—by meeting the obvious needs—helped to establish one of the most effective organizations in the world.

Applying her sympathy and practical skills, still fresh and wise in her late seventies, she made a scheme to save children a working reality. By 1948, at the close of the war, thirty thousand children had arrived in Israel. The number has risen to more than two hundred thousand since then. By 1967, one out of every ten Israelis under the age of fifty had arrived there from Eastern and Western Europe, Africa, and other countries, through the efforts of Youth Aliyah.

In 1940 she had made known her wishes for a research center for the problems of children. It was begun in honor of her eightieth birthday and renamed Mosad Szold in 1945, after her death.

On April 13, 1948, prior to the official founding of the State of Israel, Arabs killed seventy-five nurses, doctors, and technicians traveling in a caravan to Mount Scopus. Hadassah began building a medical center in Jerusalem for the second time.

Hadassah has more than three hundred fifty thousand members, is the largest Jewish organization in the U.S., and now includes a men's division. Its accomplishments in Israel are legendary: funding for hospitals and research units in neurology and ophthalmology, and for medical research centers that accomplished the first artificial laboratory cultivation of the leprosy microorganism and identified the genetic disorder mucolipidosis IV, found in some children of Ashkenazic Jews. It has opened schools and colleges; operated trauma units to deal with terrorist incidents and accidents; and continues to build and sustain the infrastructure for social welfare and modern medicine that Szold began to organize more than ninety years ago.

Lillian D. Wald

(1867–1940)

Over broken asphalt, over dirty mattresses and heaps of refuse we went. . . .
There were two rooms and a family of seven [sharing] their quarters with
boarders. . . . [I felt] ashamed of being a part of society that permitted such
conditions to exist. . . . What I had seen had shown me where my path lay.
  —Lillian D. Wald, writing in 1893 of her introduction to
  the squalor of Manhattan's Lower East Side

As a LITTLE girl, Lillian Wald was blessed with a prosperous and loving family, lived in a home full of music, books, and beauty, and enjoyed the camaraderie of sister Julia, and brothers Alfred and Gus. She had pretty clothes, a clean bed, and parents who appreciated education. They were Max D. Wald and Minnie Schwarz, whose families had emigrated from Poland and Germany after the Revolution of 1848.

Lillian was born in Cincinnati, Ohio, and raised in Rochester, New York, where her father ran an optical supplies business. The harshest event of her childhood was the death of her brother Alfred, who accidentally drowned in 1885. As devastating as that was, Lillian was sheltered from the ravages of the tailors' disease (tuberculosis), or the fatigue from continuous hunger that marred the lives of so many in her day.

She knew German, French, and Latin from her studies at Miss Cruttendeen's English-French Boarding School in Rochester and was an excellent student of math and art. She was unaware that others her age were no longer in school, but working twelve to fourteen hours a day in factories for pennies.

Lillian was disappointed that her age, sixteen, prevented her from admission to Vassar College, and that left her floundering about her future. Devoted to her sister Julia, who was now married and pregnant, Lillian enjoyed learning the skills of the nurse Julia had hired, and believed she had found her calling. Little did she know the paths she would travel as a nurse.

Enrolling in New York Hospital's Training School in 1889, she was graduated in 1891. She took her first job at the New York Juvenile Asylum, an orphanage housing one thousand children, ages five to eighteen, crammed into close quarters with not enough nurses to tend to them. Lillian was appalled at the institution's method of care, and she knew there must be a better way. She enrolled in the Women's Medical College in 1892, bent on becoming a physician, but a chance volunteer experience changed her life forever.

Wald was asked to teach hygiene and home care to immigrant women at the Louis Technical School at 265 Henry Street. Watching Lillian nurse others, a young girl took her by the hand and to her own apartment. There, lying on an unkempt mattress, was the girl's mother, gravely ill. Wald tended to the woman, one of thousands who would be touched by her nursing skills and social activism.

Her first partner in this effort was former classmate Mary Brewster, a descendent of the Puritan Elder Brewster who escaped religious tyranny on the *Mayflower*. The two decided that to really make a difference, they had to live where their clients lived, so they moved into a settlement house on Rivington Street where they established the

Visiting Nurses Service in 1893. The two had visited more than 125 families by January of 1894 and served many others at their Rivington Street quarters.

They enlisted college graduates and coworkers to teach English, art, music, history and economics, while Brewster and Wald, walking door to door, advised families about hygiene and nursed the sick, sending only the most seriously ill to hospitals for further care.

Although living apart from her family, she reached out to them and others of the German-Jewish elite to help her support the program. Her greatest benefactor was Jacob H. Schiff, grandfather of Dorothy Schiff. He first learned about Wald's work through his mother-in-law, Betty (Mrs. Solomon Loeb), who funded East Side nursing classes. Mrs. Loeb encouraged Schiff to support the women's move to a six-story building on Jefferson Street, which they called Nurses Settlement. The two women were approached by other relief agencies to join them, but they maintained their independence.

Schiff was hardly an absentee or uninformed supporter. Wald provided him with regular reports of the wretched living conditions of families where parents, and sometimes children, worked twelve to fourteen hours a day, and yet were barely able to survive. Aware of their results, and the need for a larger, permanent facility, in 1895 he bought the building at 265 Henry Street, where Wald had taught at the Nurses Settlement.

Schiff died in September 1920, ending that particular support for Wald's work, but by then she had extended her support contacts throughout the city and the country. Brewster, too, had died, but Wald, with her considerable charm and tireless energy, had surrounded herself with outstanding supporters and great thinkers of the day, and with a continually growing corps of dedicated nursing staff.

Organizing home nursing care, Wald also saw the need to elevate the profession, and coined the term "public health nurse" for those women who worked with her and others in the communities outside of hospitals. Their goals were both preventive care, through education, and hands-on health care, usually for fees based on the patients' ability to pay. (Wald never turned away anyone for lack of funds.)

In an effort to involve more people in her project, Wald lectured to prospective nurses, students at Columbia University's Teachers College in 1899, and found a wealthy patron to underwrite initial efforts of the university's new Department of Nursing and Health in 1910.

In just two years, the impact of educating more nurses was considerable. Professional standards with the National Organization of Public Health Nurses (NOPN) was started, with Wald as its first president.

The Settlement House also grew and its services became well known. More than forty-five hundred patients had visited the eighteen district nursing service centers by 1903, and the more gravely ill were housed in convalescent homes on the Hudson River. Summer field trips gave children a break from the city to visit the Settlement-owned farm in Westchester County. By 1913, it had seven houses on Henry Street, two branches, seven country homes for the R&R of families and children, ninety-two nurses who made two hundred thousand calls to homes each year, and three thousand people enrolled in clubs and classes. The branches expanded the Settlement's services to reach African Americans, Italians, and Hungarians. The Stillman House branch (later known as Lincoln House) served the African-American community, part of Wald's dictum to offer its services to all. By 1919, one hundred and one volunteers helped thirty-seven residents, and by 1932, there were twenty centers.

Despite a hectic schedule, Wald managed to pen her autobiography, *The House on Henry Street,* in 1915, which was an anecdotal retelling of the birth and growth of her Settlement House.

Nursing and social work were not enough. Wald was out to change her world. She joined the Outdoor Recreation League to raise funds for the improvement of Seward Park, which became the first municipal playground in New York City.

She campaigned the New York City Board of Education to hire Elizabeth Farrell to teach special education classes for children with physical handicaps and learning disabilities. They did so in 1900.

In 1902, Wald succeeded in getting Lina L. Rogers, a Henry Street nurse, hired as New York City's first public school nurse. In turn, Ms. Rogers led the New York City Board of Health to establish the first public school nursing program in the U.S. In her first month, Rogers treated 893 students, made 137 home visits, and helped twenty-five children recover sufficiently to return to school. The Board of Health soon hired its first twelve school nurses.

Still, there was more to be done for the schools, she believed, and in 1908, she rallied support for a school lunch program for every child in the New York public education system.

She well appreciated her own upbringing and believed that socializing was as important to the health of a community as good nursing care. In 1904, Henry Street built Clinton Hall, a public meeting and social space that was used by four to five hundred thousand people a year as a place to meet and socialize. The hall provided vocational training for boys and girls, a library and study, and a savings bank.

Sensitive to the joys and importance of theater, art, and dance, and with the support of Irene and Alice Lewisohn, Settlement House added the Neighborhood Playhouse where Ellen Terry read Shakespeare and Maude Adams presented *Peter Pan*. Yvette Guilbert acted in French plays and Mrs. LeMoyne read Robert Browning's poetry. Wald believed that inspiring a child's imagination was of paramount importance.

Wald's work also touched workers in corporate headquarters. In 1909, Henry Street and Metropolitan Life became partners in an effort to provide quality health care to employed workers, encouraging hundreds of other insurance companies to duplicate these efforts.

Wald became acquainted with Jane Addams, founder of Hull House in Chicago, and relied throughout her career on Addams's advice and counsel. They became friends, sometimes traveling together. Addams also introduced her to the dynamic Florence Kelley, a graduate of Cornell University and the University of Zurich, where she had earned a law degree.

While in Chicago, Kelley was a special investigator of child labor conditions and was instrumental in improving the conditions of workers there. In 1899 Florence Kelley became general secretary of the National Consumers' League, which Wald had helped to form, and together they championed the need for a minimum wage and limits on the work week for children and women.

In 1904, Florence Kelley and Lillian Wald founded the National Child Labor Committee and presented the idea of a federal Children's Bureau to President Theodore Roosevelt in 1905. Despite their letter-writing campaign and appearances before Congress, the bureau did not come into being until 1912, when President William Howard Taft signed it into law. As a result of her participation in the establishment of the Children's Bureau, Wald was awarded the Gold Medal of the National Institute of Social Sciences that same year.

Florence Kelley was also a part of the original meetings at Henry Street Settlement House with Henry Moskowitz, Mary Ovington, and Wald, involving the National Negro Conference that evolved into the National Association for the Advancement of Colored People. Wald also joined with the NAACP's protest of the 1915 release of D. W. Griffith's *Birth of a Nation,* in which the Ku Klux Klan was celebrated. Many leaders and progressive thinkers of the day, from Josephine Lowell, who helped found the Consumers' League, to Jacob Riis and Lincoln Steffens, were among the supporters of Wald's work and often were involved with Settlement House issues.

Wald took a six-month tour of Hawaii, Japan, China, and Russia in 1910, during which she spoke about her ideas and methods and learned more about other cultures. When she returned, she lent her support to strikers, emphasizing the need for safer working conditions, and defended workers' rights as a member of President Woodrow Wilson's Industrial Conference.

A pacifist all her life, she marched down Fifth Avenue in a women's peace parade that drew fifteen hundred women and joined the Women's Peace Party. She believed that war threatened social programs and urged a "civilized relationship between nations"; and, in 1915, she served the American Union Against Militarism (AUAM) as president.

Her anti-militarist position cost Henry Street some of its funding, but when the U.S. entered WWI, she backed down from her position to offer space at Settlement House for the Red Cross and Food Council drives, as well as the New York City office of the Children's Bureau Baby Saving Campaign. She remained, however, strongly affiliated with the Foreign Policy Organization and the American Civil Liberties Union, the offsprings of the AUAM.

When the Spanish influenza epidemic broke out in 1918, her nurses tended to five hundred cases over four days, with shifts day and night sent out to care for the ill. A call for volunteers brought in hundreds of people to tend to those felled by the devastating flu.

Even though the Wald family attended Berith Kodesh, a Reform Temple, the children received no formal Jewish training. So, as an adult, Lillian was not a practicing Jew—although most of her early nursing and social work was done for immigrant Jews. She believed it important that Henry Street make no effort to impose any religious convictions on the members attending the classes or clubs.

Wald was a member of the Ethical Culture Society begun by Felix Adler, and agreed with the idea of an evolution of organized religion to a code of ethical precepts, which the Society proposed. In her idea of the fundamental oneness of humanity, she despaired against the Americanization of immigrants, believing that their culture, traditions, arts, and ideas were important for America. About the growing anti-Semitism in 1936, she said, "wrong inflicted upon anyone is a wrong done to all."

By 1925, the long hours and personal neglect began to show. She had suffered from shingles and several incidents with influenza that caused heart problems. In 1933, she suffered a debilitating cerebral hemorrhage. She retired to her Westport, Connecticut home where, in between visits from friends, she wrote her second book, *Windows on Henry Street*, detailing its changes and progress.

Wald died in 1940 at the age of seventy-three. Rabbi Stephen Wise of the Free Synagogue led a service in the Neighborhood Playhouse; Dr. John L. Elliott led a private service at her Westport home; and several months later, Carnegie Hall hosted twenty-five hundred people to hear messages from people whose lives were affected by her social activism.

Now part of the umbrella organization, United Neighborhood House of New York, the Henry Street Settlement remains an ongoing testament to Wald's goals of social justice.

Today its programs and services aid more than twenty-five thousand people annually with shelters for the homeless and victims of domestic violence. It administers programs for AIDS awareness, literacy, child care, and household management, and offers services to the elderly. Its Abrons Art Center reaches more than one hundred thousand people involved in music, dance, theater, visual arts, and arts education programs. Two thousand youngsters participate in Pioneer Leadership, Expanding Horizons, Cadet Corps, Operation Athlete, and En Garde, a job-training program for youth who are at risk for dropping out of school or pursuing a life of crime. Posthumously, Lillian D. Wald was inducted into the Hall of Fame of Great Americans at New York Public Library in 1965, and into the National Women's Hall of Fame in 1993.

Emma Goldman

(1869–1940)

Almost from the moment she entered the anarchist movement in 1889 at the age of twenty, Emma Goldman enjoyed a notoriety unequaled by any other woman in American public life. The government thought her one of "the ablest and most dangerous" anarchists in the country. Singling her out as a special target of persecution, Washington kept up a running battle with Emma Goldman until it finally succeeded in deporting her, along with several hundred other immigrant radicals, on December 21, 1919.
—Alice Wexler, *Emma Goldman: An Intimate Life*

FEW AMERICAN REFORMERS can boast as long and substantive a list of activist credentials as Emma Goldman. A radical feminist and staunch anarchist, who vigorously advocated birth control, free love, and free speech, she was also a writer, lecturer, and popularizer of the arts. Born to ride a whirlwind, as someone once said of her, Emma Goldman stirred up more controversy than any other social or political activist of her day. Popularly known as "Red Emma" and reviled and scorned for her radicalism, she ignored the constant condemnation she received and remained the consummate rebel, determined to fight for the freedom of the individual at a time when the organization was fast becoming paramount.

Goldman was born in Kovno, Russia (now Kaunas, Lithuania), the only child of Abraham and Taube Goldman. Her father, an Orthodox Jew and a shopkeeper, who later kept an inn and managed the government stagecoach in the small village of Popelan, was disappointed at the birth of a daughter, and her mother, who had two daughters from a previous marriage, considered her an additional burden. Emma endured an unhappy childhood caught between her father's bitter and fiery temper and her mother's cold indifference. Even after two sons were born to the Goldmans, Emma's father could not forgive his daughter for her gender.

Although Goldman often later described herself as having been "born a rebel," she was also aware that it was her dismal childhood that led her to grow up "largely in revolt." Living in an Orthodox family, with a tradition-bound father, and in the Jewish Pale of Settlement, where the rights of Jews to move and to work were severely restricted and pogroms were a fact of life, shaped Goldman's cultural identity and fostered in her a sense of rebellion. However, she never felt particularly drawn toward religion and was repelled by religious orthodoxy. In her 1931 autobiography, *Living My Life,* Goldman described her childhood understanding of religion: "My people, while keeping Jewish rites and going to the synagogue on Saturdays and holidays, rarely spoke to us about religion. I got my idea of God and devil, sin and punishment, from my [German] nurse and our Russian peasant servants." As Candace Falk observes in *Jewish Women in America,* "Never escaping the public's perception of her as a Jewish woman, with the ambivalent overlay the culture placed on the term, Goldman nonetheless preferred to think of herself as a woman who could transcend the boundaries imposed by the stereotypical social constructions of religion."

When Goldman was about seven, her father, dogged by business failure, moved his family to Königsberg, Prussia, where Emma attended school. She found the teachers cruelly pedantic; but one, a sensitive German teacher, took an interest in her, cultivated her taste for music and literature, and helped her prepare for the gymnasium entrance examinations. Although Goldman passed her exams, her religious instructor refused to provide the certificate of good character necessary for admittance to gymnasium.

In 1881, the Goldmans moved to St. Petersburg. There, her father ran a grocery and Emma's formal schooling lasted only a few more months. She took a job in a cousin's glove factory, later worked in a corset factory, and also began to associate with nihilist and populist university students and to read the new radical texts that advocated political dissent. According to Goldman's autobiography, at fifteen her father tried "to marry me off," and when Emma protested that she wished to be permitted to continue her studies, Abraham Goldman "threw my French grammar into the fire, shouting, 'Girls do not have to learn much! All a Jewish daughter needs to know is how to prepare *gefüllte* fish, cut noodles fine, and give the man plenty of children.' I would not listen to his schemes; I wanted to study, to know life, to travel. Besides, I never would marry for anything but love, I stoutly maintained."

In 1885, rather than submit to her father's continued demands that she enter into an arranged marriage, Goldman immigrated to America with her half-sister, Helena. They settled in the Jewish community of Rochester, New York, and began working in a clothing factory for $2.50 a week. Goldman's treatment by factory owners happy to employ hardworking immigrants and willing to exploit them destroyed her faith in the "American Dream," fostered in her a distrust of capitalism, and formed her politics. She was also deeply affected by the execution of four anarchists without conclusive evidence in connection with the 1887 Haymarket Square riot in Chicago, an event she experienced as a moment of "spiritual birth."

The same year, Goldman married Jacob Kersner, a fellow factory worker, but their relationship faltered because of Kersner's impotence and fondness for gambling at cards. The couple separated, divorced, and reconciled, and then permanently divorced. Goldman later wrote, "I was immediately ostracized by the whole Jewish population of Rochester. I could not pass on the street without being held up to scorn." Goldman's parents, who were now also living in Rochester, refused her entry into their house. "It was only Helena who stood by me," Goldman writes. "Out of her meager income she even paid my fare to New York."

Emma Goldman liked to say that her real life began in 1889, when she moved to New York City and met Johann Most, editor of the anarchist newspaper *Die Freiheit,* and Alexander Berkman, an émigré Russian revolutionary and anarchist, who would become her lover. "All that had happened in my life until that time," she later wrote, "was now left behind me, cast off like a worn-out garment."

Goldman joined the anarchist movement, which for her—a survivor of the harsh authoritarianism of her parents, the ethical demands of Judaism, and the brutality of Russian anti-Semitism, who had quickly become disenchanted with American democracy—had an immediate appeal with its promise of a classless, nonauthoritarian society. During the early years of her political activism, Goldman endorsed the notion that the ends justified any means—including acts of violence. In 1892, after Pinkerton guards hired by Henry Clay Frick, manager of the Carnegie Steel Company in Homestead, Pennsylvania, shot and killed several workers during a massive strike, Goldman assisted Berkman in his plot to assassinate Frick. Frick survived the attack, but Berkman served a fourteen-year prison sentence. Goldman, in turn, served a one-year prison term in 1893 for advising an audience of unemployed workers in New York's Union Square that "it was their sacred right" to take bread if they were starving and their demands for food were not satisfied. In prison, Goldman took up nursing, and after her release studied nursing and midwifery in Vienna from 1895 to 1896.

By the beginning of the new century, Goldman had begun to renounce her earlier calls for violence, especially after learning that President McKinley's assassin, Leon Czolgosz, claimed to have been inspired by her. In a 1910 essay, "Anarchism: What It Really Stands For," Goldman, without disavowing its radical nature, attempted to counter the public's perception of anarchism as a philosophy of disorder and violence by describing it as "the philosophy of a new social order based on liberty unrestricted by man-made law; the theory that all forms of government rest on violence, and are therefore wrong and harmful, as well as unnecessary."

An accomplished and electrifying speaker, she traveled throughout the United States lecturing on anarchism, women's rights, and the socially and stylistically progressive works of dramatists Henrik Ibsen and August Strindberg. In 1914 she published *Social Significance in Modern Drama*. She constantly battled police and vigilante attempts to censor her. From 1906 to 1917 she and Berkman coedited *Mother Earth*, a radical monthly that raised concern among both radicals and liberals over threats to freedom of speech. Roger Baldwin, a civil libertarian and cofounder of the American Civil Liberties Union, cited Goldman's efforts on behalf of freedom of speech as the primary inspiration for his work and once said of her, "For the cause of free speech in the United States, Emma Goldman fought battles unmatched by the labors of any organization."

Influenced by Ibsen's works, Goldman trumpeted the cause of the independent New Woman and attacked the narrowness and hypocrisy of conventional marriage. She advocated "free love," by which she did not mean promiscuity but rather love unencumbered by legal and religious sanctions, and she criticized feminists who wished to banish men from women's emotional lives. At the same time, she rejected the call for woman suffrage as insignificant and a sham. A believer in voluntary motherhood and family limitation, she campaigned for over two decades on behalf of birth control, which she defined as "largely a working-man's question, above all a working-woman's question." When Goldman was jailed for lecturing on birth control and for giving the first public demonstration of contraceptives, a reporter wrote that she had been arrested for "saying that women need not always keep their mouths shut and their wombs open." One woman who was greatly influenced by Goldman's efforts to publicize birth control was Margaret Sanger, the reformer most closely associated with the birth control movement in the United States.

In 1917, Goldman and Alexander Berkman were arrested for opposing the draft and sentenced to two years in federal prison. After their release, with the aid of assistant U. S. Attorney General J. Edgar Hoover, immigration officials, who had long attempted to have Goldman deported, took advantage of wartime legislation to send her and

Berkman to Russia along with 247 other victims of the post–World War I Red Scare. In Russia, Goldman was an outspoken critic of the Russian Revolution and the Bolshevik suppression of civil liberties, much to the shock of her radical colleagues, who were unwilling to speak out against the autocratic policies of a socialist nation.

In 1921, Goldman repatriated herself to Sweden and then Germany, where she condemned totalitarianism in newspaper articles and in her book, *My Disillusionment in Russia* (1923). In 1925 she married James Colton, a Welsh collier, to obtain British citizenship. During the 1920s and 1930s she endeavored to support herself through her lectures and royalties from her two-volume autobiography.

In 1936, Alexander Berkman committed suicide. Goldman was saved from deep despair at his death by her tireless work on behalf of the doomed Loyalist cause against fascist Francisco Franco during the Spanish Civil War. In 1939 she traveled to Canada to raise money for the lost Loyalist cause. In February 1940, Goldman suffered a fatal stroke. United States officials allowed her body to be brought back for burial in the cemetery where the executed Haymarket anarchists had been buried.

Although Emma Goldman did not convert many people to the cause of anarchism, she, herself, endeavored to live up to its promise, while at the same time raising awareness of such issues as freedom of speech and birth control that would become movements in their own right. As Alice Wexler observes, "she chose to go her own way, to 'bow to nothing except my idea of right.' She never made peace either with the world or with herself. She remained restless, disconsolate, discontented, her life a kind of warfare against all the jailers of the human spirit, including the 'internal tyrants' of her own mind. She could not vanquish these tyrants, but neither did they vanquish her. In fighting her battles, in living out the contradictions of her own time, she also illuminates ours."

Rosa Luxemburg

(1870–1919)

Driven by an urge to live a complete life, Rosa Luxemburg left her country, her home, her family. She sought to make the lives of all people complete, worth living, even though she knew that we are "like the Jews, being led by Moses through the desert."
—Elzbieta Ettinger, *Rosa Luxemburg: A Life*

ON CHRISTMAS DAY, 1881, the not quite twelve-year-old Rosa Luxemburg experienced an event that would haunt her and influence her actions throughout life. After the Christmas service at Warsaw's Church of the Holy Cross, members of the congregation instigated a pogrom in the Jewish quarter of the city. For three days and three nights, the mob ransacked and looted Jewish homes, wounding and killing the inhabitants. A terrified Luxemburg heard the cries of "Beat the Jew!" while waiting for the violent storm of destruction and murder to subside. Sanctioned by the Russian authorities, pogroms were used as a way of marginalizing Polish Jews, while giving the country's Catholic majority an outlet for its frustrations under Russian rule.

The experience left a permanent mental scar on Luxemburg. The woman who would become a spell-binding orator and who would hear vast audiences cheer, "Long live Rosa!" remained terrified of the crowds she routinely addressed. "Do you know what thought obsesses and frightens me?" she wrote to a friend in 1917, "I imagine that again I must enter an overcrowded gigantic hall, the glaring lights, the ear-splitting noise, the mass of people pushing against me . . . and I feel an urge to suddenly run away! . . . I have a horror of crowds." Despite her fears, Luxemburg would struggle for the rest of her life to identify the causes for the animosity that set people against one another. Her solution would eventually extend in solidarity and brotherhood to her victimizers, and the cost of her beliefs would be to die violently with the implacable courage of her convictions.

Rosa Luxemburg is one of history's greatest revolutionary leaders. Her politics, forged in the cauldron of a Poland dominated by Russia and coveted by Germany, would lead her toward the proletarian promise of socialism and eventually to the founding of the Polish Socialist Party, the radical socialist Spartacus League, and the German Communist Party. In the crucial years of World War I, Luxemburg would endure imprisonment and later the ultimate sacrifice on behalf of her vision of equality and human worth that defied all conventional limitations of gender, class, nationalism, and even her background as a Jew. For Luxemburg, the pogrom she witnessed as a child was only the symptom of a much larger social disease infecting both the oppressed and the oppressor, which she struggled to cure.

Rosa Luxemburg was born in the small Polish town of Zamość, the youngest of five children of a Jewish merchant. As a child a hip disease kept her in bed for a year. It was incorrectly treated, and Luxemburg had a pronounced limp for the rest of her life. Although she was small and fragile-looking, she was a bright, active, self-confident child who was particularly fond of reading, especially poetry. When Luxemburg was three years old, her family moved to Warsaw, where her father became a member of leading intellectual circles. In a period when the czarist government applied systematic religious oppression in Poland, especially of the Jews, Luxemburg's considerable intellectual gifts gained her admission to the best girls' high school in Warsaw, a privilege usually reserved for Russians only.

While still in high school, Luxemburg was influenced by the first Polish socialists, and in 1887 she joined an illegal socialist "proletariat" group. In 1889, because of her revolutionary activities, she was forced to flee Warsaw for Zürich, Switzerland, home to many Polish émigrés and revolutionaries and the international headquarters of European socialism, and a city where radicals from Russia and Germany sought political sanctuary. There, she met Leo Jogiches, a Lithuanian revolutionary, with whom she lived off and on for the next twenty years, and she studied philosophy, economics, and law at the university. She earned her doctorate with a thesis on the industrial development of Poland. With Jogiches, she founded the Polish Socialist Party in 1892 and a splinter group, the Social Democratic Party of Poland, in 1894.

By the end of the 1890s Luxemburg was anxious to convert the theories of socialism and revolution to activism. Marx had predicted that Germany would be where the revolution of the proletariat would someday begin because Germany was the most industrialized nation in continental Europe. By 1898, Luxemburg was eager to go to Berlin, the center of socialist activity in Germany, but as a Russian citizen she was barred from crossing the border. To solve this problem, she married German anarchist Gustav Lübeck to obtain German citizenship. Once safely in Germany as a citizen, Luxemburg divorced Lübeck. In Berlin, she began to organize workers in the German Social Democratic Party (SPD), and with characteristic confidence wrote, "I am convinced that in six months I'll be one of the best speakers in the Party." She was, in fact, an excellent speaker, able to mesmerize audiences with her zeal and expert political analysis.

In 1904 Luxemburg served a three-month prison sentence for insulting Kaiser Wilhelm II in a public speech. The following year she returned to Poland on a false passport to organize a workers' revolt against Russian troops. She was arrested by czarist police and imprisoned but was eventually rescued by the SPD, which bribed Russian officials to release her on bail. This experience with actual revolution made Luxemburg impatient with the theorizing and abstract debate of the German socialists, and in an influential pamphlet, *The Mass Strike,* she called for full-scale action from the workers. In 1907 she was appointed instructor of economics at a school for SPD officials; at the same time she continued to write, publishing an important economics textbook in 1912, and her most famous work, *The Accumulation of Capital,* in 1914. In *The Accumulation of Capital* Luxemburg argues that capitalism is doomed to collapse as a result of imperialism; capitalist nations will be driven to expand their markets, extending their control over the world and inevitably coming into conflict with one another. Her prediction of a global war over "spheres of influence" and interlocking treaties among the great capitalist powers came to pass in August 1914.

The outbreak of the First World War was a serious setback for Luxemburg, who feared that nationalism would undermine worker solidarity. German socialists faced competing loyalties to the socialist principles and to the Fatherland, and most chose to serve the government they had long struggled to overthrow. Luxemburg was adamant and vocal, however, in her opposition to the war as the ultimate betrayal of everything that socialism stood for. As a result, she was imprisoned for most of the war, beginning in 1915, along with fellow socialists Karl Liebknecht and Clara Zetkin.

During their imprisonment Luxemburg, Liebknecht, and Zetkin organized the Spartacus League to oppose the war and foment revolution in Germany. The Spartacists, named after the slave and gladiator who led a rebellion against the Romans in the first century B.C., demanded the establishment of a dictatorship of the proletariat, opposed the postwar democratic government, and engaged in sporadic acts of terrorism. Despite her commitment to Spartacist ideals, Luxemburg advocated gradual political change and was critical of Lenin's triumph in assuming power after the Bolshevik revolution. In an editorial criticizing Lenin and Trotsky's suspension of democratic rights, she wrote that Lenin "is completely mistaken in the means he employs: decree, the dictatorial power of a factory overseer . . ." For Luxemburg, revolution must be at the will of the people and not controlled by the select few in which the majority are compelled by violence.

After her release from prison, at a meeting held during the last days of 1918, Luxemburg was instrumental in transforming the

Spartacists into the German Communist Party to oppose the moderate socialist government that assumed power when Kaiser Wilhelm II abdicated. Supporting a massive workers' strike, Luxemburg hoped that the action would bring down the government and initiate the revolution. Instead, the government cooperated with the military to suppress the strikers. In January 1919, Luxemburg and Liebknecht were arrested for taking part in a Communist uprising. They were taken from the police with the complicity of the Weimar authorities and handed over to soldiers, who interrogated, beat, and then shot them. Luxemburg's body was thrown into a downtown Berlin canal. Her murderers were eventually charged but acquitted.

The German Communist Party Rosa Luxemburg founded with such devotion to the socialist ideal grew in political strength only to perish in the flames of Nazi ambition. The communism of the Soviets would expire in its turn. Luxemburg, the astute political theorist, was certainly ahead of her time when she wrote, "Socialism by its very nature, cannot be dictated, introduced by command. . . . Without general elections, without unrestricted freedom of press and assembly, without a free range of opinions, life dies out in every public institution and only bureaucracy remains active."

A lifelong advocate of human dignity for all, Luxemburg had the courage to look beyond the usual restrictions of nationality, gender, and ethnicity in an effort to discover what unites, rather than divides, humanity. In the last public speech she delivered, on December 31, 1918, fifteen days before her death, Luxemburg spoke words that could be taken as her credo: "I do not know whether it is a duty to sacrifice happiness and life to truth. But I know this much: if one desires to teach truth, it is one's duty to teach it wholly or not at all. One who brings truth all masked and painted to humanity may well be truth's pimp, but truth's lover he is not."

Gertrude Stein

(1874–1946)

Think of the Bible and Homer, think of Shakespeare and think of me.
—Gertrude Stein, on herself, quoted in B. L. Reid,
Art by Subtraction

THE ONE WORD that cannot be associated with Gertrude Stein is "modest." A visionary force in modern literature and the most experimental of all twentieth-century American writers, Stein unabashedly declared that "Einstein was the creative philosophical mind of the century and I have been the creative literary mind of the century." If so, she is now relatively little read, an influence absorbed, if not enjoyed. The reviewer Clifton Fadiman has scornfully and wittily summarized her writing: "Miss Stein was the past master in making nothing happen very slowly." She is now largely known by her famous portrait by Picasso; by the term she coined, "the Lost Generation," used by Ernest Hemingway as the epitaph for his first novel, *The Sun Also Rises;* for her line "Rose is a rose is a rose is a rose"; for her relationship with Alice B. Toklas; and most especially for her Paris address, 27 rue de Fleurus, where Stein held court before the movers and shakers of the artistic and literary worlds between the wars. One observer remarked that she presided over her salon like "a great Jewish Buddha," as she defined and arbitrated an emerging modern art.

Critic Bettina L. Knapp, more generously than Fadiman, has described Stein as "an institution. She was an era unto herself—unforgettable, spectacular, revolutionary in every sense of the word. She invigorated language and refused to conform to the provisional culture of nineteenth-century America. . . . Virtuoso that she was, Stein mocked all literary conventions: punctuation, syntax, and grammar. By violating everything that was familiar to readers, she established new speech connections and remade language. Seemingly indifferent to the impression she made on the literati of her day, she forged ahead, dislocating, deconstructing, dismantling, fragmenting, and assaulting popular modes."

One of the leading innovators in modern literature, Stein influenced diverse literary figures such as Ford Madox Ford, E. M. Forster, James Joyce, Ernest Hemingway, and Thornton Wilder, and affected the French New Novelists and the writers of the Beat Generation. Despite all her arrogant proclamation of her own genius (she allegedly asserted that there have been "only three orginitive Jews—Christ, Spinoza, and Gertrude Stein"), egotistical, abrasive, supremely confident in her mission to revitalize language and perception, Gertrude Stein is one of the irresistible forces that created modern consciousness and revitalized language and perception.

Born in Allegheny, Pennsylvania, Gertrude Stein was the youngest of seven children of Daniel and Amelia Stein. Her grandfather was a merchant in the Bavarian village of Weikersgrubben, and her father and his four brothers immigrated to the United States in 1841, settling in Baltimore, Maryland, where in 1843 they opened a clothing store, Stein Brothers. Both of Gertrude's parents were of German-Jewish descent; and, although their parents were members of a synagogue throughout Gertrude's childhood, the Stein children were not raised as practicing Jews. Gertrude's father was a restless and often unsuccessful businessman, who moved his family back to Austria and Paris—where the four-year-old Gertrude first encountered the city that would become her home for nearly forty years—before returning to America and settling in Oakland, California, in 1879. In Paris, Daniel Stein made a fortune investing in real estate and the stock market. Gertrude, raised by governesses and tutors and emotionally neglected by her pallid, passive mother and monolithic father, formed her primary bond with her older brother, Leo.

After the death of their mother in 1888 and father in 1891, Gertrude and Leo grew even more inseparable. "Each," writes Knapp, "became increasingly dependent upon the other for moral and psychological support. Brother was the dominant force and little sister, the follower." Gertrude followed Leo to Harvard, where, because the university was closed to women, she enrolled at the Harvard Annex, soon to become Radcliffe College. There, she studied with philosopher William James, whose insistence on empirical procedures, distrust of the "intellectual method," and new theory concerning "stream of consciousness" would dominate her literary theories.

In 1897, after receiving her degree from Radcliffe, Stein followed her brother to Baltimore, where Leo was attending graduate school at Johns Hopkins. There, she entered the Johns Hopkins University Medical School with the intention of becoming a physician and a psychologist. She was a brilliant but erratic student, and in her fourth year she lost interest, failed an important course, and dropped out. Often troubled and depressed as a young woman, Stein suffered from what she called the "red deeps," tumultuous feelings in part prompted by her inability to accept the prescribed roles of wife and mother. During her time at Johns Hopkins she fell in love with another woman, a passion that was not reciprocated.

Since Leo had already left Johns Hopkins for Italy, she joined him there in the spring of 1902. That summer they went to London, where they rented a flat in Bloomsbury and divided their time between cultivating social contacts and reading at the British Museum. Gertrude disliked England and wrote about her depression while living there in a book titled Q.E.D., which was published posthumously in 1950 as Things as They Are, her first extended work of fiction. In 1903, after a short sojourn in America, she joined Leo in

Paris at the address that would become one of the most famous in twentieth-century cultural history: 27 rue de Fleurus.

For the next two decades, Gertrude and Leo collected paintings by artists such as Renoir, Daumier, Manet, and Gauguin, and cultivated their enthusiasm for the great modern painters, Cèzanne, Matisse, Braque, and especially Picasso, who would become Gertrude's lifelong friend. Their apartment soon became the most important salon in Paris, attracting hundreds of well-known painters and cultural hangers-on, who came to be seen and to inspect the Steins' impressive collection of paintings. As one of her biographers, Douglas Day, writes, "In the midst of it all sat Gertrude Stein . . . calmly authoritative, arbitrating—and imposing her own views upon—every manner of aesthetic dispute."

In a 1935 book titled *Testimony Against Gertrude Stein,* several artists, including Braque and Matisse, and the dadaist writer Tristan Tzara, denounced Stein's superficial perception of their work and of painting in general. In an outstanding example of an artist claiming his privilege to remain impenetrable and with a certain disregard for the fame gained for the moderns through exposure at the Steins' salon, Braque contemptuously insisted that, "Miss Stein understood nothing of what went on around her." But as Douglas Day observes, both Gertrude and Leo "understood enough, at least, of the new painting to know that it was of permanent significance; and they made sure that people came to 27 rue de Fleurus to see these disturbing new works."

In 1909, Gertrude Stein published her first book, *Three Lives,* in which the lives of three working-class American women are examined without the traditional use of linear sequence and climaxes. Stein attempted to duplicate in *Three Lives* what modern painters were achieving in their art, and like a Cézanne painting, the book delivers a unified pattern of tone and texture through repetition that suggests the equal importance of each element. This revolutionary approach found few readers but many admirers, one of whom was Alice B. Toklas, a Jewish Californian living in Paris. Toklas proofread the book and became Gertrude's secretary, housekeeper, lover, and companion until Stein's death.

Stein's next project was a massive, thousand-page work, *The Making of Americans,* completed in 1911 but not published until 1925. Stylistically unconventional and derived from Stein's attempt to render the "continuous present," the work is a massive family saga in which the Herslands, a fictionalized version of the Stein family, are examined to define American identity. A young Ernest Hemingway, who would later proclaim that everything he learned about writing he learned from Gertrude Stein, eventually helped in the preparation of the manuscript for publication.

In 1914, Gertrude gained notoriety with the publication of *Tender Buttons,* a volume of "cubist" or "dadaist" poetry that led reviewer Clifton Fadiman to dub her "the Mama of Dada." It is this work, in the poem, "Sacred Emily," that the line "Rose is a rose is a rose is a rose" appears. Stein would later observe, "I'm no fool. I know that in daily life we don't go around saying 'is a . . . is . . . is . . .' Yes, I'm no fool; but I think that in that line the rose is read for the first time in English poetry for a hundred years."

For a time during World War I, Stein and Toklas lived in Majorca, where Gertrude worked on her first plays and extended the experimental prose exercises in *Tender Buttons* to form the equivalent of verbal collages of mundane descriptions, bits of conversations, and random experiences. In 1916 the couple returned to Paris and entered the war effort. Stein had a Ford van sent to her from America, and, after learning to drive it, she and Toklas delivered supplies for the American Fund for French Wounded.

The postwar period in Stein's life was marked by her association with American writers, including Sherwood Anderson, F. Scott Fitzgerald, and Ernest Hemingway, for whom 27 rue de Fleurus became an essential stopover. She encouraged Hemingway to give up journalism for creative writing and to start writing prose rather than poetry. Although they had a contentious relationship and several falling outs, Hemingway often acknowledged how the famous Hemingway style—the emphasis on the concrete, stripped-down declarative sentences, on omission, the rhythm of prose, and the value of repetition—derived from Gertrude Stein. Hemingway declared that "Gertrude was always right." In 1926 Stein published *Composition as Explanation,* an essay that expresses her literary theories and which grew out of the successful lectures she gave at Oxford and Cambridge. Her first commercial success as a writer, however, came in 1933 with the publication of her best-known and most accessible work, *The Autobiography of Alice B. Toklas,* which chronicles Stein and Toklas's life together as related from Toklas's perspective but in Stein's inimitable clever style. The book's success led to a contract to publish Stein's work regularly and a well-received American lecture tour, during which she was invited to tea at the White House with first lady Eleanor Roosevelt. Stein wrote about her American experience in *Everybody's Autobiography* (1937).

In 1937, Stein and Toklas moved to a new apartment in Paris, at V rue Christine, where they lived until the outbreak of World War II. Despite their vulnerability as Jews, they remained in occupied France during the war, living in their country home in Bilignin and in the town of Culoz. The couple was largely unaffected by the Occupation; Stein, either out of self-interest, supreme self-centeredness, or naiveté, became something of an apologist for the Vichy government, viewing much of the horror of the war as her own domestic inconveniences. Despite her outspokenness concerning the rights of women and personal freedom and liberation, Stein never spoke out against the treatment of Jews under the Nazis. After the couple returned to Paris following its liberation in December 1944, they were visited by numerous servicemen eager to meet and talk with the legendary sage of modernism, "the Sibyl of Montparnasse," Stein had become in the public mind. She also made speaking tours of American bases in occupied Germany and lectured in Brussels. Her works from the 1940s include *Wars I Have Seen* (1945), Stein's account of the Occupation, and *Brewsie and Willie* (1946), a tribute to the American G. I.

By 1946, Stein was dying from cancer, and in July she was admitted to the American Hospital in Paris for an operation. Weakened from the surgery, the heavily sedated Stein looked up at Toklas, who was at her bedside, and asked, "What is the answer?" When there was no reply, she said, "In that case, what is the question?" These were Gertrude Stein's last words. She was buried in Père-Lachaise cemetery in Paris. Alice B. Toklas, who died in 1967, was buried beside her. In her will, Gertrude Stein left Picasso's famous portrait of her to the Metropolitan Museum of Art in New York City and her papers and manuscripts to the Yale University library.

Despite her enormous egoism, her arrogance, and her pretentiousness, Gertrude Stein remains one of the most influential, as well as one of the most controversial, women of the twentieth century. She placed herself at the center of what would become a remarkable era of writers and painters, and in her own way helped to shape a new aesthetic. Critic Harold Bloom has called Stein "the greatest master of dissociative rhetoric in modern writing," that is, the master of breaking down "preconceived patterns in our response, so as to prepare us for discourse that will touch upon the possibilities of transcendence." Stein's campaign for renewal of self and society began with the revitalization of language itself, to help us express ourselves and understand our world.

Melanie Klein

(1882–1960)

Melanie Klein was a woman with a mission. From the moment she read Freud's paper On Dreams *(1901) in 1914, she was enraptured, converted, and dedicated to psychoanalysis. Captivated by the concept of the unconscious, she followed its seductive lure into speculative depths from which even Freud had retreated.*
— Phyllis Grosskurth, *Melanie Klein: Her World and Her Work*

ONE OF THE first Freudian-trained psychoanalysts to work with children, Melanie Klein was an important and influential contributor to the field of early childhood development. She is especially recognized for her technique of play therapy, the first important therapeutic innovation designed to tailor psychoanalytic methods to the needs of child patients. Klein's play technique remains a standard method used by child psychologists.

Melanie Klein was born Melanie Reizes in Vienna, on March 30, 1882, the youngest child in a family of three girls and a boy. Her father, Moriz Reizes, a native of Poland, had rebelled against his rigidly orthodox family by deciding to attend medical school rather than become a rabbi. Although he had broken all ties to orthodoxy, he nevertheless agreed to an arranged marriage, which ended after the death of his father. He was in his mid-forties when, on a trip to Vienna, he met and married Melanie's mother, Libussa Deutsch, a twenty-five-year-old visiting the city from her native Slovakia.

Dr. Reizes had difficulty establishing a successful practice in Vienna because he was Jewish. He was forced to work as a dental assistant and supplemented his income by serving as a medical consultant to a vaudeville theater. Libussa Reizes operated a shop selling exotic plants and animals to help with the family finances. When Melanie was five, the family's financial situation was eased when her parents borrowed a substantial sum of money from Libussa's brother, Hermann, a wealthy lawyer. This influx of cash enabled the Reizeses to move to a larger apartment, where Moriz Reizes set up a lucrative dental practice.

Melanie was not close to her father, who was well over fifty when she was born and had little patience with his youngest child. He also frequently and overtly showed a preference for his eldest daughter, Emily, which Melanie deeply resented. However, she was impressed by her father's intellectual achievements (he was widely read and he had taught himself ten European languages) and she often turned to him for answers to questions about her schoolwork. He died when she was eighteen.

As a child, Melanie was closer to her mother, whom she admired for her beauty, courage, and devotion to her family, and to her Uncle Hermann, who showered her with attention. "I was very fond of him and he spoilt me too much," she recalled in her autobiography. "I heard him say many things, among them that, being so beautiful, a young Rothschild would come to marry me."

The Reizeses were observant Jews, what Klein would later describe as "anti-Orthodox." Libussa Reizes tried to keep a kosher household, but after facing opposition from her children soon abandoned the attempt. The young Melanie particularly liked the first evening of Passover, because, as the youngest child, it was her responsibility to ask the Four Questions at the seder. She would later write, "Since I was very keen to get some attention and to be more important than the older ones, I am afraid this attitude influenced my liking of that occasion. But there is more to it. I liked the candles, I liked the whole atmosphere, and I liked the family sitting round the table and being together in that way."

When Melanie was about nine, she developed a fascination with the Catholic Church and worried that she would some day change her religion. This was possibly due to the influence of a maid, who had come to the Reizes household from a convent and looked after the children. As Klein's biographer, Phyllis Grosskurth, observes, "While always feeling 'Jewish,' she was never a Zionist, and her way of life was in no way indistinguishable from that of a Gentile. Yet as a Jewish child in Catholic Vienna, she must have been acutely conscious that she was an outsider and a member of an often persecuted minority. Psychoanalysis became for many Jews a religion with its own rites, secrets, and demands of unswerving loyalty. Melanie Klein, when she eventually discovered psychoanalysis, embraced it as ardently as any convert to the Catholic Church."

Melanie was also close to her sister, Sidonie, who protected her from the teasing of her older sister and brother, and taught her to read and write. Sidonie suffered from scrofula, a form of tuberculosis of the lymph glands, and died at the age of nine. Melanie had a longer-lasting relationship with her brother, Emmanuel, who died in his mid-twenties of heart failure. A multitalented young man, who played the piano and wrote essays and poetry, Emmanuel planned to become a doctor until ill health forced him to abandon his medical studies. The deaths of Sidonie and Emmanuel deeply marked Klein and contributed to her lifelong tendency toward depression.

By the time she was fourteen, Melanie had decided that she wanted to study medicine at the university. First, however, she needed to move from the lyceum, which provided only a superficial secondary education, to the more academically oriented gymnasium. Her brother helped her prepare for the entrance examination and while she was attending school, introduced her to his circle of friends, a lively intellectual group, in which she blossomed. She graduated from the gymnasium but gave up her plans for further study when, at nineteen, she became engaged to her second cousin, Arthur Klein, a chemical engineering student. Later in life she regretted not having studied medicine and believed that her views on analysis would have been treated with more respect if she had earned a medical degree.

During the two years of her engagement to Arthur Klein, Melanie studied humanities at Vienna University. The couple married in 1903 and for several years lived in small towns in Slovakia and Silesia, where Arthur Klein visited factories for his work. The following year, Melanie gave birth to the first of the couple's three children. Klein's marriage was an unhappy one: she missed the intellectual stimulation she had enjoyed in Vienna and resented her husband's frequent job transfers and business trips, as well as his conjugal indifference. Adding to Melanie's unease was the interfering presence of her mother, who had come to live with them and who responded to her daughter's growing psychic distress by behaving in an overbearing and manipulative manner. Cast in the emotionally draining role of wife, mother, and needy child, Melanie Klein grew increasingly depressed.

In 1910, the Kleins moved to Budapest, where Melanie found the intellectual companionship she had been missing and where, for the first time, she discovered the work of Sigmund Freud. Her interest in psychoanalysis was sparked after she read Freud's popular 1901 work, *On Dreams* sometime around 1914. She later wrote of her experience with the work, "That was what I was aiming at, at least during those years when I was so very keen to find out what would satisfy me intellectually and emotionally." In 1914 Libussa Reizes died, which intensified Klein's depression. She began undergoing analysis with Sandor Ferenczi, a close associate of Freud, and with his encouragement began to study the psychoanalysis of young children.

In 1918, Klein attended the Fifth Psycho-Analytic Congress, where she first saw Freud in person, accompanied by his daughter, Anna, who would also go on to gain a reputation as a child psychologist. At the Congress, Sigmund Freud presented a paper called "Lines of Advancement in Psychoanalytic Theory." Klein later recalled the experience of seeing the master and listening to his words: "I remember vividly how impressed I was and how the wish to devote myself to psychoanalysis was strengthened by this impression."

In 1919, Klein produced her first paper in the field of child psychology, "The Development of a Child," which she presented to the Budapest Congress of Psychoanalysis. Soon afterward, she was given membership in the Hungarian Psychoanalytic Society. The disguised subject of Klein's paper was her son Erich, the youngest of her three children. Klein also analyzed her daughter, Melitta, and her older son, Hans. "Through her close observation of their behavior," writes Grosskurth, "she learned much about the origins of anxiety and how it impeded development, knowledge that undoubtedly contributed to her understanding of other young patients . . . tormented children whom she undoubtedly helped." All three children went on to other analysts, including Karen Horney, a supporter of Klein's theories.

At the invitation of Freudian Karl Abraham, Klein moved to Berlin in 1921. There, she began analysis with Abraham and joined the Berlin Psychoanalytic Institute as its first child therapist. In Berlin, Klein elaborated her concepts and refined her technique. She evolved her system of play therapy to supplement the usual psychoanalytic procedure, believing that the young age of her patients indicated more appropriate methods than the exclusively verbal free-association technique then used with adults. By providing her young patients with toys representing father, mother, and siblings, observing how they played with the toys, and responding to their spontaneous communication during play, Klein was able to elicit the children's subconscious feelings. Klein's technique also resulted in her discoveries of what goes on in the subconscious of the two-year-old and of even younger children, ages which had been largely ignored by Freudians, who believed that it was impossible to analyze children before the age of seven.

Life in Berlin became difficult for Klein after Abraham's death in 1925. The loss of Abraham and the interruption of her analysis was a source of deep grief, and because she now lacked his support, she found her work in Berlin to be under constant attack from more seasoned analysts. Anna Freud had begun her work with children at about the same time as Klein, but with a different approach, and there was considerable controversy and conflict between the two. The majority of members of the prestigious Berlin Society followed Anna Freud and labeled Klein's work "unorthodox."

In 1925, Klein attracted more controversy from the Freudians, when she presented a paper on her technique of child analysis at a conference in Salzburg. There, she met Freud's biographer and friend, Ernest Jones, who was impressed by the paper and agreed with Klein's explication of Karl Abraham's conclusion that the future of psychoanalysis lay with child analysis. Jones invited Klein to give some lectures in London, and she gladly accepted. The three-week series of lectures she delivered in London would form the basis for her first book, *The Psychoanalysis of Children* (1932), which presented her theories of child analysis. In 1926 Klein divorced her husband and moved to London permanently. The following year, at the invitation of Ernest Jones, she became the first European analyst elected to the British Psychoanalytical Society. In London, she continued to refine and expand her theories and technique.

An important and enduring aspect of Klein's work is her object-relations theory, which links ego development during the early years of life to the experience with physical objects that are associated with psychic drives. The very young child first relates to parts rather than complete objects; the later capacity to relate to whole objects, such as the mother or father, is marked by the child's ambivalent, usually hostile, feelings toward objects and the anxiety produced by those feelings. Klein also developed the concepts of introjection, the process whereby an external object is internalized, and projection, in which internal objects are imagined to be located in an external object.

During the 1930s, Klein began to analyze adults in addition to children. She was castigated by many Freudians for indicating the possible ways in which depressive and schizoid-paranoid states in young children relate to psychotic processes in adults. However, Klein's defection from Freudian orthodoxy led her to a greater understanding of severe mental disorders and ultimately extended the range of patients who can be psychoanalyzed. Klein stopped analyzing children in the late 1940s. She then treated adults, analyzed students of psychoanalysis, taught, and wrote. Her best-known books are *Envy and Gratitude* (1957) and *Narrative of a Child Analysis*, published posthumously in 1961. In old age, Klein became severely anemic. She died in London on September 22, 1960, due to complications resulting from a broken hip.

In 1918, Melanie Klein heard Sigmund Freud say, "We have never prided ourselves on the completeness and finality of our knowledge and capacity. We are just as ready now as we were earlier to admit the imperfections of our understanding, to learn new things, and to alter our methods in any way that can improve them." With these words in mind, Klein expanded the possibilities of psychoanalysis and left to the world a legacy of influential, provocative, and enduring ideas.

Emmy (Amalie) Noether

(1882–1935)

In the judgment of the most competent living mathematicians, Fraulein Noether was the most significant creative mathematical genius thus far produced since the higher education of women began.
> —Albert Einstein, in a letter to *The New York Times* on the death of Noether in 1935

SUFFUSED WITH A passion for mathematics, and a single-mindedness that did not pause for anything, Emmy Noether became one of the world's greatest algebraists during the twentieth century.

She enjoyed the support and encouragement of her mathematician father and the top mathematical minds of her day; yet she had to endure sexism, which prevented her from obtaining faculty positions at universities; poverty, because even when she was hired, her salary was a pittance; and later anti-Semitism, because the Bavaria of her youth became the land of the Nazis.

For much of her adult life, she was an unofficial, yet extraordinarily influential, teacher. In essence, her teaching role was a volunteer position with neither status nor salary, although much later she was given so tiny a salary she was barely able to survive. She did not care. It did not matter that all she could afford was the same cheap dish from the same cheap restaurant each evening. Only mathematics mattered.

This passion for mathematics led her to develop what is now known as Noether's Theorem, which is considered the most logical connection about nature and the law of physics that we now have. It has paved the way for mathematicians and physicists to explore protons, antimatter, and quarks.

Emmy Noether was born in Erlangen, Bavaria, in 1882 to Max Noether, an algebraic geometer and professor at Erlangen University, and Ida Kaufmann, whose family came from Cologne. Emmy had three siblings, all brothers.

Because her parents were well educated, Noether also had a very thorough education, studying German, English, French, arithmetic, and other essential subjects of the day taught at the Höhere Töchter Schule in Erlangen (1889 to 1897). Like young women of her time, she enjoyed music, dancing, and playing the clavier. Her love and further study of French and English led her, at first, to become a certified language teacher in 1900.

However, despite her credentials and enthusiasm for languages, she never taught them, but instead embarked on a pursuit of her real love, mathematics. In the early 1900s, it was rare for women to pursue such studies, even with a mathematician father on the faculty of an important university. Because she was a woman, she had to study "unofficially," and she had to obtain permission to attend every class she took. (There were two women auditors and two thousand male students at Erlangen between 1900 and 1903). She was able to obtain her permissions and studied there from 1900 to 1902; she passed her exams in Nürnberg in 1903.

In 1904 Noether was finally permitted to matriculate at Erlangen, and in 1907 she was granted a doctorate, summa cum laude, from the Mathematische Instititut after working under Paul Gordan, the "king of invariant theory." (Invariants are elements that do not vary no matter how they are measured.) Her doctoral thesis included 331 invariants of tenary biquadric forms largely reflecting Gordan's constructive approach.

As early as 1905, at age twenty-three, she worked on her theorem that solved the problem of how to prove that energy is conserved in four-dimensional space. Much of her work is used in quantum physics to study particles within atoms.

Her theorem was praised by Albert Einstein in a letter to David Hilbert that acknowledged her "penetrating mathematical thinking." Her theorem of invariants was critical to Einstein's theory of relativity.

Noether's theories helped physicists understand that nuclear particles (like protons and neutrons) contain the more fundamental building blocks called quarks. This helped physicists understand how antimatter particles, like antiprotons and positrons, could be applied to both physics and medicine. (Positron emission tomography [PET] scans use antimatter to examine brain function, for example.)

Even though her work was considered exemplary among her fellow mathematicians, sexism among administrators prevented her from obtaining her rightful place on a university faculty. And so she remained at Erlanger to assist her father.

She was still able to work on her own research, which at this point was being influenced by mathematician Ernest Fischer (1875–1954), who had succeeded Gordan at the university in 1911. It was Fischer's influence that turned Noether's theories to a more abstract approach, one posed by Hilbert in his own theorem in 1888. Fascinated by these new approaches, she attended lectures of noted astronomers like Karl Schwartzchild, and mathematicians like Hilbert, Fritz Klein, and Herman Minkowski at the University of Göttingen, a place that was to figure prominently in her future work.

Although restricted from a permanent, paid faculty position, Noether published extensively, increasing her reputation. In 1908 she was elected to the prestigious Italian mathematical society, Circolo Matematico di Palermo, and then, in 1909, to its German equivalent, Deutsche Mathematiker Vereinigung. She gave lectures in Salzburg in 1909 and in Vienna in 1913, a remarkable experience for a woman of her time.

In 1915, Noether accepted an invitation from her staunch supporters, Hilbert and Klein, to move to Göttingen, the "Mecca of Mathematics." Although she was not offered a teaching position until 1919 (and even then an unpaid one), her lectures were supported by Hilbert, who often advertised them under his own name, and "with the assistance of Dr. E. Noether. No tuition." In university protocol, *privatdozents* (certified lecturers) worked to become professors and then to become members of the university senate. Hilbert is famous for his remarks in Noether's defense that read, "I do not see that the sex of the candidate is an argument against her admission as privatdozent. After all, we are the senate, not a bathhouse."

Undaunted by the struggle to be an accepted faculty member, she spent the time researching and studying, and became such a worldclass algebraist she attracted students and younger colleagues to her very popular lectures. Many of these students would become the leading mathematicians of the period spanning the 1930s to 1960s.

For all her lecturing, supervising doctoral students, and being a part of the department as a researcher, she was never paid. Finally, from 1922 to 1933, she received a tiny salary, her first and only one in Germany, as an algebra teacher at Göttingen.

Noether's work led to the development of a second theorem. She published her findings in the paper, *Idealtheorie in Ringbereichen* (Ring Theory), in 1921, which proved how a set group of rings "obeys" associative laws. This is her most famous concept and the one called the Noetherian Ring. The Noetherian Ring satisfies what mathematicians and physicists call "the ascending chain condition" if, and only if, any nested sequence of ideals (subrings) exist. For example, the first ideal (or subring) will be nested or contained in the second one, the second ideal will be contained in the third one, and so forth. These rings become constant at some point when a bigger ideal (containing all the previous ones) ceases to become the entire ring.

After studying with her for a year in Göttingen in 1924, the Dutch mathematician B. L. Van de Waerden returned home to write the twovolume *Moderne Algebra,* of which the second is composed almost entirely of Nöether's work. Van de Waerden (1903–1996) was an algebraist, combinatorialist, and historian who recorded many of the developments in twentieth-century algebra. By including her research in his massive work, he was able to inform the world of Noether's groundbreaking theorems and attach credit to her name. Van de Waerden's book also did much to introduce Noether's theories in America.

Because of her passion, Noether is almost as well known for her influence among her students as she is for her theorems. Many of those students, like Van de Waerden, went on to develop extraordinary work in the fields of mathematics and physics because of her dedication and innovative teaching. Mathematician and colleague Hermann Weyl wrote of Noether: "Her significance for algebra cannot be read entirely from her own papers, she had great stimulating power and many of her suggestions took shape only in the works of her pupils and coworkers."

Much of Noether's theoretical work appeared under the names of other mathematicians in part because some publishers requested it, or as a way for her colleagues to promote her theories. During the late 1920s, Noether helped edit *Mathematische Annalen* and wrote about noncommutive algebras with fellow mathematicians Helmut Hasse and Richard Brauer, while continuing her personal research and sharing it with students.

Finally, the world of mathematicians sought not only to acknowledge but also to honor her contributions to their field. She taught at the University of Moscow from 1922 to 1924, and was influential to many young Soviet mathematicians. She was invited to address the International Mathematical Congress at Bologna in 1928 and again at Zurich in 1932, where she was the first woman to address its general session. In 1932 she also received the Alfred Ackermann-Teubner Memorial Prize for the Advancement of Mathematical Knowledge. (Her co-honoree was Emil Artin, who had developed the principle now called Artin's Constant.)

In a scenario that was all too familiar in the Germany of the 1930s, one of Noether's own research students, Werner Weber, began a witch hunt against Jewish members of the faculty. His first attack was on Professor Edmund Landau. The Gestapo sought to solve the Landau "problem" by ridding all its universities of "Jewish influence," and Noether found herself one of the first six professors fired from Göttingen.

Instead of cowering, she began the German Mathematical Relief Fund to help other Jewish mathematicians who had lost their jobs. Her "permission" to teach was withdrawn by the Prussian Ministry of Science, Art, and Public Education in 1933; yet she continued to teach, albeit in her home, even after she was fired. She was liberal politically, and a pacifist, and that was almost as aggravating to the Gestapo as being Jewish. It was universally acknowledged in the field of mathematics that the discipline was crippled for years because of the purge of Göttingen. "... her courage [after the Nazi regime came to power], her frankness, her unconcern about her own fate, her conciliatory spirit, were, in the midst of all the hatred and meanness, despair, and sorrow ... a moral solace," Hermann Weyl said.

Bryn Mawr College offered her a visiting professorship and, able to leave Germany in 1933, she came on a temporary fellowship. Still, she had to teach undergraduates rather than pursue her research full time. She did lecture to graduates at the Flexner Institute, now known as the Institute for Advanced Study at Princeton University. "She taught us to think in simple, and thus general, terms. ... and not in complicated algebraic calculations," said her colleague P. S. Alexandroff at her memorial service.

It is that simplicity of intellect that was Emmy Noether, the mathematician, and the woman, who paved the way toward the discovery of new algebraic patterns no one had yet been able to see.

Emmy Noether entered the hospital on April 10, 1935, for surgery on an ovarian cyst. On April 14, suffering from a tremendous fever caused by infection, she lost consciousness and died. She was fifty-three.

The University of Erlangen, commemorating the fiftieth anniversary of her doctorate, held a conference on Noether. In 1992, the city of Erlanger named a high school for her, the Emmy Nöether Gymnasium, and its curriculum emphasizes not only mathematics, but languages, and sciences. The Association of Women Mathematicians held a special symposium, which honored the centennial of her birth; and in Israel, the Emmy Noether Institute for Mathematical Research was established in 1992 at Bar Ilan University in Tel Aviv.

Today in America, women students are a regular part of the mathematics departments of universities, and several, from Berkeley to the University of Wisconsin at Madison, have "Nöetherian Rings," which are groups of women mathematics students whose goal it is to support one another in their professional work.

Mathematicians have always understood the importance of Noether's theorems, even if the culture they worked in would not allow her to personally present her papers or compensate her for teaching what became the next generation's stellar scientists and mathematicians. Emmy Noether unraveled the mystery of the principle of conservation of energy, which proved to be essential to much of what we now call modern day physics. It was a simple, yet profound, idea, not unlike the woman herself.

Rose Schneiderman

(1882–1972)

I would be a traitor to these poor burned bodies if I came here to talk good fellowship. We have tried you good people of the public and we have found you wanting. The old Inquisition had its rack and its thumbscrews and its instruments of torture with iron teeth. We know what these things are today: the iron teeth are our necessities, the thumbscrews the high-powered and swift machinery close to which we must work, and the rack is here in the "fire-proof" structures that will destroy us the minute they catch on fire.

This is not the first time girls have been burned alive in this city. Every week I must learn of the untimely death of one of my sister workers. Every year thousands of us are maimed. The life of men and women is so cheap and property is so sacred. There are so many of us for one job it matters lit-tle if 143 of us are burned to death . . .

I can't talk fellowship to you who are gathered here. Too much blood

has been spilled. I know from my experience it is up to the working people
to save themselves. The only way they can save themselves is by a strong
working-class movement.

        —Rose Schneiderman, excerpts from a speech given at
        the Metropolitan Opera House, May 2, 1911,
        concerning the Triangle Shirtwaist Fire,
        in her autobiography *All For One*

ROSE SCHNEIDERMAN MADE the speech quoted above at a mass meeting held to protest the lack of safety standards in factories in the wake of the devastating Triangle Shirtwaist Fire, which, on March 25, 1911, had claimed the lives of 146 garment workers. Present at the meeting were eminent civic and church leaders, lawyers, labor-union officials, and representatives of women's organizations. There were numerous speakers, but it was the diminutive Schneiderman whose powerful words, delivered in little more than a whisper, galvanized the audience, caught the attention of the press, and produced results. In the days following the meeting, the State Factory Investigating Commission began a successful campaign to put into place much-needed legislative reforms for the safety and well-being of workers in factories and stores, where the large majority of women worked. The Industrial Code that grew out of that campaign represented a Pyrrhic victory in Schneiderman's battle to better conditions for women workers—a battle she had been fighting since 1903 and would continue to fight until her retirement in 1955.

For more than fifty years, Rose Schneiderman was an influential leader in what she called "the most exciting movement in the United States—the fight of workers for the right to organize." During her long and extraordinary career, much of which was spent as president of the New York Women's Trade Union League (NYWTUL) and the national Women's Trade Union League (WTUL), Schneiderman worked tirelessly to improve conditions for American women in the workplace and to provide trade union women with schools, recreational facilities, and professional networks. Schneiderman's commitment to bettering the quality of working women's lives is typified in her famous 1911 declaration, "The woman worker needs bread, but she needs roses, too." It was a particularly apt statement, given Schneiderman's first name and flaming red hair, which, together with her oratorical powers of persuasion, socialist views, and staunch dedication to trade unionism, led her enemies to dub her the "Red Rose of Anarchy."

Born in Saven, a small village in Russian Poland, Rose Schneiderman was the eldest of four children of Samuel and Deborah (Rothman) Schneiderman. She spent her early childhood in Saven and in Khelm, an industrial city, where her father worked as a tailor and her mother, a skilled seamstress, made custom uniforms for Russian soldiers, baked ritual breads, and used her considerable knowledge of herbs to treat the sick. Schneiderman remembered her father as a gentle, easygoing, and intellectual man, who read books to his children and was fond of producing amateur theatricals based on Jewish themes. Her mother was more assertive and outspoken. In her autobiography Schneiderman recalled that in Saven, the family lived in one room "in the back of the house and our landlady kept a saloon in front. Not only did she sell liquor, but she also imbibed. Sometimes, when she had had a bit too much, Mother would take over for her at the bar."

Although Deborah Schneiderman never received any schooling, she taught herself to read prayer books so that she could go to synagogue on the Sabbath. A firm believer in female education, she insisted that Rose attend school and learn Hebrew, an unusual situation for girls in the male-dominated society of the shtetl. Rose began attending traditional Hebrew school (cheder) at the age of four, and at six, she was enrolled in a Russian public school. She continued her schooling on and off after the family immigrated to New York and eventually received the equivalent of a ninth-grade education.

In 1890, the Schneidermans migrated to the United States and settled in a two-room tenement apartment on the Lower East Side of Manhattan. Two years later Samuel Schneiderman died of meningitis and his wife, pregnant with their fourth child, was left to try to earn a living for the family. The family moved several times and for a time was forced to rely on the United Hebrew Charities to supplement whatever Deborah Schneiderman could earn from taking in boarders and home sewing. She eventually obtained a job in a factory sewing linings for fur capes.

The three older Schneiderman children, including Rose, were placed in Jewish orphanages during this time; when Rose returned home, she took on the tasks of housekeeping and child care while her mother was at work. At thirteen she began her first job as a cashier and sales clerk in a department store, at times working a seventy-hour week for $2.75. In 1898 she took a better-paying position as a lining-maker in a cap factory over the objections of her mother, who, Schneiderman later recalled, "thought working in a store much more genteel than working in a factory."

During a visit to relatives in Montreal, Schneiderman befriended Socialist friends of her aunt and uncle, who introduced her to the concept of trade unionism. "For the first time," Schneiderman later wrote, "I became interested in politics. I knew nothing about trade unionism or strikes and, like other young people, I was likely to look upon strikebreakers as heroic figures because they wanted to work and were willing to risk everything for it. My entire point of view was changed by the conversations I heard at their house." Schneiderman returned to the factory, where her awareness of the need for unionization grew as she realized "the hardships we were needlessly undergoing." These included employee responsibility for buying sewing machines and thread, replacing machines that broke, and less-than-adequate wages.

In 1903, Schneiderman, together with two other women at her factory, organized the shop into the first female local of the United Cloth Hat and Cap Makers' Union. She emerged as an effective leader, and her local soon grew to a membership of several hundred. Schneiderman served as the union's secretary and as one of its delegates to the New York Central Labor Union convention. The following year she became the first woman to hold national office in an American labor union, when she was elected to the General Executive Board of the United Cloth Hat and Cap Makers' Union.

Schneiderman began her association with the Women's Trade Union League in 1905 while leading a thirteen-week cap-makers' strike against employers' attempts to institute an open shop policy. Formed in 1903, the WTUL was a coalition of primarily middle- and upper-class reformers dedicated to unionizing working women and to lobbying for protective legislation. Eager to gain credibility with the working classes, the WTUL offered to help publicize the strike and sent a photograph of Schneiderman to the press, where it appeared in newspapers along with a story about the strike. After the strike was successfully concluded, Schneiderman joined the League at the urging of NYWTUL president Margaret Dreier Robins, although she was initially doubtful that an organization comprised of so many wealthy women could understand the needs of working women or accomplish much for them. Her doubts faded as she became more involved with the League and she later called her association with the WTUL "the most important influence in my life."

By 1906, Schneiderman's talents as an organizer had won her the vice-presidency of the NYWTUL. In 1908, after receiving a stipend provided to her by philanthropist Irene Lewisohn, she was able to quit her job at the factory and devote more time to union organizing under League auspices. The stipend also enabled her to continue her education. Schneiderman played a key role in organizing garment shops and conducting strikes throughout lower Manhattan, and was instrumental in paving the way for the waistmakers' strike of 1909–1910. Organized by the International Ladies Garment Workers Union (ILGWU) and known as the Uprising of the Twenty-Thousand, the strike was the largest conducted by American workers to that time and included a large contingent of workers from the Triangle Shirtwaist Company. Schneiderman helped organize picket lines, raised money for the strikers, and made numerous speeches in defense of their cause.

Although the strike ended in February 1910, with only modest concessions gained for workers, it created greater solidarity among women workers, fostered a new awareness of what unified action could achieve, focused attention on the fledgling ILGWU, and gave the NYWTUL a national reputation. However, as Robert Rothstein observes in *Jewish Women in America,* the strike "also generated tensions between Jewish women and men in the ILGWU and between working-class Jews and the middle-class Christian women who dominated the NYWTUL."

After the strike was over, Schneiderman's intention was to complete high school and go on to college, with the goal of becoming a teacher. Instead, she accepted a full-time position as an organizer with the NYWTUL, knowing that, as she later wrote, "my heart was in the trade-union movement." By 1914, however, Schneiderman was often at odds with other WTUL leaders over what she felt was a lack of wholehearted commitment to immigrant women and she resigned from the League to become an organizer for the ILGWU. As one of the few women organizers in a union composed of a largely female membership but dominated by male leadership, Schneiderman felt increasingly isolated and frustrated, especially after male organizers tried to take over the leadership of a strike she had planned. In 1917, she left the ILGWU and returned to the WTUL. In 1918, she was elected president of the NYWTUL, a position she held until 1949.

In addition to her WTUL activities, Schneiderman also developed an interest in political and educational issues. An ardent suffragist, who believed that winning the ballot would help working women obtain the protective legislation they so desperately needed, she became chair of the Industrial Wing of the New York Woman Suffrage Party; helped found the Wage Earner's League for Woman Suffrage (1911); worked as a speaker and organizer on behalf of the National American Woman Suffrage Association during NAWSA's 1913 Ohio referendum campaign; and was active in the 1915 and 1917 New York campaigns.

During World War I Schneiderman earned the enmity of conservative members of the New York State Legislature when she undertook a campaign to prevent the state assembly from suspending labor laws protecting women workers. In 1919 she helped form the short-lived New York State Labor Party and ran as the party's candidate for United States senator the following year. She lost the election, but her campaign highlighted issues such as the need for nonprofit housing for workers, better public schools, and state-funded health and unemployment insurance. In 1919 she was a member of the WTUL delegation to the Paris Peace Conference, where she helped form the International Congress of Working Women. True to her belief in education as an effective method of advancement, she was a co-organizer of the influential Bryn Mawr Summer School for Women in Industry, which opened in 1921 and was directed by Bryn Mawr president M. Carey Thomas.

In 1926, Schneiderman, by now a nationally known figure, was elected president of the national WTUL. However, the dynamism that had marked the women's labor movement and the League's involvement with it had begun to fade. Schneiderman turned her attention to promoting workers' education and on lobbying for protective legislation such as minimum wage and eight-hour-a-day laws for women workers, both of which would be enacted into New York law during the 1930s, due, in part, to her efforts. In common with several women reformers—including Frances Perkins, who would become the nation's first woman Secretary of Labor—Schneiderman opposed the Equal Rights Amendment on the grounds that it would compromise protective legislation enacted on behalf of women.

Schneiderman's long friendship with Eleanor Roosevelt, who had joined the NYWTUL in 1922, and with Franklin Roosevelt did much to shape FDR's attitudes toward labor relations during the 1930s. In 1933 FDR appointed Schneiderman to the labor advisory board of the National Recovery Administration. The only woman on the board, Schneiderman's task was to ensure that industries employing large numbers of women were adhering to codes regulating wages and hours.

In 1935, the Supreme Court ruled that the NRA had improperly delegated legislative power to the executive branch of government and declared it to be unconstitutional. Schneiderman returned to New York, where she shared an apartment with her mother in the Bronx and returned to the WTUL. She concentrated her efforts on organizing New York women laundry workers and from 1937 to 1943 also served as secretary of the New York State Department of Labor.

By the late 1940s the influence of the WTUL had waned. Many of the League's legislative aims had been accomplished, female union membership had grown to about three million, and the function of union organization and negotiation had been taken over by the American Federation of Labor (AFL) and its partner, the Congress of Industrial Organizations (CIO). The WTUL was also suffering financially. In 1950 the WTUL closed its national office in Washington, and its local chapters quickly followed suit. In 1955 members of the NYWTUL met to determine the branch's fate. Schneiderman, now seventy-three, observed, "they don't need us anymore" and advised, "Let's step out gracefully."

Schneiderman retired from public life and, apart from making radio speeches and occasional appearances for various labor unions, lived quietly in Manhattan, where she had moved after the death of her mother in 1939. Her autobiography was published in 1967 and five years later, at the age of ninety, she died in the Jewish Home and Hospital for the Aged.

In her autobiography Schneiderman noted that, "to me the labor movement was never just a way of getting higher wages. What ap-

pealed to me was the spiritual side of a great cause that created fellowship. You wanted the girl or man who worked beside you to be
treated just as well as you were." Schneiderman dedicated her career
toward realizing this ideal. Her goal was to improve all conditions of
life and to secure common justice for men and women in industry,
and she succeeded in her mission. As Robert Rothstein observed,
"the government protections that most American workers now take
for granted are the legacy of Rose Schneiderman."

Edna Ferber

(1885–1968)

It has been my privilege, then, to have been a human being on the planet Earth; and to have been an American, a writer, a Jew. A lovely life I have found it, and thank you, Sir.
— Edna Ferber, in her autobiography, *A Peculiar Treasure,* 1938

FROM THE TIME she was a teenager until her death in her eighties, Edna Ferber's singular passion was writing. Her contributions to the American novel earned her a Pulitzer Prize and her books have remained in print thirty-five years after her death, a testament to both her popularity and her keen sense of American taste.

Ferber was a writer of her time, reflecting her place in its history, and her books were hugely popular. *So Big,* which earned her the Pulitzer Prize, sold three hundred thousand copies during the 1920s, and *Giant* sold five million copies when it appeared in the 1950s. "I love the United States," she revealed in her biographies, "and I love writing about it." In her books, the heroines are strong and independent and as assertive as the various regions she depicted. She was always unabashedly American, setting her novels in intrinsically American places, from the cacophony of 1920s Chicago, to the vast ranches of Texas and the slow paddleboats rolling along the Mississippi.

Ferber was born in Kalamazoo, Michigan—a more thoroughly American start one cannot imagine. Her parents were Hungarian-born Jacob and Julia Neumann Ferber, a native of Milwaukee. The family moved frequently throughout the Midwest, and when Edna was twelve, they settled in Appleton, Wisconsin. The family, which also included sister Fannie, attended Temple Emmanuel. Edna sang in the choir every Friday night and Saturday morning. Jacob and Julia operated a small store (called My Store), but it was Julia, not Jacob, who was the brains and energy behind the business. Jacob was hopeless at business and eventually became blind.

When she was a very young girl, Edna wanted to be an actress. Her dream was to attend Northwestern University's School of Elocution; but, because she lacked the money, she instead took a job with the local newspaper. Years later, researching showboats in North Carolina for her novel, she participated in the full theatrical experience, from selling tickets to doing small roles, and she loved it.

Ferber's writing career began right after graduation from Ryan High School in Appleton. (Appleton has since honored its favorite daughter with the Edna Ferber Elementary School on Capitol Drive.) Writing a prize-winning essay won her the job for the *Appleton Daily Crescent* at three dollars a week, then a position at the *Milwaukee Journal.* Ferber worked so many hours without respite that one day she collapsed from what was soon diagnosed as anemia. Sent home to recover, Ferber used the time to pursue fiction writing, and developed a charming series of stories around the "new woman" character, a divorced working mother called Emma McChesney.

Ferber's first story, "The Homely Heroine," appeared in *Everybody's Magazine* in 1910. It was shortly followed by others, which eventually ended up in three collections of stories: *Roast Beef, Medium:*

The Business Adventures of Emma McChesney (1913); *Personality Plus: Some Experiences of Emma McChesney and Her Son, Jock* (1914); and *Emma McChesney and Company* (1915). This would end the series of thirty Emma McChesney stories, but Ferber continued to write and publish short stories in between her many novels. Those stories have been collected into *Buttered Side Down* (1912), *Mother Knows Best* (1927), and *One Basket* (1947).

Switching to the novel genre, Ferber first wrote then discarded *Dawn O'Hara*. Her mother, insisting that it was worthy of publication, salvaged it and, in 1911, it became Ferber's first published novel. With her second book, *The Girls* (1921), she earned critical praise. Her next book, *So Big,* won her the Pulitzer Prize in 1925, and from that point, her career was totally established.

Following the death of her father, and with the success of her first novels, Ferber and her mother headed to the "big city," Chicago. By the 1930s, Ferber moved to New York City, where she occasionally sat among other wits of the day at the Algonquin Round Table.

Although lightweight, her other novels remain in print, including: *Fanny Herself* (1917); *Cheerful, By Request* (1918); *Half Portions* (1919); *A Gay Old Dog* (1921); *The Girls* (1921); *Gigolo* (1922); *American Beauty* (1931); *They Brought Their Women* (1933); *Come and Get It* (1935); *Nobody's in Town* (1938); *No Room at the Inn* (1941); *Great Son* (1945); and *Ice Palace* (1958), which was a blatant campaign for Alaskan statehood.

Wit (gentle and savage) was her calling card in her personal relationships and she played it irreverently and amusingly with her longtime collaborator for the Broadway stage, George S. Kaufman. Together they were responsible for some of the most hilarious comedies ever (and still) performed, including *Dinner at Eight* (1932), which opened as a flop then became an enormous success as a film.

Kaufman and Ferber's collaboration began when Kaufman urged Ferber to make a play out of her short story, "Old Man Minick." The play was subsequently produced at the Booth Theatre in New York City, in September of 1924.

Minick is the source of a delightful anecdote of theater history. It played out of town at the Lyceum Theater in New London, Connecticut, a lovely theater with gallery, dome, and cut glass chandelier. A colony of bats had taken up residence in this elaborate house, and when the lights went on as the curtain rose, the bats started to "dip, swoop, circle, and dive all about the auditorium and on the stage it-self," Ferber wrote, causing havoc in the audience and a sudden flight, especially the women, out the door. "We were a dispirited crew," she adds, "after the laughing hysterics of the bat invasion." Winthrop Ames, *Minick's* producer, had a solution: "Next time . . . we won't bother with tryouts. We'll all charter a show boat and we'll just drift down the rivers, playing the towns as we come to them, and we'll never get off the boat."

"*What's a show boat?*" Ferber asked, only to be informed that they were floating theaters that went up and down the rivers of the South entertaining people in rural areas. "Here was news of a ro-mantic and dramatic aspect of America of which I'd never heard or dreamed," she wrote, and that was the beginning of her famous book. Like many of her works, an overheard remark, a casual aside during a conversation, would spark her interest and off she would go to re-search the story, just like the inveterate journalist she once was.

Ferber's grandniece, Julie Gilbert, noted in her book, *Edna Ferber and Her Circle,* that the collaboration of Kaufman and Ferber worked because "Ferber [wrote] about good-looking people in romantic sit-uations, while warding off physical contact in her personal life; Kauf-man worked by shunning any romantic shenanigans in his plays, yet devoting himself to them in real life." Friend of both, Margalo Gill-more termed their relationship as a "literary roll in the hay."

The collaboration of the two independently successful writers was unmatched in Broadway history. Kaufman wrote or doctored forty-four plays with sixteen partners, two of which won Pulitzer Prizes: *Of Thee I Sing* and *You Can't Take It With You.* (Ferber produced 31 works.) Kaufman and Ferber also cowrote *Stage Door* (1936), *The Land Is Bright* (1941), and *Bravo!* (1948). Their first huge hit Broad-way show, *The Royal Family* (1927), was a satiric look at the reign-ing family of theater of the time, the Barrymores. In one of many incidents of irony, Ethel Barrymore starred in Ferber's first play, *Our Mrs. McChesney,* produced in 1915, yet when Miss Barrymore was approached to play the lead in *Royal,* she turned it down.

That revived Edna's wistful desire to act. The producers, and Kauf-man (hearing Edna's query, "How 'bout me?" as a substitute for Ethel) totally ignored her. Years later, producer Cheryl Crawford hired Ferber for the role in a revival production staged in Maplewood, New Jersey, for a one-week run. The house was packed and reviews were "courtly," but hardly enough to start a second career. So she returned to her "ten-finger exercise . . ."

About the writer's life, she said, "Life can't ever really defeat a writer who is in love with writing, for life itself is a writer's lover until death—fascinating, cruel, lavish, warm, cold, treacherous, constant."

Most of Ferber's stories were pure Americana, but *Show Boat* was singular addressing miscegenation nearly three decades before civil rights, legislation, and a change in societal attitudes. Ferber referred to *Show Boat* as her "oil well" for its long life and many transitions. It began first as a book, then as a musical with lyrics by Oscar Hammerstein II and music by Jerome Kern. (The musical has been filmed three times—in 1929, 1936, and 1951—and was recently revived on Broadway to huge success.)

Several of Ferber's novels were made into films more than once: *Cimarron* in 1931 and 1960; *Dinner at Eight* in 1933 and 1989; and *So Big* in 1924, 1932, and 1953. She had twelve of her other works filmed, which were mostly minor successes.

Known to her nieces as "Aunt Ed," Ferber left them the bulk of her personal estate. She had never married, at one point referring to her thirty-one books as talking back to her like naughty children. She said she never married "because she didn't see it as part of her game plan for life."

"Being an old maid is like death by drowning—really a delightful sensation after you have ceased struggling." Whether or not this was her choice can only be conjecture, but some of the stories of her sexuality are witty. Noel Coward, a good friend and writer/actor, once commented on her tuxedo-like outfit, "Edna you look almost like a man," to which she quickly responded, "So do you."

Always proud of her Jewish heritage, she wrote, "I am an American Jewish child, a woman born in the Middle West in the middle eighties." In one infamous brouhaha, a New York society hostess remarked, "Well, there are Jews and there are Jews." The New York socialite who despaired about "those Jews" in a novel she had just read sparked Ferber to retort, "Yes, and there are Christians and there are Christians," and Ferber and several other Jews walked out of their hostess's salon without further comment.

Ferber's commentary was not always coated with wit, but in prophecy. In her first autobiography, *A Peculiar Treasure* (1939), she notes the impending crisis in Germany and connected the anti-Semitism she experienced as a child with that brewing in Europe during the 1930s. In her second memoir, *A Kind of Magic* (1963), she notes that her first visit to Israel was less than she expected. "Israel seemed a sort of Texas; without the oil."

Edna Ferber died of cancer at age 82 on April 16, 1968, in New York, at her Park Avenue home. In a lengthy obituary, *The New York Times* said, "Her books were not profound, but they were vivid and had a sound sociological basis. She was among the best-read novelists in the nation, and critics of the 1920s and 1930s did not hesitate to call her the greatest American woman novelist of her day."

In July 2002, the United States Postal Service issued a stamp with Ferber's likeness on an eighty-three-cent stamp, the new rate for three ounces, which may not cover a full manuscript but is more than is necessary for a rejection letter. The stamp, designed by Mark Summers, uses an image of the author from 1927.

Dorothy Rothschild Parker

(1893–1967)

Perhaps what gives her writing its peculiar tang is her gift for seeing something to laugh at in the bitterest tragedies of the human animal.
        —W. Somerset Maugham, in a critical essay on
        Parker's short story, "Big Blonde"

WRITING FOR HOLLYWOOD is often a ticket to wealth, fame, and acknowledgment for many writers. For Dorothy Parker, it was a time of political radicalism that marked the rest of her life.

That life began on a rainy summer day in August 1893, while her parents vacationed in West End, New Jersey. She was brought up in a Scottish-Jewish family. Her mother, Eliza A. Marton, was Protestant and her father, J. (Jacob) Henry Rothschild, was an affluent garment manufacturer and a Talmudic scholar, but not a part of the inner circle of the more famous, and wealthier, branch of the Rothschilds.

Eliza and Henry had been neighbors, yet her family delayed their union for nearly a decade, during which time, Eliza became a public school teacher. They were finally married in 1878 and became parents of four children, the last of which was Dorothy, who was born when Eliza was forty-two years old. The death of her mother (from heart disease and acute colic) a month before Dorothy's fifth birthday was a trauma that had a lasting effect on her emotional development. And the tragedy of her brother Henry's death (he was aboard the *Titanic)* when she was nineteen was devastating. But her father's death the next year, when she was twenty, had a decided financial impact; she needed to go to work. Parker never viewed herself as a practicing Jew, but often commented about herself that "I was just a little Jewish girl trying to be cute." Jewish, yes; little, yes, as she was barely five feet tall. Cute, not quite. She had a formidable mind, with the proverbial rapier-sharp wit, and she spared no one, not even herself.

Not only had she not received a Jewish education, but she also got heavily conflicted messages about religion during her childhood. Despite her father's passion for the Talmud, he had married not one but two non-Jewish women.

After the death of his first wife, he married Eleanor Francis Lewis, who was Catholic, and who sent Dorothy to the Blessed Sacrament Convent School in New York from age seven to fourteen to "reform" her from her Jewishness. The project failed as she could not contain her wit (she described the Immaculate Conception as "spontaneous combustion") and she was expelled. The tension between Eleanor and Dorothy was palpable and only ended when Eleanor died of a cerebral hemorrhage in 1903. Dorothy learned Latin, French, and English at the progressive Miss Dana's Boarding School in Morristown, N.J. To assure acceptance at the prestigious school, her father alleged that she was "Episcopalian."

As famous as she became for her quips and her considerable fiction output, her first work was playing piano for a dance school and composing light verse (she was first published in 1913). She began her writing career penning captions to photos for *Vogue* (1916–1917).

Dorothy married her first husband, Edwin Pond Parker II, in June of 1917. A Wall Street broker, he enlisted in the army and was sent overseas. They separated in 1922 and were divorced in 1928. He was an alcoholic and addicted to drugs, and this exposure may have been the beginning of Dorothy's use of alcohol to numb psychic pain, which was followed by periods of depression and several suicide attempts. Ironically, or by necessity, the drama of her life found its way into material for her short stories and verses, often a juggling act of amusement and despair. Her most famous poem, "Resume," for example, ends with the words "you might as well live."

Parker was a drama critic for *Vanity Fair* (1917–1920), but was fired for "offending too many clients." She went on to write for *Ainslee's Magazine,* and then most notably as Constant Reader in *The New Yorker,* beginning in 1925. It was *The New Yorker's* connection that led her to participate in the infamous gathering of the Algonquin Wits, which met at the Algonquin Hotel. The wits, soon to become known as the Round Table, included many of the era's theatrical and literary luminaries, including Robert E. Sherwood, Alexander Woollcott, Robert Benchley, Franklin Pierce Adams, George S. Kaufman, among others.

Parker resigned from *The New Yorker* when her first collection of poetry, *Enough Rope,* became a surprising best seller, yet she continued to contribute items to the magazine until 1957. She won the O. Henry Prize in 1929 for her story "Big Blonde," and published *Sunset Gun* (1928), a book of verse, and her first collection of short stories, *Lament for the Living* (1930).

Dorothy Parker's voice, Dean Flower wrote, was "not only the best epigrammatic poet of the century but, in her laconic short stories, [she] was at least the equal of Hemingway and Lardner . . . she . . . devised a profoundly moving art out of her lifelong unhappiness."

Part of the unhappiness was caused by a lack of money both as a staffer on magazines and as a verse writer. That was to change for at least a little while when Hollywood called. Parker wrote or cowrote more than twenty films, most of which with her husband Alan Campbell, also a writer, whom she married in 1933. Her screenwriting career brought her considerable financial success, including an Oscar nomination for *A Star Is Born,* which she cowrote with Campbell. Other noteworthy films were *Big Broadcast of 1936* and *Queen for a Day* (1951). During her Hollywood years, she also published *Death and Taxes* (1931); a second book of short stories, *After Such*

Pleasures (1932); two collections of verse and one book of stories in the forties.

Her political activities began when she was thirty-four and protested the execution of Sacco and Vanzetti in Boston. She then moved with her husband to Hollywood, where she helped to found the Screen Writers' Guild in 1934 and the Anti-Nazi League in 1936, both of which were considered to be left-wing groups at the time. She wrote about the Loyalist cause from Spain in 1937 for *New Masses* and, in her short story, "Soldiers of the Republic." Her political activism during the 1930s and 1940s against Fascism was dedicated and sincere, but based more on philosophical views than religious ones; yet after the war, she threw her energies into several organizations with a mission to aid displaced European Jews, plus the United Service Organizations (USO), the United Nations, the Spanish Refugee Appeal, and the National Council of American-Soviet Friendship.

Parker's leftist activities did not go unnoticed during the infamous McCarthy era, and she was called to testify before the House Un-American Activities Committee (HUAC) in 1951. She refused to testify, but was not subsequently charged with any violation. Like so many of the more than three hundred people in Hollywood called before the committee, the linking of her name to the HUAC meant her career in Hollywood never regained momentum.

She wrote many stories, essays, and poetry collections, including *Men I'm Not Married To*, stories and essays, (1922); *After Such Pleasures*, stories, (1932); *Here Lies*, stories, (1939); and post-humously *Constant Reader*, stories from *The New Yorker* (1970). In 1996, Scribner published *Not Much Fun: The Lost Poems of Dorothy Parker*.

Critic Edmund Wilson remarked that ". . . she has been at some pains to write well and . . . put into what she has written a state of mind, an era, and a few moments of human experience that nobody else has conveyed."

While her heyday was certainly the 1920s to the 1940s, Parker continued to work until her death. Hardly a genre escaped her wit, including seven produced plays, collections of her literary criticism, three television plays for WNEW-TV, verse, short stories, and essays.

She taught English at California State University, Los Angeles (then known as Los Angeles State College); cowrote with John La Touche and Richard Wilbur the lyrics to Leonard Bernstein's musical, *Candide* (1956); and wrote five plays, *Close Harmony* (with Elmer Rice, 1924), *The Happiest Man* (with Alan Campbell, 1939), *The Coast of Illyria* (with Ross Evans, 1949), and *The Ladies of the Corridor* (which she believed was her best work (1953). It was a commentary on the restrictions of "ladylike" behavior in American society, and considered a deeper feminist play than others of that era. It was coauthored by Arnaud d'Usseau with whom she also wrote *The Ice Age* (1955), which has not been produced.

Parker continued to write essays championing the causes of racial equality, and reviews praising the few writers she thought worthy, including Vladimir Nabokov, Norman Mailer, E. M. Forster, and Shirley Jackson. Many of her last reviews appeared in *Esquire* magazine, beginning in 1958.

Although feminists have long embraced her for rejecting "feminine writing" in pursuit of the feisty style and humor she displayed, it is no small irony that some of her best-known verses have an element of sexism.

Commenting on her participation with the Algonquin Round Table, she said it was "pretentious and shallow . . . we had to be smarty; I wanted to be cute. . . . I should have had more sense." Her chair at the Round Table, she came to believe, led the public to think of her only as a source of *bon mots* and not the author of works now considered profound, despite their appearance of irony and satire in viewing the human condition even if that is not how she viewed them. Despite neglecting her own health, she managed to outlive everyone else who sat at the Round Table.

Parker's marriage to Campbell, who was also half Jewish and eleven years her junior, was an up-and-down relationship marred by miscarriages, alcoholism, and her overshadowing him in both fame and fortune. They divorced in 1947, then remarried in 1950, only to separate again in 1953. They reconciled once more in 1956 and lived together until 1963 when Campbell died. Perhaps her verse (she never called them poems), "Unfortunate Coincidence," in which she pens the notice that no matter how romantic or deep the passion, "one of you is lying," sheds some light on her notion of romantic love.

In a number of interviews given near the end of her life, she discounted much of her work; but it is obvious from the continuous sales of her short stories and verses, in particular, that they not only are not dated, nor shallow, as she averred, but that they touch a nerve in today's readers. *The Portable Dorothy Parker* has been in print for more than fifty years, and remains the best all-in-one overview of her work.

Dorothy Parker died of a heart attack at age 74 in her rented rooms at the Volney Hotel in Manhattan on June 7, 1967.

Despite the sadness of her life, her lifelong contributions to arts and letters was substantial, and remains a benchmark style that no one yet has been able to duplicate.

At her modest funeral, attended by 150 admirers and friends who cared despite her attempts to push them away, Zero Mostel remarked, "If she had had her way, I suspect, she would not be here at all." Her acerbic suggestions for her epitaph were "Excuse my dust" and "If you can read this, you've come too close."

Perhaps, like so many artists, she had a talent to create a world where characters could reveal their own heartbreak or terror at finding themselves locked into conformity, imprisoned by societal demands or, more commonly, the binds of a bad marriage. Escaping from her own terrors, about which we can only assume, was something entirely different. She was a woman and a writer of her time, and yet she did not understand nor accept her continuing appeal to the general public. The bulk of her estate (estimated then at $20,000) was given to Martin Luther King, Jr. Upon his death, the remaining bequest was to be given to the National Association for the Advancement of Colored People (NAACP), which also was a recipient of many of her papers. Others are now held by the Houghton Library of Harvard University.

Anna Freud

(1895–1982)

Creative minds have always been known to survive any kind of bad training.

—Anna Freud

"I DON'T THINK I'd be a good subject for biography," she said, "not enough 'action'! You would say all there is to say in a few sentences—she spent her life with children!"

That rather charming self-effacing remark of Anna Freud's is but a headline to the real story. Yes, she did spend half her life with children; however, as a result, she deepened the scope of psychoanalysis, introduced child psychology as a discipline separate from adult psychology, and through her various studies, confirmed that positive parental attachment is key to the emotional stability of children.

Anna was decades ahead of her time in her emphasis on the strong role that family played in child development and that whenever possible, the environment should be changed to help the child. She was the first to provide evidence that children should be respected as individuals and that malevolence toward children was inexcusable.

The daughter of Sigmund Freud, the "father of psychoanalysis," Anna adhered to many of her father's ideas, although she believed the ego to be the "seat of observation" and wrote about this theory in her best-known book, *The Ego and the Mechanisms of Defence*, which she wrote in honor of her father's eightieth birthday. Here she outlines how human defenses work, particularly during adolescence, to repress emotions or feelings. Also, she recognized that children—even teenagers—do not always have the communication skills to articulate their feelings, so therapists need to learn different skills than those being used on adults.

According to Anna Freud, therapists need to recognize that children go through a number of stages in psychological development, just as they do in physical development. In her training of therapists, she formalized that the child should perceive the therapist as a caring, sympathetic adult figure—neither a parental substitute nor a peer—who could teach—and learn from—the child about his neurosis.

Anna Freud was the youngest of six children born to Dr. Freud and his wife Martha (Bernays) Freud, who was notorious in her indifference to her husband's field, calling it "a form of pornography."

The term sibling rivalry had not yet been coined, but it certainly existed for Anna and her older sister Sophie, who overshadowed the younger Anna in everything, until she married in 1913, leaving Anna glad that the "unending quarrel between us" was finally over.

Martha's sister Minna came to live with them to help out with the children, and this apparently further alienated Anna from her family, particularly her mother. When asked why she never wrote about the mother-daughter relationship, she said she didn't know anything about it.

Anna formed an intense attachment to her father, who himself likened her to Cordelia, the only true and faithful daughter to King Lear, and to Antigone, the Greek daughter who lovingly led the blinded Oedipus to Attica where he prepared to die.

Freud sheltered her, steered her away from male suitors, and into friendships with women. Was he protecting himself from losing his personal nurse and companion? Did he not view Anna as a daughter, but as a disciple? Some critics believe Anna was not devoted but subservient to her father (even giving him credit for her own achievements) and point to her first work, *Beating Fantasies and Daydreams* (1922) as verification of that criticism.

Anna appears to have been quite independent when younger. In 1914, at age nineteen, she traveled alone to England, beginning what would be a lifelong admiration of England, and to further study of English at which she excelled. In retrospect, her solo traveling, her learning English, and her lack of interest in pursuit of marriage seem quite extraordinary.

Anna had studied at private schools, available to her upper-middle-class family. She was graduated from the Cottage Lyceum in Vienna in 1912, trained to be a teacher, and taught at her alma mater for five years. She was by all accounts quite successful with her students and her teacher training was a critical element in her ability to train other therapists and engage them in analyzing their cases with each other. She was influenced by Maria Montessori who developed a series of small private schools based on the concept that the liberty of children allowed for their development.

At twenty-three she decided to follow her father's footsteps and become an analyst. She had read her father's work and in 1918 was analyzed by her father, a procedure now considered quite unorthodox. Then, however, the leading exponents of this new science were few, and formal training was not yet available. Her entry into the field began a professional and more intense personal relationship between father and daughter.

In addition to their work, they also shared friends like Lou Andreas-Salomé, who was to become Anna Freud's confidante in the 1920s. Andreas-Salomé was an analyst, a writer, and a femme fatale more known for her affairs with Friedrich Nietzsche and Rainer Maria Rilke than her professional work in analysis, although she did write many books and one hundred papers, many of which were confiscated by the Nazis who believed psychology was a "Jewish science." Andreas-Salomé was a serious analyst, famous for her remark, "Human life, indeed all life, is poetry."

Through her acquaintance with Sigmund Freud, Andreas-Salomé

met Anna, and introduced her to her former lover, Rilke. "The more I became interested in psychoanalysis," Anna wrote, "the more I saw it as a road to the same kind of broad and deep under-standing (sic) of human nature that writers possess." The understanding Rilke possessed was demonstrated in his "object poem," a convention he used to describe the silence of "concentrated reality." Works of art, he wrote in his *Letters to a Young Poet,* "are always products of having been in danger. Of having gone to the very end in an experience, to where man can go no further."

Anna became quite an accomplished writer herself, both in her native German and in English. Both Great Britain and American analysts have acknowledged not only the essence of her analysis but also the clear, fluid way she wrote in English.

She was invited to become a member of the Vienna Psychoanalytical Society in 1922, and, the next year, she established her practice dedicated to children, independent of her father. She addressed the Vienna Psychoanalytic Training Institute on the technique of child analysis, the first of its kind to be presented to the analytical community. She lectured teachers and parents, and compiled these speeches into *Introduction to the Technique of Child Analysis* (1927).

Anna was part of the excitement of developing a new field, and many of her techniques and theories would become benchmarks for future child analysts. "We felt that we were the first who had been given a key to the understanding of human behaviour and its aberrations as being determined not by overt factors but by the pressure of instinctual forces emanating from the unconscious mind . . . ," she wrote.

Her father, now frail from cancer, turned to Anna for help. She accompanied him for treatment in Berlin and acted as his representative for public appearances, all the while organizing conferences, conducting seminars, and pursuing her own work, which led to donning the mantle of general secretary of the International Psychoanalytical Association for seven years, from 1927 to 1934.

Anna was named director of the Vienna Psychoanalytical Training Institute in 1935, and then published what many consider her seminal work, *The Ego and the Mechanisms of Defence,* a study on how ego defends against "unpleasure" and anxiety. Her theory was a departure from the accepted viewpoints of psychoanalysts at the time, and laid the groundwork for ego psychology. More important, it established her reputation apart from her father's, a theoretician to be heard.

Observing infant behavior from feeding to playtime was critical to her work, and she was finally able to concentrate on following a set number of children for sustained periods of time at a nursery school for the poor children of Vienna that was funded by Edith Jackson, an American interested in Anna's work.

Dorothy Burlingham, another American, came to Vienna in 1925, to study. She met Anna when she brought her own four children for analysis. They became friends and she lived for a while with the Freud family, where the bond between Dorothy and Anna deepened. She became Anna's lifelong companion and collaborator in everything throughout their lives together: raising Dorothy's four children; cowriting articles; traveling to speaking engagements; and pursuing the projects at nurseries and other centers for child studies.

Anna's biographer, Robert Coles, in *Anna Freud: The Dream of Psychoanalysis*, wrote that the relationship between Dorothy and Anna was "familial in nature," and that Anna's relationship with her father had made him "irreplaceable by any other man." Whatever the reality was, it did not impact Anna's work or her reputation among analysts then or now. Some, like Melanie Klein, may have argued her theories, but no one seems to have bothered to criticize her personal life.

As the political situation in Austria worsened, Anna sought a way to leave with her father, despite the gravity of his cancer. They were befriended by Ernest Jones and Princess Marie Bonaparte who provided the necessary papers, but it was Anna who was left with the logistics of moving her family through the quagmire of Nazi bureaucracy and avoiding a second investigation of Freud by the Gestapo.

Anna somehow made it all work, and soon the Freuds were settled into a comfortable place in London, quickly realizing that though they had escaped the Nazis, they had not escaped the war. Sigmund Freud did not live to experience the Blitz and other events that occurred in wartime England. He died in 1939, Anna at his side, as she had been for the sixteen years that cancer had plagued him.

Dorothy joined Anna in London within months and they began their work in earnest. Because of the increase in orphans due to the war, Anna opened Hampstead War Nursery, which eventually cared for more than eighty children. Her aim was to help the children sustain relationships with members of their families. This became a critical part of her theories that war and trauma are not nearly as devastating to children as separation from their parents, no matter what the reason.

Some of the children were unable to be fed and clothed by their parents, who were suffering from the devastations of the war. Anna and Dorothy were astonished that the parents were more interested and grateful for the learning their children gained than the food they were served.

The Hampstead War Nursery, funded by Americans, was also unique in that its sponsors requested monthly reports. These reports give an exceptional look at the progress of Anna's theories and how the children under her care matured. In particular, this was a carefully watched study of a specific group of children, Jewish refugees and orphans.

Anna was convinced that children themselves were the keys to help therapists unlock the sources of their problems. By sharing their dreams and daydreams, through their painting, other artwork, and play, children could help therapists find the map to the darkest parts of their emotional selves and help therapists lead them out.

Anna had worked with analysts other than her father, notably Siegfried Bernfeld and August Aichhorn; however, it was Melanie Klein who most vocally challenged Anna's theories about early child development even to the length and timing of the stages. Theirs was not just an exchange of opinion, but a rather divisive set of approaches that gathered support for each of them within the British Psychoanalytical Society, which resulted in training seminars for each group, called "Controversial Discussions."

Moving between practice and theory was one of Anna's strengths, and the war presented continued practical experiences, including observing orphans from the Theresienstadt concentration camp who were under the care of her colleagues at the Bulldogs Bank home. In this case, discovering that children could find substitutes for family among their peers produced another landmark study.

By the end of the forties, Anna was training both American and English therapists specializing in child psychology. She and Kate Friedlaender developed the Hampstead Child Therapy Courses, and opened a children's clinic in which staff participated in weekly case study sessions, emphasizing both practical and theoretical viewpoints of their work.

She came to the conclusion that transference symptoms provided what she called "the royal road to the unconscious." (This theory was set down in the book *Normality and Pathology in Childhood* (1965). Examples from her work at Hampstead Clinic, the Well Baby Clinic, the Nursery School, and the Nursery School for Blind Children were analyzed in the book, along with the results of observing her mother and toddler group and the war nurseries. This was the first time such extended studies of children had been published.

Anna Freud was becoming a familiar face in the United States, traveling there from the 1950s until her death. She continued work on both her theorems and their practical applications, concentrating on the emotionally deprived and socially disadvantaged children she studied during the 1970s.

She created the phrase "in the best interests of the child," prompted by her concern about such legal issues as child custody, foster care, and adoption. While teaching at Yale Law School, she used this experience as an opportunity to help law students understand what the impact of crime was on the family.

Two Yale professors, Joseph Goldstein and Albert Solnit, collaborated with her for two important books, *Beyond the Best Interests of the Child* (1973) and *Before the Best Interests of the Child* (1979), which was revised in 1986 with Joseph Epstein, Sonja Goldstein, and Solnit.

As early as 1950, Anna was recognized for her work independent of her father and others in the field. She received honorary degrees from Clark University, University of Sheffield, Jefferson Medical College, University of Chicago, Yale University, Columbia University, J.W.Goethe University, and Harvard University. She was presented the Dolley Madison Award in 1965, the Commander of the Order of the British Empire (OBE) from Queen Elizabeth II in 1967, and the Grand Decoration of Honor in Gold from her native Austria in 1975.

The Royal Society of Medicine made her an honorary fellow in 1978, and the International Psychoanalytical Association named her honorary president. These were honors for the field, she believed, that were more important than acknowledgments for her work. The ambitious seven-volume *Writings of Anna Freud* was published in 1973 under her supervision.

Anna Freud suffered a stroke in 1982 and died on October 9 at the age of eighty-seven. A special memorial issue was produced by *The International Journal of Psycho-Analysis,* in which colleagues from Hampstead Clinic shared stories about her passion and inspiration as a teacher.

The clinic was renamed the Anna Freud Centre, and has earned a worldwide reputation for its treatment of disturbed children. In 1986, Anna's London home for forty years became the Freud Museum, following her wishes.

Marguerite "Peggy" Guggenheim

(1898–1979)

I am not an art collector. I am a museum.

—Peggy Guggenheim

IT IS PROBABLY an oxymoron to say that Peggy Guggenheim was one of the poorer Guggenheims, but having less wealth than her cousins played an important role in the drama of her life. Other aspects of her childhood that helped form her were the isolation of being schooled at home with governesses, and the death of her beloved father, Benjamin, who died aboard the *Titanic* in 1912.

The Guggenheim wealth was based on smelting and mining, and in the early 1900s, the family controlled the production of more than

131

70 percent of the copper, silver, and lead then mined in the world. Benjamin left less than his widow, Florette Seligman Guggenheim, and three daughters expected. They had to live modestly compared to the other relatives; compared to the general public they were still quite wealthy. The Guggenheim brothers (Peggy's uncles) also took their time straightening out Benjamin's estate and in 1919, when Peggy turned twenty-one, she came into what was only the first of her inheritance, a $450,000 trust fund, an estimated $22,500 in interest income for life (tied to the family investments yet well-managed throughout her life). Peggy traveled throughout the country, fell in love several times, and relished her newfound liberation.

Peggy had less than her two sisters in terms of physical beauty. She was tall and slim and wore clothes beautifully, but she was always self-conscious about her nose. That feeling was aggravated when a surgeon botched an operation on her nose (and had the chutzpah to charge her—in the 1920s—$1,000 anyway!).

Her first socialization with other girls her age did not come until her two years spent at the Jacoby School in New York City, from which she was graduated in 1915. Planning her debut took up most of the year of 1916. Once it was done, the young Peggy had time to wonder what to do with her life.

She sold military uniforms to officers at one short-lived job, and was a dental assistant and receptionist at another. Her third job was as a salesgirl in the Sunwise Turn Bookshop, a source of radical culture run by her cousin Harold Loeb. The job turned out to be pivotal to her life in ways no one could have imagined. At age twenty-three, she fell madly in love with one of the store's customers, sometime dadaist painter and writer, Laurence Vail, and had her first true affair.

Vail became her first husband and the father of her two children (Sindbad in 1923 and Pegeen in 1925). But the magic was short-lived. He was a wastrel, wife beater, drunk, and gold digger. As outrageous and ugly as his behavior often was, however, Vail did something positive for Peggy when the couple traveled throughout Europe. As a writer and self-considered king of Bohemia, he introduced her to the writers and painters who would influence the direction of her life.

Peggy divorced Vail in 1930, gave him alimony and custody of Sindbad, and was to remain lifelong friends with him.

By the time they divorced, she was already entangled in an affair with the man she would often say was the true love of her life, John Holms, also an English writer manqué. He died in 1934 after an operation, which he would have survived had he not been physically debauched by alcohol. Peggy was devastated and bereft. For a while. Then she met Englishman Douglas Garman who would choose Marx over Peggy's money. Yet she was on the verge of continuing her dilettante behavior when fate intervened to catapult her into a world she hadn't known existed: the world of twentieth-century art.

Peggy made a decision to open an art gallery in London, fueled in part by the addition of a second $450,000 trust left her by her mother who died in 1937. Her uncles Daniel, Murry, Simon, William, and Solomon kept her wealth intact; she was earning $50,000 a year in interest, a considerable sum in the late 1930s when the average Joe was earning about $1,500 a year.

She opened Guggenheim Jeune on Cork Street. The opening show featured the work of Jean Cocteau, arranged and displayed by Marcel Duchamp, who was to become her artistic mentor. Other shows soon followed displaying the works of painters Wassily Kandinsky and Yves Tanguy, and sculptors Antoine Pevsner, Henry Moore, Alexander Calder, Constantin Brancusi, Jean Arp, and the collage show of Max Ernst, Pablo Picasso, Georges Braque, and Jean Miró. The artists were, for the most part, relatively unknown at that time, but all benefited in one way or another from the exposure in Guggenheim Jeune. And Peggy benefited, too. She either received paintings from these grateful artists as gifts for the shows she mounted, or she bought them at relatively low prices.

Around this time, Peggy started an affair with Samuel Beckett that glided between his jealousy of her other lovers and into a lifetime friendship. Then she had a tempestuous affair with the very married Yves Tanguy, followed by a sadomasochist affair with a British collector of surrealist art, then an affair with a sculptor that ended with a pregnancy that was aborted. At a dinner once, she was asked how many husbands she had had. She replied, "Mine or someone else's?"

Her next relationship was one more of student and don, or daughter and father, with Herbert Read with whom she proposed to open something that had never been done before, a museum dedicated to modern art.

She was at a crossroads, again. Her gallery had folded and she was spending half her income on alimony and support for various artists. Although she didn't have the money to build her dream of a museum, she decided to gather some paintings for it "just in case" she was to find a way to finance her dream.

She headed to Paris where, for a while, she literally bought a painting a day, often for $1,000 or less. In this way, she acquired Fernand Léger, Jean Arp, and Brancusi, among others.

It was 1939. Realizing the seriousness of the coming invasion, she asked the Louvre to store her paintings, but after a cursory look, they dismissed her collection as not worth storing. Her collection included some of the seminal artists of our age: Kandinsky, Francis Picabia, Paul Klee, Braque, Juan Gris, Albert Gleizas, Louis Marcoussis, Robert Delaunay, Piet Mondrian, Jean Miró, Paul Delvaux, Georgio de Chirico, Salvador Dali, René Magritte, Victor Brauner, and Max Ernst. The Louvre didn't even look at the sculptures of Brancusi, Jacques Lipchitz, Alberto Giacometti, and Henry Moore.

She initially stored her artworks in a barn near Vichy. Then, fearing for their safety, had them moved to a small museum in Grenoble. She then discovered a loophole in shipping law, wherein she could transport the paintings as household objects, and the art sailed off from Marseilles to New York, along with her friend, André Breton and his family and Max Ernst who gratefully gave her some paintings in exchange for the safe passage of his works and himself. She fled Paris with her two children, just ahead of thousands seeking refuge from the encroaching Nazi forces.

Back in the safety and luxury of a New York townhouse large enough to display her growing collection, Peggy set about a campaign to marry Ernst. He eventually did marry her, but only offered a sexless and cantankerous companionship, at her very considerable expense. Although the war years had nearly doubled her income, she did not have enough for a museum, and could not possibly have created one until the war was resolved.

Looking for a way to stay involved in the art world, Peggy started an avant-garde gallery, Art of This Century, on West Fifty-seventh Street. She opened an all-woman show, featuring thirty-one painters, and became one of the first gallery owners to showcase women artists.

Dorothea Tanning, one of these women painters, was to be the undoing of her marriage, when she began an affair with Ernst. Peggy was devastated. To counteract the embarrassment and drama of the affair, she had an affair of her own with Kenneth McPherson (who, it turned out, liked one of her male servants more than her). Realizing that Ernst would not give up Tanning, Peggy asked him to vacate their apartment and to give up the studio she had given him. She had loved Ernst; and to recover, she poured herself into her one continuing love, her art collection.

She hired architect Frederick Kiesler to create an interior to do justice to her collection, and he complied with a mixture of curved walls, timed spotlights, and wires to hang some art from the ceiling. For the first time, paintings were shown unframed. The grand opening brought out art collectors and the press, and put Art of This Century smack dab in the middle of New York's art culture. The works of Mark Rothko, Adolph Gottlieb, Clyfford Still, Hans Hofmann, Robert Motherwell, William Baziotes, and even her daughter Pegeen, who had become quite a credible artist, were shown.

The star artist during this period was Jackson Pollock. Peggy agreed to give him a monthly allowance, against the sales of his paintings. If, the contract read, sales were low, he had to reimburse her with paintings, and that is how her eventual collection of twenty-three Pollocks first began.

Peggy took her unsold Pollocks back to Europe but was unable to sell them for more than $1,000, so she gave many to museums. She also made an arrangement with Pollock's wife, artist Lee Krasner, in which she gave Krasner one painting a year for free, making Krasner a millionaire many times over. She was to regret this generosity, as Pollock canvases continued to increase in popularity and value.

In 1948, she was invited to show her entire collection in the Greek Pavilion at the twenty-fourth Biennale Art Exhibition in Venice, and was the first to introduce Europe to American expressionist art. That show put her collection on solid footing in the international art scene, which led to showings at the Strozzina in Florence, the Palazzo Reale in Milan, and the hugely popular Pollock show in Sala Napoleonica at the Correr Museum in Venice, in 1950, which was the first exhibition of Pollock's work ever held in Europe.

Peggy had inherited additional wealth from her sister Benita and cousin Nettie Knox, but that didn't stop her from earning 1,000 lire (U.S. $300) a day from the more than eight hundred visitors who visited her palazzo/museum.

Despite all this wealth, Peggy did not give her children much in the way of financial support. Sindbad supported four children as an insurance surveyor in Paris. Always emotionally fragile, Pegeen overdosed on sleeping pills and died, the first successful attempt after four other tries in her forty-one years.

Pegeen's death haunted Peggy for the rest of her life. She had been vacationing in Mexico when she received the news. Many of Pegeen's paintings are hung in a room at the palazzo dedicated to her memory. Peggy continued to mount other shows, and, when the Tate Gallery in London requested an exhibition of her collection, she felt vindicated because it was the first time that a scholarly reference work about her art had been developed by an established museum. She lent the gallery 187 works.

Needing another project, Peggy created a foundation in 1968 to which she donated in perpetuity all her artwork, at the time 250 works valued at $30 million. Not a bad profit for an investment of barely $40,000. She subsequently agreed to will her works, and her palazzo, to the Solomon R. Guggenheim Foundation in New York, with the requirement that the works themselves remain in her palazzo "unless Venice sinks." Her objective, of course, was to fulfill the responsibility she felt for the art she had collected, and to ensure that it would be protected and viewed for generations to come. She had, after all, amassed the representations of the most innovative schools of her time: cubism, European abstraction, surrealism, and early American abstract expressionism, as these works came to be known.

Peggy had a triumphant exhibition at the family museum in 1969, and then mounted exhibits at both the Orangerie in 1974 in Paris and the Twentycentro at the Louvre, a delicious snub to the lack of vision of 1940's Louvre personnel who had dismissed her work in 1939. More than two hundred thousand people attended the show, paying nine francs apiece for the privilege.

Well into her seventies she updated her autobiography with *Out of This Century;* the earlier edition literally had been bought by her family in a futile effort to prevent the public from knowing about her affairs and irresponsible lifestyle. Her reputation greatly improved because of her art collection, and she became sought after as the experienced woman of art she became. She collaborated on an official biography with scholar Virginia Dortch, appeared in a television documentary of her life, entered into a collaboration with her grandson Nicolas (who also had an art gallery in Paris), exhibited her collection throughout Europe, and duplicated her Art of This Century gallery at the Centre National d'Art et Culture Georges Pompidou in Paris.

She enjoyed her grandchildren, her great grandchildren, her many dogs, her palazzo, and her position as one of the greatest modern art patrons and collectors of the twentieth century. Hers was the life of a grand dame; she dined in a room surrounded by her paintings, lived in the luxury of her home and magnificent garden, even slept in a room surrounded by art, including a bed with a silver Calder-designed headboard.

Surely her willingness to view the "new art" of the twentieth century with enthusiasm, support many of its creators in their attempt at expression, and amass a representative selection of the work was a feat in itself. What she leaves behind is a collection that is a monument to the best of twentieth-century art.

In December 1979, Peggy Guggenheim slipped while descending from a gondola. She broke her hip, which required an operation. Shortly afterward she suffered a stroke, fell into a coma, and died on December 23. She was eighty-one years old.

Marcel Duchamp, her mentor and teacher, once remarked that "art is a question of personality." Peggy Guggenheim's collection is stamped with the drama and shrewdness of her personality. In 2002, her collection, although considerably reduced after her many gifts to individuals and bequests to museums, was valued at more than $350 million; she had paid about $250,000 for the entire lot.

Peggy Guggenheim lived in the right place at the right time with enough cash and sensitivity to know merit when she saw it. Because of her direct support, Jackson Pollock is the modern American icon of painting that he is; because of her gifts and support, the works of Kandinsky, Ernst, Brancusi, and many other artists achieved a wider exposure than they ever could have received because she introduced their works to an interested clientele in New York, London, Paris, and Venice over a period of fifty years.

She enjoyed her collection, and in editing and fine-tuning it over the years, created a lasting tribute to the artists and their pioneering explorations of every aspect of what we now call modern art.

Golda Meir

(1898–1978)

I don't know what forms the practice of Judaism will assume in the future or how Jews, in Israel and elsewhere, will express their Jewishness 1,000 years hence. But I do know that Israel is not just some small beleaguered country in which 3,000,000 people are trying hard to survive; Israel is a Jewish state that has come into existence as the result of the longing, the faith, and the determination of an ancient people. We in Israel are only one part of a Jewish nation, and not even its largest part; but because Israel exists Jewish history has been changed forever, and it is my deepest conviction that there are few Israelis today who do not understand and fully accept the responsibility that history has placed on their shoulders as Jews.
—Golda Meir, *My Life*

Throughout her life, from her beginnings as a kibbutz worker in British-ruled Palestine in 1921, until her death fifty-seven years later, Golda Meir served her country's interests with an unflagging devotion that reflected her unswerving faith in the promise of a Jewish homeland. As the first woman prime minister of Israel, she was one of the most powerful leaders in the Middle East, and she presided over a nation that, since its birth in 1948, has not only changed Jewish history but has also greatly influenced world history.

Golda Meir was born Goldie Mabovitch on May 3, 1898, in the Jewish quarter of Kiev, Ukraine. Her parents, Moshe and Bluma Mabovitch, had eight children, five of them boys who died in childhood. Golda was the second of the Mabovitches' three surviving daughters.

Pogroms were a frequent fact of life in the anti-Semitic Russia of the late nineteenth century. In her autobiography, Meir recalled a pogrom that threatened the Jewish community when she was four years old: "I can remember how I stood on the stairs that led to the second floor, where another Jewish family lived, holding hands with their little daughter and watching our fathers trying to barricade the entrance with boards of wood . . . to this day I remember how scared I was and how angry that all my father could do to protect me was to nail a few planks together while we waited for the hooligans to come. And, above all, I remember being aware that this was happening to me because I was Jewish. . . . It was a feeling that I was to know again many times during my life—the fear, the frustration, the consciousness of being different and the profound instinctive belief that if one wanted to survive, one had to take effective action about it personally."

Survival was, in fact, the reason for Moshe Mabovitch's decision to emigrate. A skilled carpenter, who could not find enough work in Kiev for which a Jew could receive payment, he sold his tools, along with most of the family's belongings, and left for the United States. There, first in New York and then in Milwaukee, he worked to earn enough money for his family's passage to America. Bluma Mabovitch took her daughters to her hometown of Pinsk, where she peddled freshly baked bread door-to-door to earn money.

In 1906, after an arduous journey during which their luggage was stolen, Golda, her mother, and her sisters joined Moshe Mabovitch in Milwaukee. Because Golda's father was unable to adequately support his family through his work as a carpenter, her mother borrowed money to purchase a small grocery store. Golda's job was to open the store in the early mornings before she went off to school. Although she was often late for school because of her work at the store, she was an excellent student, and by the time she reached high school, she had decided to become a teacher. When her parents insisted that she enter into an arranged marriage rather than finish her studies, Golda decided to leave home. She taught English to immigrants for ten cents an hour, and, after earning enough money for a train ticket, went to live in Denver with her married sister, Sheyna. There, Golda continued high school and worked in her brother-in-law's dry-cleaning shop. The couple's home was a gathering place for tubercular Russian Jewish immigrants who had gone out west for treatment at a Denver hospital, and in the evenings Golda would listen intently to these anarchists, socialists, Marxists, and Zionists discuss politics, the future of the Jewish people, and Yiddish literature, including the works of Sholem Aleichem and I. L. Peretz. She also met and began dating her future husband, Morris Meyerson, a self-educated immigrant from Lithuania and an ardent Zionist, whom she admired for "his gentleness, his intelligence, and his wonderful sense of humor."

Golda and her sister did not get along, and, after an argument between the two, Golda moved out, left high school, and supported herself by working in a tailor shop. Meyerson, who was working sporadically as a sign painter, wanted to marry her, but at sixteen Golda felt she was too young. A year later, after receiving a letter from her father saying that she was needed at home, she returned to Milwaukee, where her parents promised not to interfere with her education. She finished high school in less than two years and went on to the Milwaukee Normal School for Teachers. At the same time, she joined the Labor Zionist Party, becoming an eloquent street-corner speaker for the Zionist cause.

In 1917, after graduating from the Normal School, Golda married Meyerson, whom she persuaded to immigrate to then British-ruled Palestine. In Tel Aviv, Golda was offered a job teaching English, but she was determined to work the land, so the couple joined the Merhavia kibbutz. There, Golda picked almonds, raised chickens, planted trees, managed the kibbutz kitchen, and studied Hebrew and Arabic. The harsh conditions on the kibbutz adversely affected Meyerson's health, and after two years at Merhavia, the couple moved to Tel Aviv and then to Jerusalem, where Golda found a job with the Histadrut (Labor Federation). The marriage faltered and Golda moved back to Merhavia for a time with the couple's six-month-old son, Menachem (b. 1924). She returned to her husband in Jerusalem and in 1926 the Meyerson's daughter, Sarah, was born. Golda stayed home to raise her children and took in washing to supplement the family's income.

In 1928, after two years of devoting herself exclusively to her family, she decided to become more active in political affairs. As she wrote to her sister, Sheyna, "My social activities are not an accidental thing: they are an absolute necessity for me." Golda's decision to abandon the role of homemaker and return to work was a difficult one, and she would later acknowledge that, "I am not sure that I didn't harm the children or neglect them, despite the efforts I made not to be away from them even an hour more than was strictly necessary." Adding to Golda's feelings of regret was the knowledge that her marriage was disintegrating. The Meyersons separated in 1941, and Morris Meyerson died in 1950.

Golda returned to the Histadrut, becoming secretary of the Women's Labor Council. In 1932 she took her children to New York, so that her daughter could be treated there for a serious kidney ailment. During Golda's two-year stay in New York, she worked with the Pioneer Women, a group of Yiddish-speaking immigrant women dedicated to Zionism, and raised money for the Jewish National Fund. Upon her return home, she was elected to the executive committee of the Histadrut and in 1940 became head of its political department, representing the Federation at international conferences. During and after World War II, Golda, David Ben-Gurion, and others smuggled Jews into Palestine in defiance of the embargo put into place by the British as part of the British Mandate that set a quota for immigration. In 1946 she replaced Ben-Gurion, then the director of the governing Jewish Agency, who had been arrested by the British. As interim director, Golda served as labor minister, foreign minister, and prime minister of the Yishuv (Jews of Palestine), and successfully negotiated the transfer to Palestine of thousands of families from British internment camps in Cyprus.

In 1947, the United Nations General Assembly voted to partition Palestine into a Jewish state, an Arab state, and a small internationally administered zone, including Jerusalem (the city would become divided into Jewish and Arab sections following the Arab-Israeli War of 1948–1949). The Jews in Palestine accepted the U.N. vote; the Arab states rejected it and prepared for war with the new Jewish state. Golda was sent to the United States to raise money for arms and during her stay managed to secure $50 million for munitions, which could only be delivered when statehood was officially declared. When she returned home she disguised herself as an Arab woman and was driven across enemy lines to Transjordan, where she failed to convince King Abdullah not to participate in the imminent war against the Jewish state.

On May 14, 1948, after the British high commissioner left Palestine, signaling the end of British rule, the declaration of independence proclaiming the State of Israel was signed in Tel Aviv. One of the proclamation's thirty-eight signatories was Golda Meyerson. (When Prime Minister David Ben-Gurion urged Israelis to Hebraicize their names several years later, Golda would choose the closest Hebrew word to Meyerson—"Meir," meaning "illuminate.") Golda wept as she realized that her lifelong dream of an independent Jewish homeland had finally been fulfilled.

During the Arab-Israeli War that followed, Golda was sent again to the U.S. to raise money, and while there learned that she had been named Israel's first ambassador to the Soviet Union. She was in Moscow in January 1949, when she learned that Israel had won the war.

After returning to Israel, Golda was elected to the Knesset (Israel's parliament) and after the first national elections were held, she served as minister of labor and development in Prime Minister David Ben-Gurion's cabinet. During her ministry Israel's workforce and number of housing units increased substantially.

In 1955, Meir decided to run for mayor of Tel Aviv on the Labor ballot, but the Tel Aviv Council's religious bloc rejected her candidacy because she was a woman. Meir was enraged at the Council's decision, as she later put it, "to exploit the fact that I was a woman, as if the women of Israel hadn't done their full share—and more—in the building of the Jewish state."

The following year she was somewhat compensated for her disappointment, when Ben-Gurion named her minister of foreign affairs, the second most important position in his government. She chaired the Israeli delegation to the United Nations and was placed in the delicate position of having to justify Israel's preemptive military strike against Egypt during the Suez Crisis. Throughout her career, however, Meir was adamant and unapologetic concerning Israel's right to defend itself, once explaining to a *Life* magazine reporter, "We have always said that in our war with the Arabs we had a secret weapon—no alternative."

She was called to the U.N. once again in 1960 to justify another Israeli action—the abduction of Nazi war criminal Adolf Eichmann from Argentina. As she later recalled, "Of all the public addresses I have made, that was the one that drained me the most because I felt I was speaking for the millions who could no longer speak for themselves."

From 1965 to 1968 Meir served as secretary-general of the Labor Party. She then retired, but on the death of Levi Eshkol in 1969 she was asked to take over as interim prime minister pending elections. The seventy-one-year-old Meir retained the post after elections were held in October. As prime minister of a coalition government, she dominated the Knesset and demonstrated toughness and touchiness together with humor and warmth, often working fifteen-hour days and running her cabinet with such remarkable efficiency that she was never outvoted on any issue. She remained strong-willed, firm, and confident during negotiations with hostile Arab nations and with the United States, Israel's greatest supporter, while retaining tremendous popularity with the Israeli people even when, in 1971, she survived a no-confidence vote engineered by her opponents in the Knesset, who felt she had made excessive concessions to Egypt in peace negotiations.

After a surprise attack by Egyptian-Syrian troops, which took place on Yom Kippur in 1973, Meir rallied Israeli forces. They managed to push back the aggressors and penetrate deep into Syrian and Egyptian territory, but Israeli troops sustained heavy losses and Meir's government was criticized for its unpreparedness. As a result of the costly war, Meir's popularity sharply declined, and she was twice unable to form a new coalition government. In 1974 she resigned, saying, "I can no longer bear the burden." She remained active in the Labor Party but became embittered when Egyptian President Anwar Sadat engaged in peace talks with the Conservative government of her longtime political rival, Menachem Begin. She died on December 8, 1978, after a lengthy battle with cancer.

Despite the criticisms that confronted her at the end of her career and her unwillingness to address Palestinian statehood, which remains a pressing and unresolved issue, Golda Meir's strength, vision, and dedication to building and sustaining a Jewish nation have earned her a place as one of history's most remarkable women. After her death she was eulogized as "a stalwart lioness" and "the conscience of the Jewish people." To Israelis, she was affectionately remembered as *Golda Shelanu*—"Our Golda." As an editorial in *The New York Times* stated, "The miracle of Golda Meir was how one person could perfectly embody the spirit of so many."

Molly Picon

(1898–1992)

I got a love of the stage because there I could make believe I was all the things I could never be in real life.

—Molly Picon, *Molly!*

ONE OF THE preeminent Yiddish-speaking actresses in the world, Molly Picon, once known as "the Sweetheart of Second Avenue," was also one of the few actresses to successfully make the transition from the Yiddish theater to the Broadway stage and Hollywood films. Born on the Lower East Side of Manhattan on February 28, 1898, she began life as Margaret Pyekoon, the daughter of Louis Pyekoon (later Picon), a Polish rabbinical student who did not finish his studies and neglected to divorce his first wife before coming to America. Margaret's mother, Clara Ostrovsky (later Ostrow) Pyekoon, was also an immigrant, who, in 1890, had arrived in the United States with her entire family, her featherbed, and her samovar from Rizshishtchov near Kiev, Ukraine, which Picon later described as "a little town that looks like a sneeze and sounds it."

Unhappy that his first child, nicknamed "Molly Dolly," was a girl, Louis was an indifferent father and husband, and when his second child, Helen, arrived, he left the family for good, marking the children forever. With their mother, the girls moved to Philadelphia, where Clara found a job as a seamstress at Kessler's Theatre. For extra cash, "Mama Picon," as she was affectionately known in the neighborhood, took in boarders and, as long as the rent was paid, looked the other way when any of them seemed not to be quite reputable.

In 1903, when Clara learned that the local Bijou Theater was sponsoring a children's contest for musical acts, she took five-year-old Margaret, dressed in red and wearing an elegant fake-fur muff, on the trolley downtown to compete. Challenged by a drunken passenger to perform, Molly sang, danced, and then imitated the drunken man himself. Impressed, the drunk passed around his hat and collected pennies from the other passengers—Molly's first payment for performing. At the contest, she won first prize—a five-dollar gold piece, which she added to her pennies and the loose change audience members tossed onstage.

Billed as "Baby Margaret," Picon began appearing in other amateur contests throughout the area, winning enough money to help with the family finances. She studied piano with Fanny Thomashefsky, the wife of theatrical manager Michael Thomashefsky and the sister-in-law of the famous Yiddish actor Boris Thomashefsky, and at age six began steady professional work with Michael Thomashefsky's Yiddish Repertory company at the Arch Street Theatre. There, she appeared for more than a decade in classic Yiddish plays and in the stage adaptation of *Uncle Tom's Cabin* (alternate performances were given in Yiddish and English). She sang in cabarets from 1912 to 1915 and continued to perform in stage acts while attending William Penn High School. She chose to drop out of school, however, when she realized she could not perform and study at the same time.

In 1918, despite her mother's concern over letting her daughter travel, Margaret, now known as Molly Picon, joined The Four Seasons, a touring English-language vaudeville act. The following year she found herself stranded in Boston after the city's board of health closed the theaters because of the influenza epidemic. The only theater that had been overlooked by the authorities and remained open was the Boston Grand Opera House, a Yiddish theater managed by Jacob Kalich, a former rabbinical student who had abandoned his studies to join a traveling theater troupe before leaving his native Poland. Kalich cast Picon as his *flaam feierdig soubrettin* (lively ingénue), beginning a personal and professional association that would last for fifty-six years. On June 29, 1919, Molly and Yonkel, as she called Jacob, were married in the back of a Philadelphia grocery store, with the bride dressed in a wedding gown made by her mother from a theater curtain.

Kalich, an educated man who spoke five languages fluently, although his English was still limited, began to manage Picon's career, writing or adapting most of her material. When Molly became pregnant, she continued to perform as usual, even doing somersaults, until her seventh month. "When I got on stage," she later wrote, "all the king's horses and all the king's men couldn't keep me from doing my best, giving 100 percent. Because I was in love, not only with Yonkel, but with the theater and especially our audiences." On August 13, 1920, she delivered a stillborn baby. "Peculiar that such a perfect love should bear dead fruit," she wrote in her diary. "A girl it was—and one must believe it's for the best." Pelvic disease left Picon unable to bear more children; however, she and Kalich would later sponsor a foster child and adopt a boy and a girl, refugees from the war.

In 1921 Kalich decided that Molly could enhance her reputation by perfecting her Yiddish and performing for audiences that were unfamiliar with her act. The couple embarked on a two-year trip to Europe, where Picon performed in the great theaters of Vienna, London, and Paris, with both Yiddish and non-Yiddish companies, including the esteemed Vilna Troupe. She also appeared in her first film, *Das Judenmadel* ("The Jewish Maiden"), directed by Otto Freister and shot in 1921 in Austria. This was followed by *Htet Eure Tochter* ("Watch Your Daughters!"), filmed in 1922.

In 1923 she and Kalich starred in *Ost und West* ("East and West"), a film written by Kalich and Sidney Goldin. In the film, Picon plays an American girl who disguises herself as a Hasidic boy and then, when out of her disguise, mistakenly marries a Talmudist (Kalich), who eventually becomes secularized. Filmed in Vienna, *East and West* was a comedy that highlighted the differences between American and European Jews, and is one of the few surviving Yiddish films from this time. *East and West* was censored when it was first shown in America, but in 1932 the film was restored with Yiddish subtitles and sound effects.

Picon's last European performance was in Bucharest, where Kalich directed her in *Tzipke,* his Yiddish adaptation of a popular American play, *Kiki.* In it, four-foot, ten-inch Molly played a plucky ragamuffin, a type of character she would later reprise, especially in her signature and most frequently acted role, *Yankele.* Picon was a success in *Tzipke,* but after a performance during which a large claque of university students shouted anti-Semitic epithets at the actors, threw cabbages at them, and started a riot, the American consul, fearing an international incident, "asked" the couple to leave Romania. After two more shows and a short vacation in France, Picon and Kalich returned to New York. There, Molly appeared in operettas scripted and directed by Kalich, with music by composer Joseph Rumshinsky. Picon frequently contributed lyrics to the songs.

During the 1920s Picon appeared on Second Avenue in numerous plays, including *Mameale, Tzipke, Shmendrick* ("Nincompoop"), *Gypsy Girl, Molly Dolly, Little Devil, Raizele, Oy Is Dus a Meyel* ("Oh, What a Girl!"), *The Circus Girl* (where she showed off her acrobatic prowess, dangling by her foot from a rope, a trick she had learned from an Arabian acrobatic troupe), and, of course, *Yankele.* Picon also starred as a Yiddish-speaking Peter Pan, a role she played for some three thousand performances during her long career.

Among Molly's many admirers during the decade was noted filmmaker D. W. Griffith, who called her "the most interesting actress in America," and who unsuccessfully tried to obtain financial backing to make a film starring her. Picon's films of the 1920s include *Mazel Tov* (1924), *Yidn Fun Sibri* (1925), and *Little Girl with Big Ideas,* a 1929 movie that marked Molly's debut in what were then called "talkies." In the film, Picon spoke English, but with a put-on heavy Yiddish accent.

In 1930, Kalich and Picon leased the Folks Theater on Second Avenue and renamed it the Molly Picon Theater. There, Molly starred in plays such as *The Girl of Yesterday* (making her entrance swinging on a rope) and *The Love Thief,* which drew nearly three thousand patrons each week. The shows were so successful that Picon and Kalich set out on a tour of the U.S., traveled to South America and South Africa, and in 1932, visited Palestine, where they lived on a kibbutz and Molly performed in Yiddish despite the country's Hebrew-only policy.

The following year Picon starred in her first American musical, *Birdie,* directed by eminent actor and acting teacher Monty Woolley and staged at the Majestic Theatre in Brooklyn. The show was, as Picon later put it, "a full-sized flop."

She and Kalich began a radio career in 1934, doing five programs a week in Yiddish. Sponsored by Jello-O and later by Maxwell House Coffee, Picon's radio shows helped to make these products popular with American Jewish housewives. At the same time, Picon, the perennial trouper, continued to perform in Yiddish and non-Yiddish plays and to do her vaudeville act. Around this time Picon decided she needed a short vacation and on the suggestion of her fellow actors headed for Ogunquit, Maine. There, she was stunned to discover that because she was Jewish, no hotel would allow her to check in.

In the 1930s, Picon appeared in two of her most notable films. *Yidl Mitn Fidle* ("Yiddle with a Fiddle"), filmed in Poland in 1937, was written by Kalich and directed by Joseph Green, with songs by Itsik and Ellstein Manger. Picon, who once again played a girl dressed as a boy, received $10,000, then the highest salary for an actor in a Yiddish-language movie. Retitled for American audiences as *Castles in the Air,* it was dubbed in English when rereleased in 1961. *Mamele* (1938), a comic melodrama based on a play by Meyer Schwartz, featured the then forty-year-old Picon as a twelve-year-old who takes care of her six siblings and widowed father. Also filmed in Poland, *Mamele* was the last Jewish film made there before the Nazi invasion.

Picon had begun to resent Kalich's inability to treat her as an adult woman rather than as a child and a student, and was pursuing roles without his management and mentorship. By the early 1940s, their marriage was in jeopardy. The couple briefly separated, then reconciled, with the understanding that Kalich would treat Picon as an equal partner, both professionally and personally.

In 1942, Kalich wrote and Picon starred in *Oy Is Dus a Leben!* ("What a Hard Life"), an autobiographical musical about their life together. Written in both Yiddish and English, it ran at the Al Jolson Theater and was the first Yiddish play presented on Broadway. The same year Picon and Kalich sponsored a foster son, George Weinstein, a teenage Belgian Jew living in London.

During World War II, Picon and Kalich performed for refugees in Canada, and after the war they were the first entertainers to visit orphanages and displaced persons camps in Europe, under the auspices of the Jewish Labor Committee. Together with their songs and skits, Molly and Yonkel brought the refugees (many of them concentration camp survivors) colorfully wrapped gifts of such luxury items as cosmetics, chocolates, costume jewelry, and sewing supplies. After one show, they were told that a three-year-old in the audience had experienced the first sound of laughter he had ever heard. Picon would later write that after hearing this, "Yonkele told me, 'Molly, that's our job. Make them laugh.'" Back in the U.S., they worked for the United Nations Relief and Rehabilitation Administration and sold bonds for Israel and the Children's Fund.

Picon's career continued to thrive after the war. She appeared in plays such as *For Heaven's Sake, Mother,* in which she played a seamstress, *Abi Gesunt* ("So Long as You're Healthy"), *Sadie Is a Lady*, and, of course, *Yankele*, in which the fifty-year-old Picon performed somersaults as the thirteen-year-old title character. (She would reprise the role at eighty). *Variety* dubbed her a "bean-sized Bernhardt" for her performance in *Pavolye, Tage* ("Slowly, Daddy"), a rewrite of an earlier Picon vehicle, *Hello, Molly.*

In 1949, Picon made her first foray into the fledgling medium of television, when she starred in *The Molly Picon Show.* In 1953 she appeared in *Make Mamma Happy,* a show bound for Broadway that flopped in previews. The same year, "Mama Clara" Picon died of a heart attack, a sad event that resulted in Molly's refusal to sing "My Yiddish Momme" for a year. In 1954 she toured Israel, playing benefit performances in Yiddish. While there, she spoke before the Knesset on the importance of preserving the Yiddish language, even among Hebrew-speaking Jews.

In 1959 Picon starred in a revival of Kalich's Yiddish drama, *The*

Kosher Widow—her last big stage success until the 1961 musical, *Milk and Honey*, which would be her only original Broadway hit. Two years later Picon scored another success, playing a Jewish housewife married to an irascible artificial fruit salesman, played by Lee J. Cobb, in the film version of Neil Simon's Broadway play, *Come Blow Your Horn*. Picon's hilarious performance earned her an Academy Award nomination for best supporting actress.

During the 1960s Picon continued to appear on the stage in plays and musicals, and was a frequent—and memorable—guest star on television shows such as *Car 54, Where Are You?*, *Dr. Kildare*, and *The Jack Paar Show*. By the late 1960s Kalich was in failing health; nevertheless he toured with Picon in *Milk and Honey* in the summer of 1969. That December, the couple celebrated their fiftieth wedding anniversary at a gala hosted by the Hebrew Actors Union at the Commodore Hotel in New York. In 1971 Kalich took a small role— his last—in the film version of *Fiddler on the Roof;* Picon played Yente the Matchmaker. After appearing in the film *For Pete's Sake* (1974), Picon stopped working to take care of Kalich, who died of cancer in 1975. After his death, she sold the couple's country house, Chez Schmendrick, in Mahopac, New York, and donated memorabilia from her home to the YIVO Institute for Jewish Research in New York City.

In 1975 Picon was honored at the one hundredth anniversary of the Yiddish theater at the Museum of the City of New York. Many of the museum's collection of scripts, programs, photographs, and costumes from Picon and Kalich's career were used in a show about the couple's life, which Molly performed at Carnegie Hall during the same year.

In 1980 the Philadelphia Public Library presented a major exhibit of Picon's work to coincide with her appearance in a revival of *Milk and Honey*. Also in 1980 she was presented with the Creative Achievement Award of the Performing Arts Unit of B'nai B'rith, and given the Congress of Jewish Culture "Goldie Award," named for Abraham Goldfaden, the father of Yiddish theater. Picon accepted her award wearing a tuxedo—it was her homage to the ragamuffin little boy characters she had played so many years ago.

Despite the onset of Bell's Palsy, the eighty-one-year-old Picon performed her one-woman show, *Hello Molly*, and published her autobiography, *Molly!* (1980). She moved to an apartment near Lincoln

Center with her widowed sister, Helen Silverblatt. They spoke Yiddish to one another for the rest of their lives together.

Molly Picon died of Alzheimer's disease in 1992 at the age of ninety-four. "The darling of the world," as critic Brooks Atkinson once called her, had charmed audiences for nearly a century and in doing so, had kept alive the vibrant language of Yiddish and the brilliance of the Yiddish theater.

Louise Nevelson

(1899-1988)

Louise Nevelson's life was the quintessential American success story—an immigrant invents a new identity for herself and achieves fame in the New World. She was uprooted twice, first from tsarist Russia in early childhood, then from Maine in 1920 when she left for New York as a young bride. Her artistic maturity coincided with the blossoming of American art in the mid-twentieth century, and although she was never embraced by any aesthetic movement, by the end of her life she was regarded as integral to the renaissance of American sculpture, and her work was in the collections of the world's major museums.

—Laurie Lisle, *Louise Nevelson: A Passionate Life*

A PIONEER IN the art of sculpture, Louise Nevelson spent three decades struggling for recognition of her work. She was determined to fully devote herself to the search for her personal artistic vision and, to that end, willingly sacrificed marriage, motherhood, and even financial security. Today she is considered one of the major sculptors of the twentieth century and toward the end of her life, she received more public commissions than any other American sculptor.

Nevelson is known for her monumental box assemblages of complex, rhythmic abstract shapes. Her sculptures, constructed from odd pieces of wood, found objects, cast metal, and other materials, and completely covered with black, gold, or white paint, have a uniform tone that gives them a mysterious, dynamic quality and accentuates the structural importance of the shadows within them. Nevelson, who, as Laurie Lisle observes, "regarded herself as an original self-creation," also favored a wardrobe that was almost as dramatic and unique as her sculptures. She fringed her eyes with layers of thick, black eyelashes made of fur and costumed herself in wildly unconventional ensembles that might typically consist of a Chinese embroidered robe over a denim workshirt and a Mexican skirt, topped by a head-scarf or jockey cap. Nevelson's unmistakable style in sculpture and dress, as well as her outspokenness, energy, and resilience, made her immediately recognizable as an artistic presence and a celebrity, and expressed to the world her fierce individualism. As she once said, "It's a hell of a thing to be born, and if you're born you're at least entitled to your own life."

Nevelson was born Leah Berliawsky in Pereyaslav, a shtetl town fifty miles southeast of Kiev, in the present-day Ukraine. Her parents were Isaac and Minna Zeisel (Smolerank) Berliawsky. Called by the diminutive, Leike, Nevelson was the second child in an Orthodox family that would eventually include one son and three daughters. Nevelson's birth date is difficult to pinpoint with any accuracy. The Russians did not record Jewish births, but Minna Berliawsky, who observed the Jewish calendar, knew that her oldest daughter was born during the seven-day Succoth harvest festival, on the nineteenth day of the month of Tishri. Since Succoth falls on a different day each autumn, and the Julian and Gregorian calendars differ by thirteen days, no one could ever agree on Nevelson's birthday, with the result that it continually fluctuated, and included dates in September, October, and December. The adult Nevelson finally settled on September 23, after consulting a rabbi and asking him to conclusively determine when Succoth had occurred in the year of her birth. The Berliawsky's next-door neighbor was the sister of writer Sholom Aleichem, and when Aleichem called upon them and saw baby Leah, he described her as "built for greatness," an interesting compliment, given Nevelson's sculpture, as well as her later artistic fame.

In 1902, Isaac Berliawsky immigrated to the United States, an event which greatly affected two-year-old Leah, who refused to speak for nearly two years. "While she remained mute," writes Lisle, "her powers of observation were strengthened, since she had to grasp things by watching rather than by asking. Her memories from that time were later expressed as heightened visual ones, like the vibrant hues of the vegetable colors with which her grandmother dyed wool. Other recollections would not emerge until she had blossomed as a sculptor in the 1950s, like her creation of *Forgotten Village*, a sculpture that seemed to evoke a half-remembered Russian shtetl."

In 1905 Isaac sent money and steamship tickets to his wife, so that she and the children could join him in Rockland, Maine, where he had settled. Although Minna Berliawsky was hesitant to leave her home, she was observant of the Jewish tradition that a wife must follow her husband. Anti-Semitic violence was also increasing, and she was fearful for the lives of her children. After a long journey by cart, train, and ship, Nevelson's mother, brother, and little sister arrived in Boston in March 1905. There, they were met by a Russian-born relative, Joseph Dondis, who helped the children anglicize their names. Leah became Louise; her older brother, Nachman, became Nathan; her sister, Chaya, was renamed Annie. The following year, Minna Berliawsky gave birth to her fourth child, a daughter who was named Lillian.

In Rockland, Isaac Berliawsky began as a junk dealer and grocer, and eventually became a well-to-do landowner and builder. But the family's transition from a Russian shtetl into what Nevelson would later describe as "a WASP Yankee town," was difficult. The Berliawskys spoke Yiddish, did not mingle with the nearly thirty other Jewish families in Rockland, and, as immigrants and Jews, were excluded from much of the community's social life—all of which increased their sense of isolation and alienation.

Nevelson learned enough English to attend first grade in Rockland's public grammar school in the fall of 1905, but predictably it took time for her to gain any real fluency in the new language. Ostracized by the other children, Nevelson felt shy, tongue-tied, and self-conscious throughout her school years. She continued to speak Yiddish at home, but as her fluency in English grew so did her feeling that she was losing her cultural origins as well as her native language. "As Yiddish became for Louise a hidden tongue," writes Lisle, "she became accustomed to using an intimate private language and a more formal public one, which laid the groundwork for both her sense of secrecy and her eventual reliance upon a personal aesthetic vocabulary."

Nevelson's feelings of isolation and her shyness were somewhat mitigated by what she later claimed was a happy home life. "I adored my parents," she told her biographer and friend, art dealer Arnold Glimcher. "My mother was freethinking and had strong socialist ideas. My father believed in equal rights for women." The Berliawskys stressed the value of education, and encouraged their children's interest in the arts.

In addition to her schoolwork, Nevelson took private dancing, piano, and voice lessons. She also drew and painted in watercolor and oils, and early on expressed her artistic sense of fashion by wearing her own creations. Once, when the Rockland librarian asked nine-year-old Louise what she wanted to be when she grew up, she replied, "An artist, no a sculptor; I don't want color to help me." She was a mediocre student, but she excelled in her high school art classes and became determined to attend Pratt Institute in New York City. Her chance to fulfill her dream of studying in New York, not as a poor student, but as a wealthy society matron, came in 1917, when she met thirty-seven-year-old New York businessman Charles Nevelson, a partner in Nevelson Brothers Shipping Company. The Nevelsons were German-speaking Lithuanian Jews from Riga, Latvia. The couple became engaged in 1918, after Louise's graduation from high school. They were wed in Boston in 1920, and following a honeymoon in Cuba settled in an apartment on Central Park West in New

York City. Two years later, Louise Nevelson's only child, Myron (Mike), was born.

During the 1920s, Nevelson, now a New York socialite, wife, and mother, plunged into a study of all the arts. She took voice lessons from Metropolitan Opera coach Estelle Liebling and private drawing lessons from the well-known artist William Meyerowitz, and in 1924 began to study acting at the International Arts Institute in Brooklyn with the Italian actress Princess Norina Matchabelli. She also attended lectures given by the Eastern mystic Krishnamurti, and throughout her life she continued to study metaphysics in an ongoing search for self-awareness. In 1929 Nevelson enrolled full time at the Art Students League, where she studied painting and drawing with the artist Kenneth Hayes Miller. At the same time, she began to feel increasingly stifled by her marriage, and by the *haut bourgeois* behavior of the Nevelson clan. "My husband's family thought they were terribly refined," she later wrote. "Within their circle you could know Beethoven, but God forbid if you *were* Beethoven. You were not allowed to be a creator, you were just supposed to be an audience."

In 1931, Nevelson gave herself what she later called "the greatest gift I could have, my own life." She left her husband, entrusted her son to her family in Maine, and went to Munich, Germany, to study with legendary art teacher Hans Hoffman. Soon after Nevelson arrived, however, Hoffman left for the United States to escape the rising tide of fascism. Nevertheless, Hoffman's cubist teachings greatly impressed Nevelson and profoundly affected her work. After a short stay in Munich, where she became part of the café community of artists and writers, she was invited to Vienna to appear in films as a bit player. Nevelson's experience with the shadowy and illusory appearance of the movie sets, as well as the lighting and the look of the films would add another dimension to her artistic vision. After permanently separating from her husband, she pawned her jewels and went to Paris. While studying there, she became entranced by Picasso's work, as well as the power of the African sculpture in the Museé de L'Homme. She returned to New York in 1932 to continue her studies and to begin working as a sculptor.

The 1930s were difficult years both financially and professionally for Nevelson. She resumed her study of art with Hans Hoffman, who was now teaching at the Art Students League, and assisted the charismatic socialist Mexican artist, Diego Rivera, in his Rockefeller Center WPA mural project. Rivera introduced Nevelson to the art of pre-Columbian Mexico, and the two became friends, although Nevelson later admitted she had felt competitive with him, recalling, "I thought I could be as good an artist as Diego, so why should I play second fiddle to him? I had my future in front of me, and I was very confident that I could fulfill it." Nevelson also began studying sculpture with sculptor Chaim Gross. Her sculptures during this period were small human, animal, or abstract figures modeled in plaster or clay. In 1935 she showed her work for the first time in a show titled "Young Sculptors" at the Brooklyn Museum. It was around this time that her son came to live with her while he finished high school. Despite their long separation, Nevelson was able to establish a close relationship with Mike that lasted for the rest of her life. Like his mother, Mike Nevelson became a sculptor.

In 1937, Nevelson took her first and only steady job, as a WPA-funded teacher at the Educational Alliance School of Art. In 1939 Congress cut off funds for such WPA projects, and she was laid off. By 1941 she had gained a small amount of recognition for her work, but had achieved no significant success and was in acute financial distress. With a courage born of desperation, she stormed into the prestigious Nierendorf Gallery and insisted that Karl Nierendorf look at her work. He agreed, visited her studio, and, impressed, arranged her first solo exhibition. Nierendorf became Nevelson's close friend and a major source of professional support. When he died suddenly of a heart attack in 1947 Nevelson sank back into obscurity. After making two trips to Mexico from 1949 to 1950, she produced *The King and Queen* and *Magic Garden,* two etchings that reflected the monumental and totemic Mayan art and architecture she saw there. Both would be incorporated into her sculptures of the 1950s.

A small inheritance enabled Nevelson to buy a house on East Thirtieth Street in Manhattan. There, for the first time, she was able to live and work in one place. In 1952 she started the Four O'Clock Forum, a discussion group that included such artists as Mark Rothko and Max Weber, who were seeking a new abstract form different from the abstract expressionist style that dominated the art scene. In 1955 Nevelson began to exhibit again when her sculptures, constructed of orange crates painted black, were featured in the first of several one-woman shows at the Grand Central Moderns Gallery.

In 1957, Nevelson began to assemble "found objects"—moldings, jagged scraps of crates, furniture legs—within stacked boxes to create rich encrusted walls. With her "Moon Garden + One" exhibition in 1958, which featured her matte black sculpture wall, *Sky Cathedral,* Nevelson fully came into her own style. Critics called *Sky Cathedral* "marvelous"; Nevelson characteristically called it "a feast—for myself." Art collectors began to show interest in her work, and she was offered a contract with the prestigious Martha Jackson Gallery. Louise Nevelson was at last financially secure.

When Nevelson was invited to exhibit in the Museum of Modern Art's "Sixteen Americans" show in New York in 1959, she created a massive all-white environment, *Dawn's Wedding Feast,* which she defined as "a marriage with the world." In 1962, she produced the all-gold wall assemblage, *Dawn,* which she had filled with furniture sections, baseball bats, and rifle stocks. The same year she represented the United States in the sculpture section of the Venice Biennale. In 1967 she presented a major retrospective exhibition of her work at the Whitney Museum of American Art in New York. During this period Nevelson also created what Laurie Lisle has called "a sculptural kaddish," titled *Homage to Six Million I,* a massive black wall dedicated to the memory of the Jews slaughtered during World War II. A second *Homage* was dedicated at the Israel Museum in Jerusalem. In the remarks she wrote for the ceremony, Nevelson said she hoped that her wall would be "a living presence of a people who have triumphed. They rose far and above the greatest that was inflicted upon them." Among Nevelson's other notable works are *Ice Palace I* (1967), a Plexiglas sculpture; *Bicentennial Dawn* (1976), a large three-part white wooden sculpture; *Mrs. N's Palace* (1977), her largest assemblage; and *Shadows and Flags* (1978), a group of huge steel sculptures created for the newly named Louise Nevelson Square in downtown Manhattan.

In 1978, she was elected a member of the elite American Academy of Arts and Letters, occupying the chair originally held by the nineteenth-century sculptor Augustus Saint-Gaudens, and in 1983 was awarded the academy's gold medal for sculpture. Two years later she received the National Medal for the Arts.

Louise Nevelson died of a brain tumor at her home on April 17, 1988. A memorial service arranged by Arnold Glimcher was held in the Medieval Sculpture Hall at the Metropolitan Museum of Art in New York City. In 1994, she was once again eulogized during a commemoration of the Nevelson-Berliawsky Gallery of Twentieth Century Art at the Farnsworth Museum in Rockland, Maine.

Nevelson has earned her place among the pantheon of major twentieth-century sculptors for her unique view of sculpture as environmental and transforming, and for her innovative use of materials. As an artist and a woman who succeeded in living her life and pursuing her work completely on her own terms, she has been a source of inspiration for the women artists who came after her. As art critic Robert Hughes observed in a *Time* magazine cover story on the artist, Louise Nevelson has redefined "the assumptions that surround the role of women in art. In that respect, she belongs to the culture as a whole, not just to the art world and its concerns."

Dorothy Schiff

(1903–1989)

Dorothy Schiff had a remarkable journalistic career. Almost forty when she gained control of the New York Post, and lacking experience in the newspaper business, she transformed the paper from a money-losing venture into a profitable and successful enterprise. Under her leadership the Post supported liberal causes, including civil liberties during the McCarthy period and the early years of the civil rights movement. A determined and often courageous woman, Dorothy extended her influence beyond the corporate office to create an instrument of social change.

—Kevin J. O'Keefe, newspaper critic and author of
*A Thousand Deadlines: The New York City Press
and American Neutrality, 1914–1917.*

PART OF AN affluent family that prized being the first Jewish family listed in the New York Social Register, Dorothy Schiff had a shaky foundation for her role in life as the first woman publisher of a newspaper in her hometown. Through her relationships with both Eleanor and Franklin Delano Roosevelt, and her second husband, George Backer, she became much more involved and aware of the social issues of her day. Nonetheless, she was not naive about how and why she came to own a newspaper. "Influence, not power, is what interests me," she said, commenting on the allegation that she confused gossip with political commentary. "It's only because I'm Dorothy Schiff of the *New York Post*; otherwise I wouldn't be there."

Dorothy Schiff was born into a wealthy Republican family, on March 11, 1903, in New York City. Her parents were investment banker Mortimer Leo Schiff and Adele Neustadt Schiff. Her father loved racehorses more than banking, and both he and his wife coveted a spot on the city's social register, so much so that they gave up their Fifth Avenue mansion, a gift from Mortimer's father, and settled on the Oyster Bay estate, Northwood, on Long Island in an area known as The Cove, long the bastion of WASP wealth. Mortimer bought a thousand acres in 1900 and hired Charles P. H. Gilbert to design a Tudor-style home, which was completed in 1906. The Schiffs reached their dream of inclusion into the Social Register in 1904, and when they moved into their new home they also moved into an arena of social activity they were to relish for years. Dorothy's grandfather, Jacob Schiff, had been an émigré from Frankfurt in 1865. The elder Schiff was an accomplished banker and financier who was a director of Kuhn, Loeb & Co. He was a devout Jew who set up Hebrew schools in all five boroughs of New York City, and contributed generously to the International Ladies Garment Workers Union, most of whose members were then eastern European Jews. He was also a founder of Temple Emanu-El. This conflicted heritage of social-climbing parents, and a devoutly religious grandfather, left its mark on Dorothy. Although she and her brother underwent bat and bar mitzvahs, she dallied with Christianity, converting to the Episcopal faith but later reverted back to Judaism. In the end, she favored the establishment of Israel, was impressed by its dedication and the kibbutz movement, and supported many Jewish-related causes in her later years.

Dorothy and her brother were educated at home, more out of their mother's phobia of germs and fear of "infection" than any particular public curriculum; this experience, Dorothy wrote in her auto-biography, left her feeling isolated both by her exceptional wealth, and by her Jewish heritage. She was graduated from the private Brearley School in 1920, then attended Bryn Mawr, where she was such a poor student that she flunked every course. As many women of her era did, she sought marriage as an escape, and she found her route through the affections of a bond salesman, Richard B. Hall, who was, importantly, listed in the social register. She was seventeen years old.

This alliance produced a son, Morti, and a daughter, Adele, but the marriage did not survive Hall's drinking, philandering, or his re-grettable anti-Semitism. What finally made the divorce possible was her inheritance of fifteen million dollars from her parents; her father died in 1931 and her mother a few months later in 1932.

Dorothy quickly segued into another marriage, this time with a writer and liberal Democrat who was a city councilman, George Backer. Backer was well connected in the arts and politics of the day, and introduced Dorothy to the luminaries of the Algonquin Round Table and to the power brokers of the New Deal. She quickly switched allegiance from her family's Republican Party to become a supporter of Franklin Delano Roosevelt and the Democratic Party.

Close friends with both Eleanor and President Franklin D. Roosevelt, Dorothy Schiff purchased land adjacent to their estate on the Hudson River and built a more modest home she dubbed Red House, in a style she called "Franklin the First." Eleanor Roosevelt encouraged her work with the National Association for the Advancement of Colored People (NAACP) through which Dorothy would meet, and work, with African-American leaders including Mary McLeod Bethune and Walter White.

Dorothy and George had a daughter in 1934, Sarah Ann, and lived on her share of the Northwood estate, some three hundred acres. Following a bout with depression, she moved back to New York City where both political and community events drew her to boycott German goods, which sparked her interest in both political and so-cial welfare organizations. She was named to the New York City

Board of Child Welfare (1937–1939) by Mayor Fiorello LaGuardia, and devoted much of her time and effort as a member of the boards of directors of the Henry Street Settlement (1934–1938), Mt. Sinai Hospital (1934–1938), and the New York Women's Trade Union League (1939). She also served on the Social Service Committee of Bellevue Hospital, the Ellis Island Investigating Committee, and was the secretary-treasurer of the New York Joint Committee for the Ratification of the Child Labor Amendment.

Backer had been friends with Franklin Delano Roosevelt, who had urged him to buy the *Post*. Roosevelt had previously urged his friend J. David Stern to buy the paper, but Stern's tenure as publisher proved disastrous. At Backer's prodding, Dorothy Schiff bought the floundering *New York Post* in 1939 and installed Backer as president and treasurer. She became the vice president and treasurer. (The paper is the oldest continuously published daily in the United States. It was founded on November 16, 1801, by Alexander Hamilton and a consortium of Federalist supporters.) It was not an immediate money maker; in fact, it lost two million dollars in its first year under Dorothy Schiff's ownership.

In 1943, she took control of the paper—not only to save her investment, but also her personal fortune—and in doing so became New York's first woman newspaper publisher. She ended her marriage and professional collaboration with Backer in 1943, and married the feature editor, Theodore O. Thackrey, whom she promoted to executive editor. A miscarriage and a decided difference in political opinions sounded the death knell for their marriage, which ended in 1950. (He liked Wallace, she endorsed Dewey, and they were both wrong; Truman won.) Despite the failed marriage, Thackrey has been credited for helping the *Post* first become profitable in 1949. Schiff became the owner, publisher, and chairman of the board of directors of the newly constituted New York Post Corporation in 1945 and acquired the *Bronx Home News*, a daily newspaper, which merged with the *Post* in 1948. She launched a Paris bureau and established the *Paris Post* to compete with the *International Herald Tribune*, only the second American newspaper to be published in the French capital. The *Paris Post*, edited by Paul Scott Mowrer, was published from May 1945 until 1948, from an office at 6 Boulevard Poissonniere, until labor difficulties forced its closing.

Schiff appointed thirty-three-year-old James Wechsler as the paper's editor in 1949. The Washington correspondent, whom many journalism analysts view as the head of the *Post*'s golden age, was brash and brilliant and gave the *Post* its decidedly livelier and more liberal slant. He developed the paper's national reputation for investigative reporting in its crusade against Westbrook Pegler, broke the Richard Nixon "slush fund" story, and revealed that television's quiz show contestants had been cheating with the cooperation of the shows' producers.

Her own column, "Dear Reader," contained commentary that was so popular she won election as an anti-Tammany candidate for the Democratic State Committee from the Ninth Assembly District in 1951.

During the 1950s, Schiff made the *Post* her primary focus, and launched critical coverage of Walter Winchell, Joseph McCarthy, and J. Edgar Hoover. She came to believe that "narrow-mindedness, prejudice, and all the things it is the business of liberals to fight" was the primary mission of her newspaper.

The *Post*'s stance against McCarthyism brought counterattacks, from vandalism on the newspaper's building to summoning Wechsler to appear before the Permanent Committee on Investigations. Her vigorous and wholehearted support of Wechsler greatly enhanced her personal and professional reputation.

Despite her enthusiasm for Wechsler, in 1961 she came to view the necessity for dividing his responsibilities into two distinct areas: giving him a political column and supervision of feature columnists, and hiring Paul Sann as executive editor to broaden general news and sports coverage.

In the early 1950s she had met a Jewish-German industrialist, and Zionist, Rudolf G. Sonneborn, to whom she was married from 1953 to 1974; they had no children. They traveled to Israel and remained together despite his slow recovery from a massive stroke in 1959.

Throughout her tenure Schiff brought a wide spectrum of columnists, reporters, and feature writers to her *Post* pages, including Langston Hughes, Murray Kempton, William Shannon, Jimmy Cannon, Sylvia Porter, Victor Riesel, and Max Lerner. Columnists William F. Buckley, Tom Braden, Pete Hamill, Jimmy Breslin, James Thurber, Nora Ephron, Joseph Lash, Norman Poirier, Anthony Scaduto, and Robert Spivak were also part of the *Post* family of writers.

Celebrity columnists included, at one time or another, Eleanor Roosevelt, Jackie Robinson, Arthur Schlesinger, Jr., and Orson Welles.

Schiff caused an uproar when she switched her political support from New York Governor Averell Harriman to Nelson Rockefeller only twenty-four hours before the election. In a feature, "Notice to Readers," she wrote that she had gone against her editors because of Harriman's "snide insinuation that Nelson Rockefeller is pro-Arab and anti-Israel." The change in support helped launch Rockefeller's national political career.

Dorothy Schiff became editor-in-chief in 1962 and in this pivotal position, she was the decision maker when the *Post* was shut down by a strike of the International Typographic Union, Local #3, from December 8, 1962, through March 3, 1963. Fearing further losses, she took the controversial step of withdrawing the *Post*'s membership in the Publishers Association (alienating her from her fellow publishers) and made her own arrangements with the union.

The 1970s were a shaky time for newspapers across the country, with drops in circulation because of the increasing dependence on television for news, which was fostered by a growing suburban population, and the escalating costs of paper and labor. Still, the *Post* was vocal in its support of the early efforts of the Civil Rights struggle, hiring Ted Poston to cover the movement, making it one of the first major newspapers to hire an African-American journalist. Schiff also hired many other crusading columnists and talented news reporters, and took the bold step to be one of the first American newspapers to protest the war in Vietnam.

In 1976, the year in which the *Post*'s circulation reached a low of 489,000, she sold the newspaper to Australian publisher, Rupert Murdoch, for an estimated $31 million. "The reason has been widely misconstrued. It was not sold for 'estate purposes.' Evening papers in urban areas have not survived. The *Post* had a deficit in 1975, and was a heavy loser in 1976, I could no longer meet the deficits," she said.

Dorothy Schiff died of cancer at her New York apartment in 1989 at the age of 86. The *New York Post* has since been sold several times, but it remains one of New York City's major dailies.

Ayn Rand

(1905–1982)

My philosophy, in essence, is the concept of man as a heroic being, with his own happiness as the moral purpose of his life, with productive achievement as his noblest activity, and reason as his only absolute.
—Ayn Rand, on her philosophy of objectivism

As a LITTLE girl in Russia, Alyssa Rosenbaum lived a relatively affluent life, the result of her father holding a rare position in the country at the time: a chemist with his own shop.

The family home in St. Petersburg represented this station, with maid, cook, and a governess for Alyssa and her two sisters, Nora and Natasha. Her mother, Anna Borisovna Rosenbaum, hosted frequent parties, was supremely social, and valued friendship and the arts, particularly theater and ballet. She was proud of Alyssa's intelligence, but concerned about her lack of social graces and girlfriends her own age. Alyssa's father, Zinovy Zacharovich "Fronz" Rosenbaum, was busy at work and considered remote, until his daughter became a teenager and engaged him in frequent discussions of ideas, especially political.

She was taught French and German by her governess and given French children's magazines to enjoy, especially those in which good triumphed over evil. One hero was Cyrus, from *The Mysterious Valley,* Maurice Champagne's story of the British soldiers in India. Cyrus became a personal inspiration. He was a man of action and intelligence and great courage, a model for what was to be Rand's "heroic man," immortalized in her future novels.

Her family could afford travel to Austria and Switzerland, and during these travels she first expressed her goal to be a writer. What she would write about, she declared, was "how people could be not as they are."

In 1917, the Russian Revolution began, ripping the power from Czar Nicholas II, who was overthrown by the Duma, headed by Prime Minister Alexander Kerensky. The fight of the people against the aristocracy was the fight for the freedom of the individual, she surmised, and for the first time, she understood that politics could be a moral issue about where the power to govern over others would lie.

When Kerensky abdicated his role as leader, Communists seized private businesses (including her father's shop), and what followed for the Rosenbaum family was acute poverty and a move to Odessa, a city in the Crimea region that was not yet under Communist control. The area, however, soon became a battleground. Food was almost impossible to come by, and the family was forced to exist on a diet of onions and millet.

Now a teenager, Alyssa excelled in school, especially in logic and mathematics, and was fascinated with a course in American history, which introduced her to the idea that the freedom of the individual that was supported by American democracy was actually working— something she had long believed in.

While a teenager, she also changed her belief system to atheism, primarily because she could not accept a concept of God that would degrade man. While never denying her Jewish heritage, she dismissed all religion and forms of mysticism as something to be opposed. Her philosophy that altruism is a vice certainly could be painted as opposite the values of traditional Jewish culture, yet it is no small irony that her passion for the freedoms of America was shared by hundreds of thousands of Jews, just like her, who left Europe to pursue these freedoms in the United States.

An avid reader (she had taught herself to read by age four), she fell in love with the works of Victor Hugo, who wrote *Les Miserables;* Edmond Eugene Alexis Rostand, who wrote *Cyrano;* and the philosophical writings of Frederich Nietzsche, who shared her belief that man's purpose is the pursuit of his own personal happiness. The values and beliefs she formed from these writers during her teenage years were to remain unchanged throughout her life.

The family returned to St. Petersburg (renamed Petrograd in 1914) where she was graduated from the University of Petrograd (later known as Leningrad University) in 1924 with a degree in history. Alyssa was nineteen. Despite the change in the political climate, movies were still being shown, and she studied screenwriting at the State Institute for Cinema Arts in 1924.

In January 1926, thanks to Chicago relatives who offered to finance her trip, Alyssa left Russia, never to see her parents or Russia again. When she arrived, she presented herself as Ayn Rosenbaum. She had heard of a Finnish writer whose first name was Ayn (which rhymes with line) and she co-opted it not because she loved the books, but because she loved the name itself. She later changed her last name to Rand; taking it from her typewriter, a Remington-Rand. When she married, she kept her name, and fully expecting success, she did not reveal her Russian name until much later in life for fear that there might be repercussions to her remaining family there.

Ayn loved to see movies in Russia and was familiar with many American films, particularly the glamorous ones of Cecil B. DeMille. With an introduction to his publicity agent, Rand soon left her Chicago relatives to pursue a screenwriting career in Hollywood, but the contact could offer her nothing job-wise. By pure serendipity, she saw DeMille in his car and stared at him so long he asked her why. "I just arrived from Russia," she said, "and I'm very happy to see you." Charmed, he took her to the set of *King of Kings* to watch the filming and by the end of the week, he hired her as an extra.

Timing nodded again. On the set she met a handsome actor, Frank

O'Connor, who was to become her husband, and later the physical prototype of her hero Howard Roark of *The Fountainhead*. They married on April 15, 1929, and although the marriage may have been spurred on by her desire for a permanent visa, the couple remained married for fifty years. Rand reaffirmed her enthusiasm about America and became a naturalized citizen on March 13, 1931.

During the thirties, with the Great Depression crippling the economy, Rand found various jobs in and outside of the film industry. She used the cushion of a regular salary to begin writing her first novel, *We the Living*. She was able to sell *Red Pawn*, a screenplay, to Universal Studios for $1,500, although it was never produced. But that money allowed her the time to reshape her novel, one of the very first to reflect the truth of what was happening in Russia.

She also wrote *Penthouse Legend,* which was produced on Broadway in 1935 retitled as *Night of January 16*. It was only a moderate success. When *We the Living* was finally published, it was not an immediate success but gained momentum as the years went by. It would eventually sell millions. It was a credible beginning of what would be her greatest strength as a novelist, the ability to develop a strong narrative and, more important to her, offered a glimpse of her growing personal philosophy about man against the state, and the effort to create a character that would become her archetypal man.

Her next published novel was *Anthem,* a futuristic look at a society in which the individual is an outcast. It was also a love story, an action thriller, and, of course, a treatise of her political philosophy. First published in England because American publishers systematically rejected it, it eventually found its audience back in the U.S. after a few years. In *Atlas Shrugged,* Rand dramatized her total philosophy in the character of John Galt, who leads a strike of the creative and productive people against the devastated welfare state that America has become in the novel. In this work, she has Galt echo her philosophy by saying, "I swear—by my life and my love of it—that I will never live for the sake of another man, nor ask another man to live for mine." Again the reaction by critics was mixed, but some thought it both stimulating intellectually and entertaining, again a "novel of ideas." By the eighties it had sold more than five million copies. (In 1991, the Library of Congress reported that the one-thousand-page *Atlas Shrugged* is second to the Bible as the "most influential in the lives" of the LOC readers.)

In 1947, as the momentum about fighting Communism was fueling up with the House Un-American Activities Committee's penetration into the film industry, Rand testified before the committee and wrote "Screen Guide for Americans" in the November issue of *Plain Talk*. Her actual experience under Communism, and her hate of it as a political system, were the underpinnings of her willingness to testify. She did not "name names" but was asked to analyze films, particularly *Song of Russia,* for alleged propaganda. She was a difficult and no-nonsense witness who reiterated her message that a government should not control its people. "I don't believe the American people should ever be told any lies, publicly or privately. I don't believe that lies are practical. . . . [When we were an ally of Russia] why weren't the American people . . . told that Russia is a dictatorship but there are reasons why we should cooperate with them to destroy Hitler and other dictators . . . why pretend that Russia was not what it was?"

She worked on developing her other most popular book, *The Fountainhead,* over a period of six years (1936 to 1942), taking time out to write plays, including a staged version of *We the Living.* She was challenged by the ending for *Fountainhead,* in which her main character was an architect. To learn more about the field, she worked as a file clerk for six months in the office of Ely Jacques Kahn, an established New York architect. This work, too, was rejected by many publishers until an editor, Archibald G. Ogden, championed her work to his company, Bobbs-Merrill.

The Fountainhead was published in 1943, and Rand and O'Connor moved back to Los Angeles, where she wrote the adaptation for the screenplay that would star Patricia Neal and Gary Cooper (who resembled Frank O'Connor). The film was released in 1949 and is a classic of modern filmmaking, although its philosophical message remains controversial. The character Howard Roark was her key to dramatizing her philosophy that supported freedom, the self, and reason. In the conclusion of the book, Roark says, "I do not recognize anyone's right to one minute of my life. Nor to any part of my energy. Nor to any achievement of mine. . . . I am a man who does not exist for others."

Critics gave mixed reviews but few could deny that her "novel of ideas," was often brilliantly told. By 1948, the "noncommercial, intellectual" book had sold more than four hundred thousand copies, and by the mid-eighties, had topped four million copies. Rand was beginning to make many readers believe they could conjure the courage of a Roark to make some effect in their own lives.

One of those readers was Nathan Blumenthal, whom Rand met in 1950, along with Barbara Weidman, who was to become his first wife. The couple became close friends with Frank and Ayn, who eventually moved to New York permanently because of this friendship with the much younger couple. (Nathan, who eventually changed his name to Nathaniel Branden, was twenty-five years younger than Ayn.)

Nathaniel and Ayn, despite their age difference and perhaps because of their shared philosophical visions, became lovers from 1954 to 1958. "It's a rational universe, she said, "this had to happen."

Branden was instrumental in helping her make the segue from novelist to cult figure and spokesperson for the philosophy of objectivism that she created. He celebrated her writing by establishing the Nathaniel Branden Institute and producing lectures and teaching courses about her work all over the country. They rekindled their affair from about 1964 until 1968, when she discovered that he was having another affair with a younger woman.

In personal conversations and in an open letter to her objectivism readers, she, in effect, dismissed Branden from her inner circle, closed down the Institute, and created a permanent split among the followers of the objectivist movement that had developed around her writings. It was at this point that she lost the possibility of making objectivism accepted in America as a viable philosophical movement.

During the 1960s, Rand lectured at many of the top universities in the country, including Harvard, Johns Hopkins, Yale, Princeton, and Columbia, the University of Wisconsin, and MIT. She was a frequent presenter at the annual Ford Hall Forum in Boston.

Rand also wrote nine nonfiction books about her ideas, including *For the New Intellectual: The Philosophy of Ayn Rand,* 1961; *The Virtue of Selfishness: A New Concept of Egoism,* 1964; and *Philosophy: Who Needs It,* 1971.

Despite the intensity with which she championed self-responsibility, honesty, and independence, Ayn had her personal demons. She was afraid to fly, phobic about germs, wore a "good luck watch," and never learned to drive a car. And while she championed capitalism as the only moral economic system, she was always frugal and did not invest her money in purely capitalistic ventures. In the two decades since her death, the nonprofit Ayn Rand Institute has kept alive her objectivism message and acquired considerable income from the sale of her books and related writings.

Ayn Rand had been a lifelong smoker, and lost a lung to cancer in the early 1970s. She also suffered from gallstones and a deep grief over her husband's death, which occurred in 1979. Frank greatly admired his wife's philosophical stance and her forthright honesty. He supported her efforts to write novels, often editing her material, and affectionately called his petite wife Fluff. Frank died of complications from dementia, being cared for primarily by Rand during the last three years of his life.

Rand's last public appearance was a speech to the conference of the National Committee for Monetary Reform in December 1981.

Rand died on March 6, 1982 as a result of a heart attack. Her casket abutted a six-foot floral dollar sign. In keeping with her atheistic beliefs, the only commentary at the gravesite was the reading of Rudyard Kipling's poem "If." She was buried alongside her husband, whom she called her "greatest value."

Her novels have sold more than twenty million copies, and continue to sell over two hundred thousand copies a year, influencing new generations about her philosophy through the medium of the "novel of ideas."

Among those leaders who have followed her philosophy are Robert Bleiberg, publisher of *Barron's;* Alan Greenspan, U.S. Federal Reserve Board chairman; Margaret Thatcher, former prime minister of Great Britain; Supreme Court Justice Clarence Thomas during his tenure as head of the Equal Employment Opportunity Commission; and Billie Jean King, American tennis champion.

The Ayn Rand Institute currently champions her philosophy of objectivism, and is the main source for sales of her books and lectures. It was organized by Leonard Pelikan, her literary heir.

Hannah Arendt

(1906–1975)

A political theorist with a flair for grand historical generalization, Hannah Arendt exhibited the conceptual brio of a cultivated intellectual, the conscientious learning of a German-trained scholar, and the undaunted spirit of an exile who had confronted some of the worst horrors of European tyranny. Her life was enriched by innovative thought and ennobled by friendship and love. Although her books addressed a general audience from the standpoint of disinterested universalism, Jewishness was an irrepressible feature of her experience as well as a condition that she never sought to repudiate.
     —Stephen J. Whitfield, "Hannah Arendt," in Paula E. Hyman
          and Deborah Dash Moore, *Jewish Women in America:
          An Historical Encyclopedia*

HANNAH ARENDT IS regarded as one of the twentieth century's most brilliant and original political theorists. She was one of the most celebrated intellectuals of her generation and her best-known, sometimes controversial, works, *The Origins of Totalitarianism, The Human Condition, Eichmann in Jerusalem,* and *On Revolution,* written in a post–World War II climate of uncertainty and reevaluation, are classics of political history and philosophy that have lost none of their relevance.

Born in Hanover, Germany, Hannah Arendt was the single child of Paul Arendt, an electrical engineer and amateur classical scholar, and Martha Cohn Arendt, both of whom were from middle-class Jewish families of Russian descent and had been born in Königsberg in East Prussia. The Arendts were Social Democrats and Reform Jews, who admired Hermann Vogelstein, a prominent leader of liberal German Jewry. They were critical of the Zionists, but at the same time they cultivated a friendship with Kurt Blumenfeld, the future president of the German Zionist Organization. In an interview, Hannah Arendt recalled that "the word 'Jew' never came up when I was a small child" and that she was raised to be "completely a-religious," only aware of her Jewish identity because of the anti-Semitic remarks she heard from other children and her high school teachers. As Arendt's biographer, Elisabeth Young-Breuhl observes, it would later be Kurt Blumenfeld "who awakened and fostered her sense of her Jewish identity and introduced her to the renewal of Jewish consciousness the Zionists had undertaken."

When Arendt was a small child, the family moved back to Königsberg, where, in 1911, Paul Arendt was institutionalized with tertiary syphilis. He died in 1913, as did Arendt's grandfather, Max Arendt, with whom she also had been very close. Martha Arendt was left to raise her child alone during World War I, a frightening experience, given the periodic battles waged between German and Russian troops on the nearby eastern front. Broadminded and progressive, Arendt's mother supported the Left in the turbulent political postwar era and instilled in her daughter an admiration for socialist leader Rosa Luxemburg. In 1920, Martha Arendt married Martin Beerwald, a merchant with two teenage daughters.

Hannah Arendt was a precocious child, who learned to read before entering kindergarten. While attending the gymnasium (secondary school), fifteen-year-old Hannah became offended by a teacher's remark (the text of which was not revealed in Arendt's later telling of the story) and led her classmates in a boycott of his classes. Expelled for this breach of conduct, Arendt studied with a private tutor and from 1922 to 1924 prepared for the final examination for entrance to the university by auditing courses at the University of Berlin.

At the University of Warburg, Arendt wanted to take Rudolf Bultmann's New Testament seminar and needed permission from the theologian to do so. During her interview with Bultmann, she informed him categorically that "there must be no anti-Semitic remarks" in the class. Bultmann calmly and gently assured her that together they would handle any such remarks if they occurred. Also on the Warburg faculty was philosopher Martin Heidegger, whose lectures would become the basis for his *Being and Time,* the chief source for the later Existentialist movements in Germany and France. Arendt studied philosophy under Heidegger and the two had a brief, intense love affair, which ended in 1925, when Arendt went to Heidelberg to study with psychiatrist-turned-philosopher Karl Jaspers. The fatherly Jaspers became Arendt's mentor and under his supervision she completed her dissertation, *The Concept of Love in St. Augustine.* The philosophies of both Heidegger and Jaspers would later influence Arendt's works. Arendt received her doctorate in 1929 and the same year married Günther Stern, who would later become a well-known writer under the pen name Günther Anders.

During the early 1930s, as fascism was on the rise and growing anti-Semitism was a cause for concern, Arendt turned her attention to the history of German-Jewish relations. She focused on a period of cultural détente during the eighteenth century, when Jewish salon hostesses dominated Berlin literary life. She began writing a biography of one such hostess, titled *Rahel Varnhagen: The Life of a Jewish Woman,* in which she explored her subject's repudiation of her Jewishness, her conversion to Christianity, and her final acceptance of her Jewish identity toward the end of her life. Arendt was interrupted in her work by the events that followed the rise to power of the National Socialists in 1933 and the book was not published until 1958. Although Arendt was not a participant in the Zionist movement, she was sympathetic to Zionism, and in 1933, at the behest of Kurt Blumenfeld, she began collecting German anti-Semitic propaganda, with a view toward publicizing abroad the plight of Jews under the Nazi regime. This activity resulted in Arendt's arrest by the Gestapo. After a week's imprisonment, she was released, and shortly thereafter, she left Germany for Paris. There, she worked for various Jewish organizations, including Youth Aliyah, arranging for the immigration of Jewish children to Palestine.

In 1936 Arendt met Heinrich Blücher, a self-educated, working-class non-Jewish Berliner, who had been a member of Rosa Luxemburg's Spartacus League. After divorcing their spouses, Arendt and Blücher married in January 1940. The couple became close to celebrated literary critic Walter Benjamin, who helped shape Arendt's sense of European history and her understanding of how nineteenth-century nationalism had played a role in the outbreak of World War I, fostered an openly anti-Semitic climate, and contributed to the current armed conflict. When the German army invaded France in the spring, Arendt and Blücher were detained, then separated and sent, along with other German exiles, to different internment camps in the south of France. After six weeks, Arendt managed to escape and reunite with her husband, and in May 1941 the couple secured visas and sailed to New York, where Arendt's mother later joined them.

During the 1940s Arendt worked to learn English while embarking on her career as an American intellectual. She wrote essays for such Jewish journals as *Jewish Social Studies* and *Jewish Frontier*, and contributed a political column to the German-Jewish weekly, *Aufbau* (Reconstruction), in which she argued on behalf of a Jewish army to fight Hitler and expressed her hope that Jews and Arabs would coexist in a postwar state in Palestine. Arendt would later express her disappointment at the failure of a binational state in Palestine, which caused a distancing between her and the organized Jewish community. The continuing existence of Israel remained a source of concern to her, however, and she was relieved when the Jewish Defense Forces triumphed and disaster to the country was averted in 1967 during the Six-Day War.

From 1944 to 1946, Arendt was employed as a research director for the Conference on Jewish Relations and as a part-time history teacher at Brooklyn College. For two years, beginning in 1946, she worked as an editor for Schocken Books, a German-Jewish publishing firm that had reestablished itself in New York and Palestine. Meanwhile, Arendt and Blücher had developed friendships with such New Left writers and editors as Philip Rahv, Alfred Kazin, and Mary McCarthy, and during this time Arendt wrote for *The Partisan Review, The Review of Politics,* and *The Nation.* After the war, Arendt also directed Jewish Cultural Reconstruction, an initiative dedicated to recovering and relocating European Jewish cultural treasures stolen by the Nazis during the Holocaust.

In 1951, the same year she acquired American citizenship, Arendt published *The Origins of Totalitarianism,* which firmly established her as a major historian and political theorist. Based on a series of articles, this original, unprecedented, and extremely influential three-part work traces the genesis of Nazi and communist state theories back to the collapse of the eighteenth-century European nation-states with their stable class structures and the decline of Enlightenment ideals of human rights, explores the rise of nationalism, imperialism, and anti-Semitism during the nineteenth century, and follows the progress of ideology and racism into the twentieth century. An expanded edition, which included an analysis of the Hungarian revolution of 1956, was published in 1958. Heinrich Blücher, who had become Arendt's political mentor despite his lack of formal schooling, contributed greatly to the book. Blücher became a highly respected teacher of philosophy at the New School for Social Research in New York City and at Bard College in upstate New York.

The success of *The Origins of Totalitarianism* made it possible for Arendt and Blücher to move out of the rooming house they had occupied for many years into an apartment. Easier financial circumstances also made it possible for Arendt to pursue other writing opportunities. While she appreciated the book's success, she was, writes Young-Breuhl, "uncomfortable with the publicity she received. She was, and remained, reticent, uneasy in public, and very protective of her privacy. She had a wide and appreciative circle of acquaintances—many would have agreed that she was the most incisive, intelligent person they had ever met—but few ever came to know her well."

Arendt's acclaimed second major work, *The Human Condition,* published in 1958, explores humanity's historical-political shift from private and active public realms to a hybrid liberal social realm. In 1961 she further developed the thesis she had offered in *The Human*

Condition in a series of six essays, published as *Between Past and Future*. In *On Revolution* (1963), Arendt focuses on the American political model of local township government. "Arendt never sought a science of politics that could be laid down, gridlike, on events," observes Young-Breuhl. "She looked, rather, for large patterns in political life—such as the shift away from valuation of action to valuation of labor, which she thought marked the twentieth century—in the light of which particular events could be considered. Her technique was to explore the broad concepts that she felt defined 'the human condition,' such as life itself, existence with others or plurality, natality, mortality, existence in a cultural world, and on the earth. She then analyzed these concepts in their interactions through history until the present day."

In 1961, Arendt was sent to Jerusalem by *The New Yorker* to cover the trial of Nazi war criminal Adolf Eichmann. In 1963 the pieces she wrote on the trial appeared in the February and March issues of the magazine. Controversy over her analysis of Eichmann and his role in the Holocaust was growing as Arendt prepared the essays for book publication as *Eichmann in Jerusalem: A Report on the Banality of Evil*. Arendt argued that Eichmann was essentially an ordinary, thoughtless bureaucratic tool of Nazi state evil and not an inherently despicable man invested with the individual power to kill millions, and she raised questions about the ability of the existing legal system to adequately adjudicate cases in which a defendant is charged with "crimes against humanity." She further outraged many readers with her assertion that the complicity of the European Jewish Councils in the Nazis' deportation program contributed to the implementation of the Final Solution and the ultimate destruction of nearly all of European Jewry. Arendt was demonstrating the insidiousness of the Nazi regime and its methods, but the book's critics interpreted her arguments as an attempt to blame the victims for their fate. Arendt, who became alienated from some of her friends because of *Eichmann in Jerusalem*, was shocked by the ferocity of the book's detractors, although she faced the controversy with courage. She included a response to the debate over Eichmann, titled "Truth and Politics," in a revised edition of *Between Past and Future* (1968).

During the mid-1960s, Arendt wrote only essays. She also edited a two-volume work, *The Great Philosophers*, which appeared in 1962 and 1966. Her later works include *Men in Dark Times* (1968), diverse portraits of modern men and women of courage, such as Karl Jaspers, Rosa Luxemburg, and Walter Benjamin; and *Crises of the Republic* (1972), a collection of essays of the late 1960s and early 1970s. At her death, Arendt left the nearly completed manuscript for two volumes of a three-volume work, *The Life of the Mind,* an analysis of the thought process. The first two volumes, titled *Thinking* and *Willing,* as well as the third volume, *Judging,* for which Arendt left only notes, were edited by her closest American friend, writer Mary McCarthy, and published as an incomplete work in 1978.

A teacher as well as a writer, Arendt served on the faculties of a number of American universities and colleges, including the University of Chicago, Cornell, Columbia, and the University of California at Berkeley. In 1959 she became the first woman to hold the rank of full professor at Princeton, where she taught a course in politics. From 1967 until her death, she was a professor at the New School for Social Research in New York City.

Hannah Arendt died of a heart attack in her New York City apartment at the age of sixty-nine; her ashes are buried at Bard College, where her husband taught. (Blücher had died in 1970.) In *The Life of the Mind,* Arendt wrote, "Death not merely ends life, it also bestows upon it a silent completeness, snatched from the hazardous flux to which all things human are subject." Throughout her life and career, Arendt accepted the hazards and instability of the human condition, and in the process articulated a new science of political philosophy that ultimately reflected her abiding concern with personal and public moral integrity. Her works, required reading for a thorough understanding of nineteenth- and twentieth-century political history, continue to instruct us on the wisdom of rational political and cultural discourse.

Estée Lauder

(1908–)

First comes the shy wish. Then you must have the heart to have the dream.
Then, you work. And work.
> —Estée Lauder, from her autobiography, *Estée, A Success Story*

WHEN SHE WAS a dewy-faced teenager, peddling her uncle's face
creams, Josephine Esther "Esty" Mentzer often dreamed of a glamorous, exciting life away from her hometown of Corona, Queens—a
rural area that was the dumping area for garbage and ash from other
New York City boroughs in the early 1900s.

Her ambition was fired by a chance remark a patron made to her
at the Florence Morris Beauty Salon where she had her first cosmet-

ics concession. When young Esty complimented the woman about her blouse and asked where she bought it, the woman replied that a salesgirl like her could never afford such a blouse. The pain of that reply still stings, she admits, yet "I wouldn't have become Estée Lauder if it hadn't been for her." From that point on, she was determined to have all the finest jewelry, art, and homes possible. And, she did.

The road from Queens to developing the world's largest cosmetic products corporation, with more than thirty-five thousand employees worldwide, was paved by a strict adherence to the ethics of hard work and creating a quality product. However, it was a willingness to be creative in marketing that made the difference between running just another company and heading an empire.

Esty Mentzer was born July 1, 1908. Her parents were Rose Schotz Rosenthal, a French Hungarian who brought six children to her marriage to a man ten years her junior, and Max Mentzer a Czechoslovakian immigrant. He had traded in his horse riding skills to be a custom tailor; but, failing to be successful at that, he opened a hardware store at which he excelled. He also had a knack for buying eccentric properties like cemeteries.

Esty and her siblings lived in Queens except for a brief stay in Milwaukee to escape the terrors of a polio epidemic in the early 1920s. Unfortunately, when they returned, older sister Renée contracted the disease but later regained the strength of her legs.

From her mother, Esty learned the importance of carrying a parasol and wearing gloves to deflect the sun's rays. She learned merchandising at her father's hardware store and at her half brother's dry goods store, Plafker and Rosenthal.

Her mother's brother, John Schotz, was a chemist, who had developed Dr. Schotz's Viennese Cream, Schotz Crème Pack, All-Purpose Crème, Super Rich All-Purpose Cleansing Oil, and Skin Lotion. He introduced the young teenager to his scientific methods, and found in her a ready and very willing student. She believed she had found a calling. She would experiment with his core group of products for more than twenty years until they reached her exacting expectations.

Esty was never without samples in her purse to pass out to anyone she thought "needed a sparkle to their face." She hit the beauty salon circuit in Miami and New York, visited resorts in the Catskills and Long Island, and encouraged everyone she met to tell their friends, which became the basis of her "Tell-A-Woman" marketing scheme.

At nineteen, she met Joseph Lauter, whose parents had emigrated from Galicia, in Eastern Europe. They were married on January 15, 1930. They had their first son, Leonard Allan, in 1933, but the marriage became strained when Lauter tried and failed in a number of business ventures. The marriage, which was also compromised by her constantly marketing her creams, dissolved into divorce in 1939 although she kept in touch with her husband because of their son and their basic friendship.

The early 1940s proved to be very fruitful for the ambitious Esty, who had renamed herself Estée. She moved to Miami where she tapped into the vacation crowd, firing up another audience for her "Tell-A-Woman" appeal. Estée introduced her products at hotel and private beauty salons. She met other men, including Charles Moskowitz, an executive with MGM, and had an affair with a man savvy about the fragrance and beauty business. He was Arnold Lewis Van Ameringer, sixteen years her senior (she was then in her thirties) and very married.

When he refused to leave his wife and marry Estée, she returned to New York, and remarried Joseph Lauter in 1942. This reunion produced a second son, Ronald, who was born in 1944. Estée had learned a lot during the time she'd been away from Joseph, and this marriage was to be a true partnership, personally and professionally. Many years later she would admit, "Whether you are a businesswoman or a housewife, attention must be paid to your mate."

Joseph, who agreed to change the spelling of his name to Lauder, is credited with the decision to keep the company's products in department stores and not capitulate to pressures to market them, as their competitors did, in drugstores and similar venues. He was largely responsible for managing the firm's finances and supervising the huge production facility in the Melville, Long Island, factory. Estée, of course, was manager of sales and marketing.

Estée's association with Van Ameringer did not fade entirely, and she called upon his expertise (some say he helped her financially) when she took her first step into the fragrance field with what was then a totally different kind of product, a perfumed bath oil she named Youth-Dew. It was a huge success from the beginning, sparked by the introduction of hundreds of samples and Estée's innovative marketing tactics. She was not above doing little tricks, like spilling a bottle on the floor of the cosmetic area, recognizing that the scent would remain for hours.

Customers tried it and liked it, as Estée instinctively knew they would. In its premier year, 1953, Youth-Dew grossed $50,000 in sales; by the sixties it grossed $30 million, and by 1984, with its extended product line the Youth-Dew scent sold $150 million. It continues to sell exceedingly well.

What has been an enduring part of her success is selling exclusively through upscale department stores. After months and months of trying, she finally got her products into Saks Fifth Avenue. In typical Estée fashion, she offered to help the daughter of a Saks Fifth Avenue buyer who had problem skin. The young girl tried Estée's creams, they worked, her mother was thrilled, and she bought Estée Lauder products for Saks. Afterwards, it was all uphill. Estée could rely on the stores to house the products and hire the personnel to sell them; however, she trained the personnel herself. Another marketing technique she employed was to create the image of The Estée Lauder Woman, whose persona was classic elegance. In print ads she is always shown in a beautifully appointed room, or a softly lit outdoors area. And, in an interesting twist, her whole upper torso or her entire body was photographed, even if it was an eye or lip cosmetic that was being promoted. In the nearly forty years since this campaign began, the company has used only eight models: Phyllis Connors and Karen Harris were the first, in 1962, followed by Karen Graham, Shawn Casey, Willow Bay, Paulina Porizkova, Elizabeth Hurley, and Carolyn Murphy. Each was chosen to project beauty, elegance, and style.

Estée also seemed to understand intuitively and practically that packaging was critical to the image of her products. She would have her packagers transform a seashell, an embroidered shawl, a pair of cinnabar earrings into paper, packaging, art, or other elements so the packaging tied in with the theme of the product.

"Lauder blue," a shade as unmistakable as Tiffany blue, has been her primary packaging color. Even the type fonts used in advertising and packaging are a signature of the company, created just for their use in marketing. All of these marketing tools are part of her intense drive for perfection and exclusivity that translated from the ingredients in her products to the containers, boxes, and advertising. Today, this is nearly standard procedure, but in the 1950s through the 1970s, her ideas broke new ground.

Giving away samples of her products in the early years evolved into what became the most phenomenally successful marketing strategy of all, the Free Gift With Purchase. Risking her entire advertising budget, she placed $500,000 in a campaign to offer a "free gift" with each purchase. The entire industry followed suit, but none as extravagantly or as consistently as Estée Lauder in her signature line.

Estée Lauder has always believed that giving away samples is a surefire way to build sales; she pioneered the custom of providing products for favors at charity balls. This had the impact of powerful, intimate promotion to guests, and brought with it press coverage that always mentioned her products by name, thus influencing thousands of people to try the products that celebrities used. As an additional bonus she made glittering connections for her own personal social life. She visited the White House under several administrations, and even partied with the Duchess and Duke of Windsor and Prince Rainier and Princess Grace of Monaco, among other celebrities in film, theater, and society.

Estée was the first to break away from standard industry pricing, and market a cream for what was then the highest price ever charged, $115 per pound: Re-Nutriv. That it became a huge seller was attributed to its quasi-scientific claims, and like all her products, worked for her dedicated market who appreciated Lauder's message of top quality and feminine style, without regard to fashion or trendy gimmicks.

Another clever marketing ploy was the creation of other lines without any mention that they were owned by Estée Lauder. In that way, the companies carved out their own business personalities with products targeted to specific audiences. The three top performers are Clinique, Prescriptives, and Origins, which was developed by her grandson William.

By the sixties, Estée was well entrenched in her dream, which had come true. She lived in a mansion in Manhattan, had homes in tony Palm Beach and in the South of France, and pursued the jet set social whirl not only for the prestige of it, but also because it was a great way to promote her products.

Her sons Leonard and Ronald were involved in the family business from the time they were youngsters, and both attended the Wharton School of Finance and Commerce at the University of Pennsylvania. They have been instrumental in expanding the company internationally and establishing global brands.

Among Estée's many honors are the Insignia of Chevalier of the Legion of Honor, in 1978, and the Medaille de Vermeil de la ville de Paris, in 1979, for efforts to raise funds to restore the Palace of Versailles.

She also has been awarded the Crystal Apple from the Association for a Better New York (1977), the Albert Einstein College of Medicine Spirit of Achievement Award, the Golda Meir Ninetieth Anniversary Tribute Award, as well as honors from the Girl Scout and Boy Scout councils and honored by most of the major department stores. She has contributed to the Manhattan League, National Cancer Care, and Jewish charities and causes.

The Estée and Joseph Lauder Foundation, established in 1962, has funded children's parks throughout New York City and made substantial donations to both the Whitney Museum of Art and the Museum of Modern Art. It also has contributed to Memorial Sloan Kettering Hospital. For ten years, Estée Lauder, Inc. has raised public awareness of breast cancer in an annual promotion that has raised millions and helped to save women's lives.

From 1946 to 1995 Estée Lauder, Inc., was totally family owned, which was the key reason it could afford to ride out the competition, make changes when it wanted, and launch the variety and scope of its separate product lines. However, changes in the world market and the urge to acquire other firms forced a change. By 1985, almost half of all Estée Lauder products were sold outside the United States, in more than seventy-five countries.

The company went public on November 17, 1995. By 2000 the company had acquired Aveeda, Bobbie Brown Essentials, Stila, M.A.C. (Make-Up Artists Cosmetics Limited), Stila, Tommy Hilfiger, and Jo Malone fragrances. The family still controls a majority of the stock worth in excess of $6 billion. The company controls more than 45 percent of the cosmetics market in U.S. department stores, and sells in more than 120 countries. Estée Lauder retired from the day-to-day operations in 1972, but she kept her sure and steady hand in much of the decision making until 1994, when a fall broke her hip and she retired from the public eye.

The magic of a face cream created by an uncle attentive to the curiosity of a young girl was the beginning of a long and fruitful life for little Esty Mentzer. She created a persona—Estée Lauder—that is now synonymous with elegance and beauty. She worked hard to create a company based on products of quality and, with her success, has supported countless community services and causes. One of these causes is the effort to educate students about the practices of international business. When her husband Joseph died in 1982, at the age of eighty, the family established the Joseph H. Lauder Institute of Management and International Studies graduate program at the Wharton School of Finance and Commerce.

Estee Lauder died, at age ninety-seven, in April 2004. In ceremonies held at the White House on June 23, 2004, President George W. Bush awarded her a (posthumous) Medal of Freedom, the highest civilian honor in the United States.

Pauline Trigère

(1908–2002)

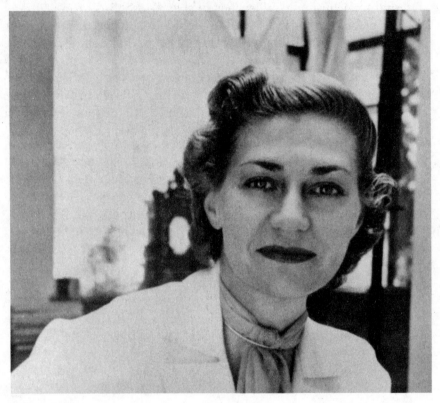

Fashion is what people tell you to wear, style is what comes from your own inner thing.

—Pauline Trigère

AT A RECENT Golden Globe Awards ceremony, actress Julianna Margulies wore a black gown she purchased at a vintage dress shop. The dress received rave reviews from fans and fashion mavens, even though it was more than forty years old. But, then, it was a Trigère.

Paris-born Pauline Trigère was the woman whose designs revealed style over fashion, cut and designed to fit the woman not the trend of the day. She was a striking example of her philosophy, with large

188

tinted glasses, sleek hairstyle framing her face, and always her own Trigère designs on her slim body. And, always, she wore her signature turtle pins, sometimes on a pant leg, sometimes on a sleeve. She became a passionate collector of le tortue (turtle), amassing a collection that finally numbered in the hundreds.

Trigère was never known to wear anything but her own designs and her dynamic personality when appearing in public. And although she stood only five feet, four inches, she appeared taller, more sophisticated, more elegant than anyone else in the room.

"Trigère's fashions were very elegant, timeless fashions one could wear for decades," said Jean Druesedow, director of the Kent State University Museum. "The details of finely done button holes, darts, which she did brilliantly, are too expensive to do these days, so students must learn to design the line into the cut, as Trigère could do so ably. When she visited with our students, she would take a fine fabric, like a double-faced wool, and cut the coat on the student model. It was a revelation to many of our students. She was very realistic and her teaching method was to be very frank and forthright. She would say, for example, on your first job, expect to be picking up pins, but keep your ears and eyes open."

Museums have recognized the importance of Trigère's fashions, and examples of her work can be found at the Kent State University Museum, the Metropolitan Museum of Art, the Phoenix Art Museum, the New Jersey Shore Museum, and the Fashion Institute of Technology (FIT).

Trigère's father, Alexandre Triger, was a tailor who had manufactured military uniforms in his native Russia. After arriving in Paris, he designed clothing for top department stores like Galleries Lafayette and Bon Marche.

Her mother, Cecile, had a boutique in the Pigalle apartment where Pauline and her brother Robert grew up. The young Pauline studied at the Collège Victor Hugo and, upon graduation, dreamed of becoming a surgeon. But medical school was not an option. So, back to the family trade she went getting a job at the Martiel et Armand salon in the Plàce Vendôme. It is here that she learned how to design and construct women's clothing with the élan for which she became famous. Her clothes had more than style, they had craft, the details that only an experienced tailor could provide.

Pauline married Lazar Radley, a coat and suit manufacturer, and had two sons, Jean-Pierre and Philippe. Legend has it that her husband had given her special brooches, lavish diamond clips, at the birth of each son which was to have an impact on her designing career a few years later.

Paris in the late 1930s was fraught with tension as the Nazis spread from Germany to other points in Europe, and emigration was the hope of all Jews, including Trigère. Fortunately, Pauline, her sons, and her brother and mother were able to immigrate to Chile in 1937, stopping at New York City along the way. They loved it, and stayed. That's when the last e was added to their name, adding an inevitable French touch, and more important, avoiding being called "triggers." Interested in pursing her designing career, she called upon Adele Simpson, who got Pauline work with Hattie Carnegie. But it was the tail end of the Depression, and Carnegie was eventually forced to lay her off. As World War II was beginning, European couture fashions were in limited supply in the United States. Seizing the opportunity, in 1942, Trigère pawned her diamond clips, borrowed money and fabric, and was able to create eleven dresses for her initial collection.

With her brother Robert's help, she packed the eleven samples carefully into a suitcase and sent them with Robert on a bus—the only transportation they could afford—and he showed her dresses to the country's top shopkeepers. Six of them accepted the line, and Trigère, Inc. was born.

The savvy sextet who had immediately recognized her talents were Nan Duskin of Philadelphia, Becky Blum of Chicago, Elizabeth Quinlan of Young Quinlan in Minneapolis, Amelia Gray in Los Angeles, Martha Phillips of New York's Martha, and her former employer, Hattie Carnegie. That first collection was a hit. Trigère bought back the clips, and began her fifty-plus-year career, the only American-based designer to have had such a long career. New York made Pauline Trigère, she said, and in 1944, she demonstrated her thanks by becoming a U.S. citizen.

Throughout her career, she created many unique designs: the first jumpsuit, the spiral jacket, the mobile collar, and the first use of cotton and wool for evening wear. Her coats remain elegant, simple, and extremely flattering. Although she infused them with her French style, she added an intrinsically American practicality with the first reversible coat, the first sleeveless coat, coats with detachable scarves, and the cape-collared coat.

Her dresses were flattering to a woman's shapely figure, cut to fit in a simple elegant way, and made of the finest fabrics available, from Bengal silk to flowing jerseys, taffeta, and charmeuse satins, all cut to drape, flow, and caress the body as it moved. Perhaps her most famous dress style, and one that has been interpreted and reinterpreted by thousands, was the black dress with a sheer top. It was classic yet sexy, comfortable yet sophisticated enough for any event. Pure Trigère.

As simple as her coats and as elegant as her dresses were, her evening gowns were complex, often with elaborate sleeves, yards of fabric for skirts, and lavish adornments from precise pleating to beads, lush gold, and gemstones—and all real. The most remarkable aspect of her designs is that they never look dated, whether from her first collection or her last. Her fashions have become a popular feature of online auctions that have not only brought back attention to her fashion, but also brought top dollars for owners of these vintage clothes.

Her clothes were favorites among stars of the 1940s and 1950s, including Lauren Bacall, Anne Baxter, Bette Davis, Lena Horne, Claudette Colbert, Paulette Goddard, Ethel Merman, Kitty Carlisle, Josephine Baker, the Maguire Sisters, and the Duchess of Windsor. Later on, luminaries such as Angela Lansbury, Joan Rivers, Rita Gam, Dina Merrill, Evelyn Lauder, Beverly Sills, and Mrs. John Hay Whitney would also wear her fashions.

She stayed mainly with classic A-line designs, especially her deceptively simple coats, often without cuffs, closures, or collar. Yet the spirit of the sixties made an impact on her, and she designed a rhinestone-encrusted bra to wear under an evening jacket in 1967. In classic Trigère style, it was elegantly feminine, sexy but not raunchy.

Her salon was the choice destination for any aspiring designer, and during her long career, many top names learned from her timeless design and tailoring acumen. She also was protective of her friends and defended fellow designer Geoffrey Beene against the vitriol of *Women's Wear Daily* publisher John Fairchild, whose criticisms of Beene she deemed unwarranted. For her stance, Fairchild practically blackballed her from *WWD* despite a charming full-page ad she took out in her defense.

That hardly stopped her. She was trailblazing in many directions
She was the first fashion designer to hire a black model (in 1961), a
hugely independent and risk-taking feat that was met with some
shock, but others quickly followed suit to the point where ethnic
models are as common as white models used to be. Her company,
now known simply as Pauline Trigère, had grossed $2 million in
1958; but by 1988, she was too broke to mount a full collection.
Licensing, branding, and cookie-cutter fashion had made their in-
roads into the industry and she did not follow suit. Many of her best
boutique shops had died out with their owners and some of the very
upscale department stores, like I. Magnin, had either closed, or dras-
tically changed how they showcased couture. Still, she had a loyal
clientele of individuals who kept her busy until 1994, when she
closed her shop for good.

Keenly aware of her place in history, she donated her sketchbooks
from 1944 to 1994, plus many of her fashions, to the June F. Mohler
Fashion Library, part of the Shannon Rodgers and Jerry Silverman
School of Fashion Design and Merchandising at Kent State University.

Trigère herself never sketched, a not-uncommon characteristic of
fine designers. She would have artists draw the sketches after she had
draped and cut an item, and completed its detailing. Much of the
sketches were the work of Lucie Porges, a Viennese refugee from World
War II who became artist-in-residence for the house of Trigère for
nearly four decades.

She often regretted not licensing her name on everything. However,
the Trigère name was synonymous with fine craftsmanship, detailing, and innovative design, a style that defied the concept of a common "brand." During the 1970s, she mentored students of fashion
design at Kent State University, Parsons School of Design, the
Fashion Institute of Technology, and Marist College, which gave her
an Honorary Silver Needle Award for her support of future generations of designers.

All the top fashion honors have been hers: fashion awards from
Neiman-Marcus and Filene's; the National Cotton Award; the Medal
of Silver from Paris (1972); the Medal of Vermeil (1982); and three
Coty Awards (1949, 1951, and 1959). She also was inducted into
the prestigious Coty Hall of Fame in 1959, the first woman to win
the honor, and she did it less than twenty years after her business
was launched. In 1992, the Fashion Institute of Technology (FIT)

celebrated her fifty years in American fashion, a milestone no other living designer has yet achieved, on or off Seventh Avenue.

The crown jewel among the awards was given in 1993. In front of a standing ovation of 2,000 people, she was presented the Hall of Fame Award from the Council of Fashion Designers of America, the highest honor in the industry.

She was one of eight designers recognized in 2001 with a plaque along the Fashion Walk of Fame, sponsored by the Fashion Center Business Improvement District, the only permanent monument to the fashion industry in America. The plaques are installed along Seventh Avenue between Thirty-fifth and Forty-first streets and honor Anne Klein, Oscar de la Renta, James Galanos, Donna Karan, Bonnie Cashin, Charles James, and Giorgio di Sant'Angelo. In 2001, the Order of the Legion d'Honneur, the highest national order of France, was awarded to Trigère by Richard Duqué, the French consul general in New York, who called her a living French-American legend.

In 1994, after closing the doors on her couture business, she formed P.T. Concepts, marketing scarves, ties, and jewelry. She was asked to design accessories for senior citizens by Gold Violin, a shop and online source, adding a totally Trigère touch to ordinary products, like pillboxes, walking sticks, travel bags, wheelchair accessories, hearing aid pouches, and eyeglass cases. This was only an extension of her mission that practical could always be made more elegant, and elegant could be made practical.

Pauline Trigère died in 2002 at age ninety-three. She had for years refused to reveal her age, but in 1998, she invited friends and family to celebrate her ninetieth birthday and the word was out. At ninety, she told everyone she wanted to be cremated wearing her signature red lipstick. A friend asked her who will know? *"I'll* know," she replied.

Understanding that "inner thing" of style and translating that message to her work are part of the legacy of Pauline Trigère. She was willing to make changes in her life but not willing to capitulate to terror whether it be Nazis or criticisms from the fashion press. She valued the integrity of fine workmanship over mass market appeal. And, she knew when to take a business risk yet she never risked stopping completely. She was designing up to her last day.

Anna Sokolow

(1910–2000)

The artist should belong to his society, yet without feeling that he has to conform to it. He must see life fully, and then say what he feels about it. Then, although he belongs to his society, he changes it, presenting it with fresh feelings, fresh ideas. Art should be a reflection and a comment on contemporary life.

—Anna Sokolow in *Modern Dance: Seven Statements of Belief,* edited by Selma Jeanne Cohen, 1966

ANNA SOKOLOW SOUGHT to awaken in her audience an awareness of the world through dances that examined the issues of the day: the Great Depression, the Holocaust, the turbulent sixties and its alienated youth, and her Jewish culture. In a career spanning more than seventy years she created dances performed in theaters throughout the world; inspired dancers with her passion and tremendous knowledge; and taught hundreds of actors how to be comfortable enough in their own bodies so they could touch the humanity of their characters and help the audience understand the playwright's intent.

Anna was born in Hartford, Connecticut, on February 9, 1910, to Sarah (Kagan) and Samuel Sokolow, emigrants from Pinsk, Russia. Like so many men of this time, her father had difficulty switching from the role of scholar to breadwinner, and so her mother eventually took over those responsibilities, in addition to caring for the couple's four children. When the family moved to New York City, Sarah found work as a garment worker. Samuel developed Parkinson's disease and, unable to care for him, the children, and work, Sarah had to admit her husband to a charity hospital. Her two oldest children, Rose and Anna, went to school, but son Isadore was forced to abandon his education to help support the family, while little sister Gertie was placed in an orphanage until her mother was able to support her.

Sarah's involvement in the garment industry politicized her and she became active in the Socialist Party, joined the International Ladies Garment Workers Union, and marched in various protests, with Rose and Anna in hand. Sarah introduced her children to the vibrant Yiddish theater of the early 1920s, the Workman's Circle dances, and created a Jewish home that was kosher and observed the Sabbath and all holidays.

Concerned that Anna and Rose would be alone while she worked, Sarah took them to the Emanuel Sisterhood of Personal Service, which provided a hot lunch and activities for the children. It was at the Emanuel Sisterhood that Anna "fell madly in love with dance" after taking a class taught "in the style of" the great Isadora Duncan. She attended these classes from age ten through fifteen. Realizing they had nothing left to teach her, her teachers were able to enroll Anna in the dance program conducted by Blanche Talmud, Bird Larson, and Irene Lewisohn at the Neighborhood Playhouse, established by Lewisohn and her sister Alice, patrons of dance and theater, at the Henry Street Settlement House.

The program taught everything from dance to pantomime, diction, and voice, all of which Sokolow would incorporate in her future choreography. The Playhouse eventually left the Henry Street facility and opened the independent, professional School of the Theater in 1928. Anna dropped out of school to do odd jobs, including tying teabags in a factory, yet her exceptional talent had not gone unnoticed by the Playhouse administrators.

Believing in her promise, they offered her a full scholarship and membership in the school's Junior Festival Players. Her education expanded to movement, singing, theater craft and, of course, dancing, this time under Michio Ito, Benjamin Zemach—expert in Hebrew dancing—and the demanding dancer/choreographer Martha Graham and composer Louis Horst, who were revolutionaries of the dance world of the time.

After this training she joined Graham's professional dance group in late 1929, continuing her studies and dancing locally in pieces like Graham's *Primitive Mysteries* (1931) and *Celebration* (1934). "It was staggering," Sokolow said. "I just knew I was in the presence of something great."

A tough taskmaster, Graham did not pay her "disciples," and was equally stringent about praise. Later in life, Sokolow recognized Graham's contribution to her development; but at the time, impassioned with a fever to dance about her heritage (in sharp contrast to Graham's "Americana" themes), Sokolow resigned in 1938 to pursue her own dreams to become a choreographer.

From Horst, for whom she worked as a paid ($25 per week) assistant, she learned to appreciate music and a variety of dance forms. "The way I found out [who I was] was not with Martha Graham but with Louis Horst." She sought his advice and counsel for years afterward.

In the early 1930s, many Jewish women dancers formed the unstructured movement called "radical dance," in the belief that dance could, and should, be more than entertainment; they believed that dance should be an agent for social change. To achieve this goal, they dramatized the economic, social, and political concerns of their time, spurred on by growing reports of fascism in Europe and the spiraling depression in the United States.

Sokolow's first major composition, *Anti-War Trilogy*, was performed at the 1933 First Anti-War Congress, sponsored by the American League Against War and Fascism. The theme of fascism and the perils of war were also captured in *Inquisition '36, Excerpts from a War Poem*, and *Slaughter of the Innocents*. The oppression of industrial workers was dramatized in *Strange American Funeral* and juvenile delinquency was the theme of *Case History No.—*. Not all was serious about her work; she attempted satire in *Romantic Dances, Histrionics.*

In her twenties, Sokolow was the youngest American choreographer to lead her own professional dance group, Dance Unit, and at only twenty-six she staged the first full-evening concert of her own works at New York's 92nd Street YMHA in 1936. In 1937, Sokolow received one of the first fellowships from the Bennington School of Dance. She shared the honor with Esther Junger and José Límon, and all three benefited enormously from this support during a time of financial struggle.

Eager to discover the avant-garde possibilities in dance in the Soviet Union, Sokolow traveled there in 1934, but it was a disappointing visit. What was an inspiration was Mexico.

After seeing Dance Unit perform in New York in 1939, Mexican painter Carlos Mérida invited Sokolow and her company to perform in Mexico City. Her work was an immediate success and the enthusiasm of audiences encompassing all strata of Mexican society increased the performances from the six originally scheduled to an unprecedented twenty-three.

Based on this popularity, and a lack of modern dance culture in Mexico, the Mexican Ministry of Fine Arts invited Sokolow to develop a modern dance company under their aegis. In only eight months, the Ballet Bellas Artes (Fine Arts Ballet) debuted in March 1940. She was instrumental in developing La Paloma Azul (The Blue Dove), which lasted but one season, yet laid the foundation for an indigenous Mexican modern dance movement. "Las Sokolovas" was the affectionate name she gave her dancers, and she became "la fundadora de la danza moderna de Mexico," or "the founder of Mexican modern dance."

Sokolow was impressed by the reigning painters of Mexico, especially Diego Rivera, José Clemente Orozco, and Silvestre Revueltas. "For the first time in my life," she said, "I knew what it felt like to be an artist." She would commute between New York and Mexico City for the next nine years, choreographing numerous works with Mexican/Spanish themes that she had discovered in the artists and in her travels in Mexico, but she longed to return to her Jewish roots for her art.

At the end of World War II, Sokolow created her intensely powerful *Kaddish* (1945) in which she expressed mourning through the
simulated wrapping of leather tefillin straps on her wrist and implied
chest beating. Nothing like this had ever been shown in dance before. As powerful and as poignant as *Kaddish* was, considering the
terrors of World War II, it was not until 1961, that Sokolow could
address the Holocaust. The superbly dramatized dance, *Dreams,* incorporated images of the concentration camps as "an allegory of
time and helplessness." It is still performed and still elicits the same
dramatic impact on audiences, many of whose members sit in stunned
silence at its completion.

A number of her works celebrated Jewish women, from the biblical Ruth, Miriam, and Deborah to twentieth-century figures such as
Hannah Senesh and Golda Meir. *Songs of a Semite,* which premiered
in 1943, was named after a book of poems by Emma Lazarus and
presented a lonely Jewish woman who gained strength from remem-
bering the courage of her biblical foremothers.

Sokolow premiered many of her works at New York's 92nd Street
YMHA, most often to an audience from her Lower East Side beginnings. She staged events in support of State of Israel bonds, combined poetry with her dances, and became a force in the world of
dance.

Broadway and off-Broadway were also a part of her lexicon of
dance design. In 1935, her *Anti-War Cycle* appeared on the program
with Clifford Odets's play *Waiting for Lefty,* and she directed the
dances for a Broadway production of André Obey's *Noah.* For the
WPA's Federal Theatre Project, she choreographed the revue, *Sing
for Your Supper,* which entertained hundreds, and employed many
actors, singers, and dancers eager to work in those depression-tinged
years.

Sokolow created a lively jitterbug duet for the musical version of
Elmer Rice's *Street Scene* in 1947 (score by Kurt Weill and lyrics by
Langston Hughes) that many believed was a delightful departure
from her more serious efforts. Sokolow created dances for a produc-
tion of Leonard Bernstein's *Candide,* Kafka's *Metamorphosis,* Marc
Blitzstein's *Regina,* and provided choreography for a season for the
New York City Center Opera.

Although much of her staging was reworked due to clashes with directors and writers, her inventive choreography for the 1967 original Public Theater production of the rock musical *Hair* is evident.

Broadway choreographer Jerome Robbins called on Sokolow in 1951 to help the Inbal Dance Theatre, a Yemenite Jewish ensemble in Israel. Sponsored by the American-Israel Cultural Foundation, Sokolow visited Israel in 1953 and was greatly impressed by the indigenous Yemenite dancers' movements and rhythms but understood that her goal was to instill the techniques and professionalism that would make them able to perform in commercial venues. For three years, she worked with the group, and when Inbal made its European debut, it was a huge success.

One of the Yemeni dancers, Ze'eva Cohen, returned with Sokolow, who helped Cohen study at The Juilliard School where Sokolow taught. Cohen danced in *Session for Six,* created by Sokolow in 1964, along with Martha Clarke, Dennis Nahat, Michael Uthoff, Paula Kelley, and John Parks—all of whom have had spectacular dance careers. "I certainly didn't expect to be affected so deeply, [by Israel] but [the] minute the plane landed I was overwhelmed with an indescribable feeling about being there. I didn't have any kind of strong Zionist background, but going there changed my point of view. [Israel] is now one of the deepest things in my life." The "deepest thing" inspired her to return almost each summer for more than twenty years.

She taught dancers and actors and, in the early 1960s, created the Lyric Theater to help Israeli modern dancers bring theater, music, and dance together in a professional way. It was short lived, but was recognized as a strong contribution to the art of dance in Israel. Sokolow continued to choreograph for major dance companies in Israel, including Batsheva Kibbutz Dance Company.

In 1951, Sokolow staged and performed in a theater dance production of S. Ansky's play, *The Dybbuk* (the ghost), a combination of mime and dance that also marked the beginning of the end of her public performances as she concentrated more and more on choreography.

Her "vocabulary of movement" was realized in *Lyric Suite,* performed with Alban Berg's music, which was a completely atonal score. It premiered in Mexico in 1953, and then was performed at the 92nd Street YMHA in 1954. Having created a dance that combined music with "non-narrative" choreography was an exciting

break, and former mentor Horst said, "Now, Anna, you are a choreographer!"

Sokolow continued to experiment with music, especially that of
jazz composers Teo Macero and Kenyon Hopkins, and was among
the first to set choreography to "serious" jazz music. Her *Opus '65*
became the prototype for what later became called "rock ballets."
She wanted her dancers to act, and utilized mime as a strong tool.
Among her works of this period were *Act Without Words* (1969),
based on the work of Samuel Beckett, and *Magritte, Magritte* (1970),
a suite of eight movements evoking the images of the surrealist
painter, accompanied by poetry. Not everything was serious, as noted.
She fused recitation, dance, and music into the birth of jazz in her *A
Short Lecture and Demonstration on the Evolution of Ragtime as
Presented by Jelly Roll Morton* (1952).

Rooms, a stark drama about the isolation of the city dweller, was
depicted by a series of dancers, each reaching into space, sitting in
chairs that are both close to one another yet unknown or unrelated
to one another. The piece was developed originally at the Actors
Studio in 1955. That year, it was seen by more people than had seen
all of her live productions when it became the first modern dance
choreography shown on national television.

New York Times critic Clive Barnes wrote, "No one would go to
Miss Sokolow for a good laugh—yet far more importantly no one
would go to her for a good cry. . . . Sokolow's belief in humanity
shines through her pessimism. Her pity and her compassion give her
taut and tortured dances a justification."

Like so many dancers and choreographers, then and now, it was
not always easy to make all your income from dancing, so Sokolow
turned to teaching. She taught throughout her life, beginning at the
92nd Street YMHA, the Neighborhood Playhouse, and at the Group
Theatre; then in the 1940s and 1950s, with Elia Kazan at the Actors
Studio. In 1958, she began decades of teaching actors and dancers at
the Juilliard Dance Division. "My first aim is to free the actor from
his self-consciousness," she said. "I make him forget about the clichés
about having to smoke, to touch, to handle something. It may seem
to the actor that he is learning how to move and how to use his
body, but what he really learns is to be simple, honest, and human."

Sokolow later taught internationally, first continuing her associations with Mexico and Israel, then in the Netherlands, England, Japan, and several other countries.

Her honors were many. She was one of only six American choreographers to receive $10,000 grants in 1967 from the National Council of Arts (now the National Endowment for the Arts), and later a National Endowment for the Arts' Choreographic Fellowship; the Lifetime Achievement Award from the American/Israeli Cultural Foundation; and a Fulbright Fellowship to Japan. Mexico awarded her its highest civilian honor in 1988: the Encomienda Aztec Eagle.

Her peers also acknowledged her. A 1961 citation from *Dance Magazine* read: "To Anna Sokolow, whose career as concert dancer, choreographer, and teacher in this country and on the international scene has been distinguished by integrity [and] creative boldness, and whose recent concert works have opened the road to a penetratingly human approach to the jazz idiom."

The 92nd Street Y cited Sokolow in 1975 for contributions to the world of dance and to the Jewish people; in 1986, it held a three-day conference in her honor called "Jews and Judaism in Dance." The Samuel H. Scripps American Dance Festival Award for lifetime contribution to American dance was given to her in 1991, and in 1998 she was inducted into the National Museum of Dance's Hall of Fame.

Gerald Arpino, artistic director of the Joffrey Ballet, speaking at her eighty-fifth birthday celebration, said, "I became a dancer because of the pure joy and spirit of dance. I remained in the field ever since because pioneers such as Anna Sokolow showed me the deep commitment and intense humanism that dance is capable of expressing. Her indomitable spirit, her courage, her uncompromising truths are beacons not only for the dance world but also for all humankind." Her work is in the repertoire of the Joffrey Ballet, the Netherlands Dance Theater, Ballet Rambert, the José Límon Company, the Boston Ballet, the Pennsylvania Ballet, and other companies around the world. Anna Sokolow died in her New York City home on March 29, 2000. She was ninety years old.

The Players' Project continues to perform the full repertoire of Anna Sokolow's choreography, including works she designed up until 1997. Many of these works reflect her idea that dancers should be actors as well. The company tours nationally and internationally, and produces a full season in New York annually.

"[M]y works never have real endings," she said. "[T]hey just stop and fade out, because I don't believe there is any final solution to the problems of today. All I can do is provoke the audience into an awareness of them. The artist should belong to his society yet without feeling that he has to conform to it. . . . Then, although he belongs to his society, he can change it, presenting it with fresh feelings, fresh ideas."

Barbara Tuchman

(1912–1989)

The writer of history, I believe, has a number of duties vis-à-vis the reader, if he wants to keep him reading. The first is to distill. He must do the preliminary work for the reader, assemble the information, make sense of it, select the essential, discard the irrelevant—above all, discard the irrelevant—and put the rest together so that it forms a developing dramatic narrative. Narrative, it has been said, is the lifeblood of history. To offer a mass of undigested facts, of names not identified and places not located, is of no use to the reader and is simple laziness on the part of the author, or pedantry to show how much he has read. To discard the unnecessary requires courage and also extra work, as exemplified by Pascal's effort to explain an idea to a friend in a letter which rambled on for pages and ended, 'I am sorry to have wearied you with so long a letter but I did not have time to write you a short one.' The historian is continually being beguiled down fascinating byways and sidetracks. But the art of writing—the test of the artist—is to resist the beguilement and cleave to the subject.

—Barbara Tuchman, "In Search of History," in
Practicing History: Selected Essays, 1981

HISTORIAN *AND* LITERARY artist Barbara Tuchman performed a great public service by turning the past into best-selling books accessible to millions of readers. With her characteristic clarity, Tuchman would observe that "The unrecorded past is none other than our old friend, the tree in the primeval forest which fell without being heard." She saw her vocation as supplying that unheard sound. The winner of two Pulitzer Prizes, Tuchman specialized in telling the story of the past with the eye and understanding of a novelist, shaping the formless past into riveting and revealing drama.

Barbara Tuchman was born Barbara Wertheim in New York City, the daughter of an international banker and a leader in New York City's Jewish community. Her grandfather was businessman and diplomat Henry Morgenthau; her uncle, Henry Morgenthau, Jr., was Franklin Delano Roosevelt's secretary of the treasury; while a cousin, Robert Morgenthau, gained prominence as a U.S. federal attorney. At the age of two, Tuchman witnessed one of the first naval engagements of World War I as she traveled by ship to visit her grandfather, who was serving as the U.S. ambassador to Turkey.

Her interest in the past was first stimulated by her childhood reading of Lucy Fitch Perkins's "Twins" series that described children of various nationalities during different historical periods. "After the Twins," Tuchman recalled, "I went through a G. A. Henty period and bled with Wolfe in Canada. Then came a prolonged Dumas period, during which I became so intimate with the Valois kings, queens, royal mistresses, and various Ducs de Guise that when we visited the French *châteaux* I was able to point out to my family just who had stabbed whom in which room. Conan Doyle's *The White Company* and, above all, Jane Porter's *The Scottish Chiefs* were the definitive influence. As the noble Wallace, in tartans and velvet tam, I went to my first masquerade party, stalking in silent tragedy among the twelve-year-old Florence Nightingales and Juliets."

Tuchman was educated at New York's Walden School and then Radcliffe College, where she studied both history and literature. Her summers were spent with her family in Europe, and she accompanied her grandfather at the World Economic Conference of 1933 in

London, where economists and statesmen wrestled with finding a solution to the worldwide economic depression. After graduation, she took a job as researcher and editorial assistant with the Institute of Pacific Relations and worked for a year in Tokyo as an assistant to the Institute's international secretary. Her subsequent experience as a foreign correspondent in Tokyo for *The Nation,* the magazine owned by her father, resulted in one of her earliest articles, a piece exploring Japanese characteristics, which was published in the prestigious *Foreign Affairs* magazine when she was only twenty-three. She returned to the U.S. after a month in China via the Trans-Siberian Railway. In 1937 she covered the civil war in Spain, experiences which stimulated her first book, *The Lost British Policy: Britain and Spain Since 1700,* published in 1938. In it she surveyed the relationships between the two nations while calling for Great Britain's involvement on behalf of Republican Spain.

In 1940, she married Manhattan physician Lester R. Tuchman, and, after a two-year stint on the Far East desk for the Office of War Information during World War II, Barbara Tuchman focused her attention on raising the couple's three children.

In the early 1950s she embarked upon her career as a historian. "It was a struggle," she recalled. "I had three small children and no status whatsoever. . . . To come home, close a door and feel that it was your place to work, that was very difficult, particularly when you were—well, just a Park Avenue matron." Adding to the challenge was the issue of being a woman in a field dominated by men and pursuing her interests without any graduate training. However, Tuchman did not feel that her lack of academic credentials was a drawback. "I never took a Ph.D.," she once said. "It's what saved me, I think. If I had a doctoral degree, it would have stifled any writing capacity." She felt strongly that academic historians "who stuff in every item of research they have found, every shoelace and telephone call of a biographical subject, are not doing the hard work of selecting and shaping a readable story." Accordingly, Tuchman approached the task of writing history as if she were a more traditional storyteller: "There should be a beginning, middle, and an end. Plus an element of suspense to keep the reader turning the pages."

In 1956, Tuchman published her first major historical work, *Bible and Sword: England and Palestine from the Bronze Age to Balfour,* a study that includes an analysis of British policy concerning Palestine, stimulated by events surrounding the recent emergence of the State of Israel. The study is incomplete, since Tuchman became overwhelmed with a sense of outrage at the British indifference toward the Jews in Palestine, the violent Arab reaction, and the Arab-Israeli war that followed the creation of Israel. As she recalled, "When I tried to write this as history, I could not do it. Anger, disgust, and a sense of injustice can make some writers eloquent and evoke a brilliant polemic, but these emotions stunted and twisted my pen. . . . Although the publisher wanted the narrative brought up to date, I knew my final chapters as written would destroy the credibility of all the preceding, and I could not change it. I tore it up, discarded six months' work, and brought the book to a close in 1918." It became a crucial lesson (for Tuchman as a historian), which taught her that a primary duty "is to stay within the evidence," to keep her own emotions in check, and "to tell what happened within the discipline of the facts."

Tuchman's first popular success was *The Zimmerman Telegram* (1958), a gripping and dramatic chronicle of Germany's attempt to incite Mexico to enter the war against the United States during World War I. It is the first in a trio of books centered on the Great War, prompted no doubt by her early memories of the conflict.

In 1963, she became the first woman to receive the Pulitzer Prize for general nonfiction with her book *The Guns of August,* an account of the opening weeks of World War I. Tuchman succeeded in untangling and then reweaving the complicated diplomatic maneuverings of the time into an epic story of the futility and calamity of war. "There is much of battle orders, of tactical, strategic, and logistical problems in the pages of *The Guns of August,*" writes reviewer Ernest S. Pisko, "but such is the skill of the author that these technical issues become organic parts of an epic never flagging in suspense."

She followed *The Guns of August* with *The Proud Tower: A Portrait of the World Before the War* (1966), which examined the cultural and political forces that led to the conflict (and the creation of the modern world). As one reviewer commented, Tuchman "has the storyteller's knack for getting the maximum dramatic effect out of the events which crowd her pages." In all three books, Tuchman shows her remarkable ability to discover the telling detail, to trace the significant thread that brings the past alive, and to create memorable and rounded historical characters. She was awarded a second Pulitzer Prize for *Stilwell and the American Experience in China, 1911–45,* published in 1971. In it, the career of General Joseph W. Stilwell, who served in China in various capacities from 1911 to 1944, is used for a wider exploration of the relationship between the United States and China.

With her next historical work, *A Distant Mirror* (1978), Tuchman moved from the twentieth century to the tumultuous fourteenth. Following the career of Enguerrand de Coucy, a French knight, nobleman, and son-in-law of the English king Edward III, the book explores the politics, manners, and mores of a medieval century devastated by the Hundred Years War and the Black Death. *A Distant Mirror* was described as an "ambitious, absorbing historical panorama," and Tuchman was praised for her thorough scholarship while suggesting the relevance of the distant age to the contemporary world, as indicated in the book's title. Like the twentieth century, the fourteenth century was a period of almost continuous warfare and widespread political instability, producing a crisis of confidence in all institutions, particularly the church. The bubonic plague that swept across Europe and Asia, killing nearly a third of the population, is compared to the possible devastation a nuclear war might cause today. The following year Tuchman became the first woman to be elected president of the American Academy and Institute of Arts and Letters.

In 1984, *The March of Folly: From Troy to Vietnam* examined in depth the "folly" of four events in Western history: the episode of the Trojan horse; the corruption of the Renaissance popes, which led to the Reformation; England's treatment of her American colonies; and America's involvement in Vietnam. The book represented a departure for Tuchman, who said of it, "I've done what I always said I would never do, and that is to take a theory before I wrote a book. My other books were narratives, and I tried not to adopt a thesis except what emerged from the material. It's what I don't believe in when writing history, actually."

Her final history, *The First Salute* (1988), attempts to put the American Revolution in the context of international politics and diplomacy. It had been on the national best-seller list for four months when Tuchman died of complications following a stroke.

Tuchman has been criticized by academic historians for some of her theories and conclusions, and for her narrative selectivity. Yet she clearly achieved something different from what is usually done by the scholarly historian. As Jim Miller of *Newsweek* pointed out, "Most academics lack the talent or inclination to write for a general audience. Into this vacuum has stepped Tuchman. . . . Her imaginative choice of topics and flair for words have enabled her to satisfy the popular hunger for real history spiced with drama, color, and a dash of uplifting seriousness."

Tuchman embraced the role of the historian, not as a collector of dry historical artifacts or esoterica, but as a compelling teacher and synthesizer who linked the lessons of the past with the world of her audience. Few writers have mastered the art of historical narrative as expertly as Barbara Tuchman, or have left such a standard to follow.

Bella Abzug

(1920–1998)

In a perfectly just republic, Bella Abzug would be president.
—Gloria Steinem

WHEN EMANUEL SAVITSKY died in 1933, he left behind his wife
Esther and two daughters, Bella and Helene. A sweet-natured man
who ran the Live and Let Live Meat Market in the Bronx, Emanuel
had filled their home with music and a clear understanding that war
was never a solution to conflict.

In her first act of rebellion, young Bella stood in the synagogue
daily for a year to recite the mourner's prayer, the Kaddish, taught to
her by her maternal grandfather, Wolf Tanklefsky. In Orthodox syn-

agogues, then and now, women are seated separately from men, and tradition has it that only a son could recite the Kaddish. Bella did not accept this. Grief is grief, duty is duty, with no nod for gender, and so she recited the Kaddish each day and no one objected. She was twelve years old.

"In retrospect," she wrote, "I describe that as one of the early blows for the liberation of Jewish women. But in fact, no one could have stopped me from . . . honoring the man who had taught me to love peace, who had educated me in Jewish values . . ."

Bella had a very thorough Hebrew education, from Florence Marshall Hebrew High School to Talmud Torah, an afternoon program she attended after high school. She was encouraged by her teachers to join Hashomer Hatzair (the young guard), a Zionist group that supported the founding of Israel as a Jewish homeland.

Leadership seemed to be a natural trait of hers even early on. She was class president at Walton High School and student government president at Hunter College, both good training for the skills she would later use in the U.S. House of Representatives and in organizing agencies of change.

Bella became impassioned about the law and, following her graduation with a degree in political science from Hunter College, she won a scholarship to Columbia Law School, where she became editor of its Law Review. Harvard, her first choice, had turned her down because they did not admit women at that time. (Harvard finally admitted women in 1952.)

Attending Columbia meant she could live at home, and the subway only cost her five cents. This made her sensitive all her life to the importance of low-cost public transportation.

On a vacation to Florida in 1942, Bella met Martin Abzug. After they returned to New York, they continued to see each other while Bella finished law school, then were married in 1944. Martin, whose family owned A Betta Blouse Company, worked as a stockbroker and a novelist while Bella pursued the law.

For more than twenty-five years she practiced law, specializing in civil rights and liberties, labor law, and tenant rights. Her most famous case was defending Willie McGee, a black man, against the charge of raping a white woman with whom he had had a relationship for years. The case ended with his execution, despite her appeals and pleas. Traveling to Jackson, Mississippi, while she was pregnant, brought her to a place so inhospitable she could not even find a room or hotel to accommodate her. She ended up sleeping in a locked stall in the women's room of the bus station rather than subject herself to the rage of the local Ku Klux Klan. (The pregnancy ended in a miscarriage.) She and Martin later had two daughters, Eve (Eegee) Gail, born in 1949, who is a sculptor and social worker, and Isobel Jo (Liz), born in 1952, an activist and political consultant.

During the period of the House Un-American Activities Committee (HUAC), Abzug was one of only a handful of attorneys who fought against the committee's effort to blacklist people, under the infamous chairmanship of J. Parnell Thomas. Abzug took the courageous stance of defending labor leaders, teachers, and activists whom the committee alleged were Communist sympathizers.

Her first grassroots activity led to the founding of the Women's Strike for Peace (WSP) in the 1960s, which aimed to prevent nuclear testing and later became a movement to protest the war in Vietnam.

Life was not always politicking or defending the law. Abzug enjoyed her long marriage and children, and had many friends. Whenever interviewed, she always gave credit for this balance to her husband's willingness to share household responsibilities and his enduring respect for her professional work.

In 1970, at the age of fifty, when most people are slowing down, Bella entered the political arena and was elected a representative from Manhattan's 19th district. She campaigned with the slogan, "This woman's place is in the House—the House of Representatives." When she took her seat in 1971, she became the first Jewish woman to serve in the House of Representatives, and the first representative ever to be elected on a platform for women's rights and peace.

On her first day, Abzug introduced a resolution calling for the withdrawal of U.S. troops from Indochina. The motion was defeated, but she remained an impassioned critic of the Vietnam War, and the first to call for President Richard Nixon's impeachment. She introduced the first legislation supporting gay and lesbian civil rights, and actively protested the Zionism-with-racism equation that was part of a U.N. General Assembly resolution in 1975. (It was later repealed in Nairobi in 1985).

Her very first vote was for the Equal Rights Amendment, and she went on to champion the Equal Credit Act that permits women "fair access" to consumer credit, Title IX regulation, and equal opportunity for federally funded education institutions.

As chair of the Subcommittee on Government Information and Individual Rights, she broke down the barriers of secrecy in government and coauthored three bills that have impacted the public's right to know: the Government in the Sunshine Act, the Right to Privacy Act, and the Freedom of Information Act, which has helped both the press and historians gain access to information previously withheld by government agencies, including the FBI and the CIA. She also cowrote the pivotal Water Pollution Act of 1972.

During her tenure in the House, she was an assistant Democratic whip to Thomas P. "Tip" O'Neill, Jr., Democratic Speaker of the House. Abzug also served as chair of the subcommittee on government information and individual rights and chair of the House subcommittee on government and individual rights.

Her fellow congressmen may have been divided about her politics, but no one ever denied she was the hardest working member of the House. She was tenacious, understood both grassroots and high-level politicking, and her legal background made her a formidable negotiator and author of legislation.

In a 1997 interview in the online publication GEMNET/GIST, Abzug said, "You can't continue to have a world without equal participation of men and women. That's my central thesis. Can I prove that women will change the nature of power rather than power will change the nature of women? I can't prove it, but it's something that in my heart I have always believed would happen."

Progress has been slow, but many of the changes begun during her terms of office are still in effect at this writing. Since Abzug's election to Congress in 1970, the numbers of women in public office have increased. There were ten women then, now there are fifty-eight; there was one woman senator, now there are nine; there were no women justices sitting on the Supreme Court, now there are two—one of them Jewish. There were no women cabinet members in 1970, but today there are four. Even the military profile has changed. In 1970, the military was only 3 percent women and had no female admirals or generals; today the military is 14 percent women, with twenty admirals and generals. And today, more than 50 percent of all law students are women.

Brash, bossy, brazen, and yes, loud, Abzug understood that to be heard one first had to be noticed. One technique she employed was always to be seen wearing a hat. "When I first became a lawyer only about 2 percent of the bar were women. People would always think I was a secretary . . . ask me to get coffee. . . . In those days, professional women in the business world wore hats. So I started wearing hats," she told an interviewer in 1987. Her involvement in women's issues, civil rights, and environmental concerns reads like a timeline of progress in these categories for the latter part of the twentieth century. The first national organization to benefit from her considerable (she would say LOUD) voice and political acumen was Women Strike for Peace, which campaigned against nuclear war (1961).

Others were the National Women's Political Caucus (cofounder, 1971); United Nations' Decade of Women conferences (1975 onward); National Women's Conference (presiding member, 1977); First National Women's Conference in Houston (presiding officer, 1977); and Women USA (cofounder, 1979). She was inducted into the National Women's Hall of Fame in 1994.

Not all went smoothly. She was appointed cochair of the National Advisory Committee on Women in 1978, but was fired by President Carter when the results of the committee criticized him for cutting funding for women's programs.

In the latter part of her career she devoted much of her time to the Women's Environment and Development Organization (WEDO), which she cofounded in 1990 and later served both as president and cosponsor of its First Conference on Breast Cancer in 1997. Abzug herself had been diagnosed with the disease.

Abzug was greatly involved in the U.N.'s work around the world with women, the environment, and civil liberties. She served as a leader of the United Nation's Fourth World Conference on Women in Beijing (1995).

In particular, her championing of women's rights in the international realm empowered thousands of women to take responsibility for their lives and those of their families and communities. One of the accolades heard following her death was from women introducing themselves at UN activities, as "I'm the Bella Abzug of my country."

Her Jewish heritage was never far from her conscience nor her activities, and she supported assistance for Soviet Jews and aid for

Israel. Her district was, of course, in New York, and her membership on the Committee on Public Works and Transportation helped bring more than six billion dollars to the state for use in sewage treatment, economic development, and mass transit, including financing buses directly designed for the elderly and provisions for people with disabilities.

It has been more than thirty years since she served in the House, and fought for social changes within the framework of the various organizations she helped to organize. Most of those changes are so much a given these days, that it is sometimes difficult to imagine our life without being sensitive to the needs of the disabled, the elderly, and being aware that women can and should have a say in their own lives, at work, and at home.

Abzug published two books: *Bella!: Ms. Abzug Goes to Washington*, a diary of her first year as a Congresswoman, 1972, edited by Mel Ziegler, and *Gender Gap: Bella Abzug's Guide to Political Power for American Women*, coauthored with lifelong friend Mimi Kelber, in 1984.

She resumed private law practice in 1980 after unsuccessful attempts at regaining public office, once for senator in 1976 against Daniel Patrick Moynihan. She ran again for Congress from Westchester County in 1986 but lost. No loss, however, was as great as the death of Martin, her husband of forty-two years, also in 1986.

Abzug gave her last public speech before the United Nations in March 1998, and died later that month from complications of heart surgery. She was seventy-seven years old.

Not insignificantly, she had been born a month before women's suffrage came into effect in the United States in 1920, and she died on the last day of Women's History Month, a celebration unimaginable at her birth.

"She didn't knock politely on the door. She didn't even push it open or batter it down. She took it off the hinges forever," said Geraldine Ferraro at Bella Abzug's funeral.

The U.N. General Assembly staged an unprecedented memorial meeting in Bella Abzug's honor in the chamber of Secretary-General Kofi Annan. He pledged "that the doors Bella opened would remain open from this day forth . . ."

Gerda Lerner

(1920–)

History, a mental construct which extends human life beyond its span, can give meaning to each life and serve as a necessary anchor for us. It gives us a sense of perspective about our own lives and encourages us to transcend the finite span of our lifetime by identifying with the generations that came before us and measuring our own actions against the generations that will follow. By perceiving ourselves to be part of history, we can begin to think on a scale larger than the here and now. We can expand our reach and with it our aspirations. It is having a history which allows human beings to grow out of magical and mythical thought into the realm of rational abstraction and to make projections into the future that are responsible and realistic.

—Gerda Lerner, *Why History Matters: Life and Thought*

IN THE MID-1960s, when Gerda Lerner—then well into her forties and already a published author—was pursuing a graduate degree in history at Columbia University, she decided to write her dissertation on women's history, a highly unusual choice at a time when the women's movement was still in its infancy and women's studies was a concept yet to be realized in colleges and universities. Her advisors were skeptical but Lerner insisted. The result was *The Grimké Sisters from South Carolina: Rebels Against Slavery,* which was published in 1967. The following year, while Lerner was teaching at Sarah Lawrence College, she began and directed the first program to offer a graduate degree in women's history. Lerner would go on to organize programs designed to train future feminist historians and to earn a reputation as one of the world's foremost scholars in the field of women's history—no small achievement for a woman who, at eighteen, was forced to flee Nazi-occupied Austria after a harrowing series of events, and who arrived in the United States alone and without speaking English.

Born Gerda Kronstein in Vienna, Lerner was the elder of two daughters of Robert and Ilona Kronstein. Her father was a pharmacist and businessman, and Lerner grew up in a comfortable, assimilated, middle-class family. She would later write that she and her sister "were raised in the best traditions of German culture and regarded ourselves as liberal Austrians." She was sent to Sabbath services in the Orthodox synagogue and her family observed the Jewish holidays, but her mother did not keep a kosher home. Cultural self-identification was always present, however. When Lerner brought home the first B grade she had ever earned, her father told her angrily, "Jews don't get B's." Lerner attended a public school in which one day a week was given over to religious instruction. As she writes in *Why History Matters: Life and Thought* (1997), "the class divided into two groups—*them,* thirty or more Christians; and *us,* three or four embarrassed Jewish children who were gathered in another room . . . so that we might be instructed by a rabbi imported for that purpose." When the Kronstein family vacationed at Austrian mountain resorts, Lerner's father "impressed us with the need not to act 'too Jewish' . . . it told me we were outsiders and

ought to try to hide our deviant, disgraceful status as best we could."
Lerner's sense of being an outsider extended to her exclusion within
the Jewish religious community because she was female, so much so
that she provoked a family crisis by refusing to have a bat mitzvah.
In her autobiography, *Fireweed,* Lerner sums up her sense of identity
succinctly: "I consider myself a Jew belonging to the Jewish community, the Jewish tradition, sharing a common fate. I do not believe
that fate is inextricably linked with religion."

The persecution of Austrian Jews that took place soon after the
Anschluss (the incorporation of Austria into Germany) in 1938 would
contribute to Lerner's later assertion that "I am a historian because
of my Jewish experience." A business acquaintance, who was also a
Nazi sympathizer, warned Lerner's father that he was about to be arrested; shortly thereafter, he fled Austria for Liechtenstein. A few
weeks later, a group of storm troopers raided the Kronsteins' apartment, demanding to know the whereabouts of Robert Kronstein. To
punctuate their demand, one storm trooper threatened Lerner's
twelve-year-old sister, Nora, with a pistol. Another man mistook
Lerner for an Aryan servant because of her light brown hair and blue
eyes; when she told him who she was, he called her "a Jewish pig"
and insisted that she tell him where her father had hidden his money.
After ransacking the apartment and continuing to terrorize the family, the storm troopers left, only to return less than a month later to
arrest Lerner and her mother. They spent six terrifying weeks in
prison and were released only after Robert Kronstein agreed to sign
over his property and his business to the Nazis. Lerner and her
mother and sister were forced to sign their own deportation orders
and they escaped to Liechtenstein a few days before the events of
Kristallnacht—the night of violence against Jews and destruction of
Jewish property that took place on November 9, 1938. Lerner was
the only member of her family to obtain a United States visa, and in
1939 she immigrated to New York.

In New York, Lerner taught herself English while working as a
waitress, sales clerk, office clerk, and X-ray technician. She also began
writing, and during the 1940s published two short stories, "The
Prisoner" and "The Russian Campaign," which concern Nazi brutality and the characters' attempts to resist it. After marrying film editor Carl Lerner in 1941, she moved with him to Hollywood, where
they remained for many years before returning to New York. In

1943 Lerner became a naturalized U.S. citizen. She continued to write while raising the couple's two children, Stephanie (b. 1945) and Daniel (b. 1947), and at the same time became politically active in the Congress of American Women, a progressive grassroots women's organization. She also participated in events sponsored by the Emma Lazarus Foundation and worked to support the United Nations. Lerner's only novel, *No Farewell,* a story about Vienna on the eve of the *Anschluss,* was published in 1955. The following year saw the production of *Singing of Women,* a musical written by Lerner and Eve Merriam.

In 1958, Lerner entered the New School for Social Research in New York to resume the formal education that had been cut short by the war. She received her Ph.D. in history from Columbia University in 1966. While she was pursuing her graduate degree, she collaborated with her husband on a screenplay, *Black Like Me,* which became a 1964 film he directed. The critically well-received film chronicles the true story of a white reporter who attempts to pass for black so that he can experience racism first hand in order to write about it.

During Lerner's academic career at Sarah Lawrence College from 1968 to 1980, she published books and articles that would provide the framework for the development of women's history as a recognized field of study and advance the concept that class and race were central to an understanding of the role gender has played in significant historical events. Her 1969 article, "The Lady and the Mill Girl," is an influential study of class differences among women in the early nineteenth century. Her superb 1972 collection of writings of African-American women from the time of slavery to the present was published as *Black Women in White America: A Documentary History.* Reviewer Joyce Jenkins, writing in the *Saturday Review,* praised the book as the first "to treat in depth the grossly neglected segment of American history." Lerner's other works of the 1970s include *The Female Experience: An American Documentary* (1976), which reorganizes history around issues pertaining to women, and *The Majority Finds Its Past: Placing Women in History* (1979), a collection of Lerner's writings and speeches, which also contains directions for research in women's history.

Lerner temporarily departed from the subject of women's history in 1978, when she published *A Death of One's Own,* a moving account of Carl Lerner's battle with brain cancer and death in 1973.

Lerner also worked to make women's history accessible to those out-side the college academic community. In 1976 and 1979 she served as educational director for summer programs that offered training in women's history to high school teachers and leaders of women's or-ganizations. The idea for Women's History Week, which would evolve into Women's History Month, grew out of the 1979 program.

After teaching at Sarah Lawrence College, Lerner moved to the University of Wisconsin, where she became Robinson-Edwards Pro-fessor of history and started a graduate program in women's history. In 1981 she became the first woman in fifty years to be elected presi-dent of the Organization of American Historians. She retired from the University of Wisconsin in 1990.

During the 1980s and 1990s the focus of Lerner's work shifted from American to European women's history. In *Women and History, Volume I: The Creation of Patriarchy* (1986) and its companion vol-ume, *Women in History: The Creation of Feminist Consciousness, from the Middle Ages to 1870* (1993), she traces the roots of patri-archal dominance from prehistory through the nineteenth century and chronicles the sporadic attempts of women to resist the male-dominated culture of the past. Historian Londa L. Schiebinger noted in the *Journal of Interdisciplinary History* that the two volumes "provide a powerful history of the insidious workings of patriarchy and the toll that being left out of history has taken on women and their creativity."

Lerner did not entirely abandon her commitment to the history of American women during this time, however. Between 1990 and 1993 she directed a project called "Documenting the Midwest Ori-gins of Twentieth-Century Feminism," which resulted in a compre-hensive record of the beginnings of the women's movement in the 1960s. In 2002 Lerner published her autobiography, *Fireweed*, in which she presents her life in the context of the historical events she witnessed and experienced. The book ends in 1958, "the year," she writes, "that marked the major transitions in my life: from outsider to insider, from writer to historian, from activist to theoretician."

The recipient of numerous awards, Lerner was able to add two more during the 1990s, both of which would have special meaning. In 1995 she returned to Austria to receive the Kathë Leichter Preis, the Austrian state prize for excellence in women's history. The fol-lowing year the Austrian government awarded Lerner with the

Austrian Cross for Science and Art. It was a fitting honor for a survivor of Nazi persecution, and an appropriate tribute to a historian who has explored her own past and that of the world's women with precision and perception, and who, as she asserts in *Fireweed*, has "finally found the wholeness that embraces contradictions, the holistic view of life that accepts multiplicity and diversity, a view that no longer demands a rigid framework."

Betty Friedan

(1921–)

I never set out to start a women's revolution. I never planned it. It just hap-pened, I would say, by some miracle of convergence of my life and history, serendipity, one thing leading to another.

What I am sure of, though, is that ideology has to come from personal truth, has to test against real life. Personal life, personal truth is not an ab-stract concept; the life it comes from and feeds back into is real. So what, in my personal truth, made me—and gave me the power to—help bring about that wonderful massive change in society?

—Betty Friedan, *Life So Far: A Memoir*

IN 1957 BETTY FRIEDAN, a freelance writer, wife, and mother of three children, sent out questionnaires to two hundred of her former Smith College classmates. Her goal was to try to discover whether they shared her dissatisfaction with her primary role as wife and mother. The answers she received convinced her that she was not alone in suffering from a psychic distress she would come to define as "the problem that has no name."

After several years of intensive research into the origins of, as she later wrote, "the strange discrepancy between the reality of our lives as women and the image to which we were trying to conform," Friedan produced a book in which she analyzed that image and exposed it as a fantasy of post–World War II happy suburban female domesticity created and reinforced by educators, sociologists, psychologists, and the media. She called the image and the book *The Feminine Mystique*. Published in 1963, *The Feminine Mystique* was a groundbreaking treatise that sounded a clarion call for change in the status of women unlike any other written work of feminist thought at a time when women were ready to listen. Friedan's analysis of a postwar society that subordinated women and repressed their desires for greater opportunity and fulfillment beyond the traditional roles of wife, mother, and homemaker was readily absorbed into the hearts and minds of American women and sparked a revolution that would result in the revitalized women's movement of the 1960s and 1970s. Friedan would continue to adhere to the "personal truth" that had moved her to research and write *The Feminine Mystique,* and go on to become one of the most influential leaders of the movement she helped to set in motion.

Betty Naomi Goldstein was born in Peoria, Illinois, the oldest child in a family of two daughters and a son. Her father, Harry Goldstein, a jeweler, had immigrated to the United States to escape the pogroms of Eastern Europe. The oldest of thirteen children, Goldstein had received no formal American education and started his business career selling collar buttons at a street corner stand. Friedan's mother, Miriam Horowitz Goldstein, whose family also had escaped persecution in Eastern Europe by immigrating to America, worked as a journalist after attending college but gave up her career when she married. Friedan writes in her autobiography, *Life So Far,* "I somehow sensed that if my mother had a profession that absorbed her, if she was really as strong and confident as she seemed, bullying us or the women's committee, she wouldn't make life so miserable for my father or us kids, she wouldn't find everything we did, every present, so inadequate."

In her memoir, Friedan writes of her experiences growing up Jewish in a family that celebrated aspects of the Christmas holiday, such as exchanging gifts, in a town where parochialism was an aspect of life and where anti-Semitism was present in all its subtle insidiousness. She attended a high school in which students were rushed for sororities and fraternities, but "No Jewish kids were ever invited to join those sororities or fraternities, which ran high school social life in Peoria." She writes that her mother "didn't think of herself as Jewish, she didn't send me to summer camp, something was wrong with *me* that I didn't get into a sorority." She records that her father "would sometimes say, bitterly, about the equality of opportunity and freedom from prejudice America promised, 'only until six o'clock when the store closes'—for in social life in Peoria, Jews were not free and equal."

For Friedan, who often felt lonely and isolated, "Peoria was the world then to me, and how I hated that world. It seemed so unfair to me, so unjust, to be barred from places the others enjoyed just because we were Jewish. I hated being different, an outsider." On reflection, Friedan has acknowledged that, "I expect I also learned the value of community in Peoria, not only because of the cold pain of being excluded from it but because of the way, in a town like Peoria, people organized the community to solve problems, provide services, innovate kinds of enrichment that were not always or only for profit."

Friedan's sense of exclusion did not prevent her from excelling in school, however. A voracious reader in childhood, she was an academically gifted student who founded a literary magazine in high school (funded by Peoria merchants), won a dramatic award (for a time she aspired to become an actress), and graduated as valedictorian of her class. Although there were quotas for Jewish college applicants during that time, Friedan's academic standing and the fact that she came from a town like Peoria rather than a large city, resulted in her acceptance at Seven Sister schools such as Vassar, Radcliffe, and Smith, as well as Stanford University. She decided to attend Smith, where, she later wrote, "What had made me different in Peoria made me accepted, welcomed by the other bright girls, one of the crowd, finally, as I had longed to be, in spite of being Jewish." She studied psychology and, after graduating summa cum laude in 1942, won two research fellowships to the University of California at Berkeley. Unwilling to commit to a doctorate and a career as a psychologist, Friedan left Berkeley for New York City.

Women were encouraged to make up the labor shortage caused by men who had left to fight in World War II, and Friedan was able to find work as a journalist, first for the Federated Press, a news agency for labor unions and liberal and radical newspapers, and then for *U.E. News,* the official publication of the United Electrical Workers. In 1947 she married Carl Friedan, and a year later gave birth to the first of the couple's three children. After twelve stormy years together the Friedans divorced.

In the 1950s, Betty Friedan lost her job as a newspaper reporter after requesting her second maternity leave. She continued to write, however, submitting articles to women's magazines. Concurrent with Friedan's growing feeling of discontent was a notion, popular in American society during the 1950s, that the educational system was not adequately preparing women for their proper roles as wives, mothers, and homemakers. To that end, some colleges and universities featured a required course called "Marriage and Family Life." When Friedan and her Smith classmates met to discuss her questionnaire results during their 1957 college reunion, they canvassed Smith seniors about their aspirations. Friedan writes, "Try as we might, we couldn't get these fifties seniors to admit they had become interested in *anything,* at that great college, except their future husbands and children, and suburban homes. . . . It was if something was making these girls defensive, inoculating them against the larger interests, dreams and passions really good higher education can lead to."

With this in mind, Friedan submitted an article to *McCall's* titled "Are Women Wasting Their Time in College?" in which she suggested that "maybe it wasn't higher education making American women frustrated in their role as women, but the current definition of the role of women." *McCall's* and *Redbook* rejected the article, and Friedan refused to allow the *Ladies' Home Journal* to publish it after she saw that it had been rewritten to show the opposite viewpoint of her findings. She continued to research her subject, interviewing professional women and suburban housewives. She then decided to expand the piece into a book. "Neither my husband nor my publisher nor anyone else who knew about it thought I would ever finish it," she later recalled.

Five years after signing the contract with her publisher, Friedan completed *The Feminine Mystique*. W. W. Norton, who published the book in February 1963, brought it out in a modest printing of two thousand copies. Over the next ten years the book sold three million hardcover copies and many more in paperback. Friedan received hundreds of letters from women who told her that they had no idea, until they read her book, that anyone else shared their feelings. In *Life So Far,* Friedan recalls, "Many men whose wives had made those feminine mystique renunciations had bought the book for their wives, and encouraged them to go back to school or work. But then, of course, it was threatening to women who'd made those painful choices and had to get up the courage to take themselves seriously in a new way." The book was also greeted positively by older members of the women's movement, such as Women's Party activist Alma Lutz, who declared that *The Feminine Mystique* offered "a glimmer of hope that some of the younger generations are waking up."

The Feminine Mystique was seen as a new unifying force in a second wave of twentieth-century feminism, and the newly famous Friedan emerged as a leading figure in the women's liberation movement that followed. In 1966, while attending a conference of the State Commissions on the Status of Women in Washington, D.C., Friedan and others met to form the National Organization for Women (NOW) to support and lobby for the civil rights of women. At the meeting, Friedan wrote NOW's statement of purpose, the first sentence of which reads, "to take the actions needed to bring women into the mainstream of American society now, exercising all the privileges and responsibilities thereof, in truly equal partnership with men." As Friedan would later assert, NOW was founded to promote "actions, not just talk." She was elected NOW's first president and held the post until 1970. That year, Friedan co-organized the Women's Strike for Equality, which took place on the fiftieth anniversary of the ratification of the Nineteenth Amendment guaranteeing women the right to vote. In 1971 she helped organize and convene the National

Women's Political Caucus, which was formed to encourage women to participate in the political process, both as candidates for public office and as electors.

During the 1970s Friedan focused her energies on writing, also teaching and lecturing at various colleges and universities. She wrote articles for a wide range of magazines and a column for *McCall's*, "Betty Friedan's Notebook." In 1975 she was named Humanist of the Year by the American Humanist Association and received an Honorary Doctorate of Humane Letters from her alma mater, Smith.

The following year she published her second book, *It Changed My Life: Writings on the Women's Movement,* in which she recorded and assessed the progress of the women's movement and provided a journal of her experiences. Concerned with the splintering of the movement into special-interest groups, Friedan called for an end to polarization and a new emphasis on "human liberation."

Her third book, *The Second Stage* (1981), offered a reformist view of feminism based on the acceptance of men and the family in the quest of women for equality. Published at a time when women were entering the workforce in record numbers, having children, and beginning to face the daunting task of balancing the demands of career with the pursuit of family life, *The Second Stage* reflects Friedan's concern with the emergence of the superwoman myth—the image of the woman who is expected to cope effortlessly with both a career and a family. Friedan suggested that this "feminist mystique" was as much a fantasy as the feminine mystique was in an earlier era. Her perceived revisionism caused a backlash among some feminists, who felt that Friedan had strayed from the basic goals of the movement she had helped to establish. Other critics applauded her call for an end to polarization and her new thesis, seeing in it a new, more humanistic direction for feminism.

In the 1980s Friedan's activism shifted to issues concerning aging and ageism. Research for a book on age discrimination resulted in the publication of *The Fountain of Age* in 1993. In it Friedan analyzes and deconstructs what she has termed "the mystique of aging," the negative image American society has created for men and women over sixty-five. Six months before the publication date, Friedan developed an infection in her aortic valve that called for a transplant. The surgery was successful, and Friedan returned to an active life of teaching, writing, and traveling. Her autobiography, *Life So Far: A Memoir,* was published in 2002.

Betty Friedan has had an immeasurable effect on the lives of American women, first with *The Feminine Mystique* and later through her activism on behalf of women's needs and concerns and the writings that followed her groundbreaking seminal work. Her life is a testament to the words she wrote in *The Feminine Mystique:* "Who knows what women can be when they are finally free to become themselves?"

Rosalyn Sussman Yalow

(1921–)

*. . . The world cannot afford the loss of the talents of half its people if we
are to solve the many problems that beset us . . .*
          —Rosalyn Yalow, about the role of women, in her acceptance
          speech for the Nobel Prize in 1977

THE WOMAN KNOWN as the Madame Curie of the Bronx, Rosalyn
Sussman Yalow, and her longtime research partner, Solomon A.
Berson, were the first to apply nuclear physics in clinical medicine.
They developed radioimmunoassay, a method of detection that the
Nobel Prize committee referred to as "the most valuable advance in
basic clinical research" up to that time.

Their discovery, in 1959, is the reason why the ability to detect changes in the blood—from hepatitis to illicit drugs—is possible. By measuring minute changes in the chemical analysis of human blood and tissue, this radical application can be used in more than one hundred ways.

Some of the analyses possible are: detecting and curing some forms of mental retardation; detecting and altering growth hormone disorders; screening blood for foreign substances; determining effective dosage levels of drugs and antibiotics; diagnosing high blood pressure; and testing and correcting hormone levels in infertile couples.

Her route from the Bronx to Stockholm for her Nobel Prize began on July 19, 1921, when she was born to Simon Sussman, and Clara (Zipper) Sussman. Despite their lack of formal education beyond grade school, her parents (like so many immigrant parents at the time) understood the advantages and purpose of education and encouraged Rosalyn and her older brother Alexander to pursue their studies. Rosalyn, who could read before entering kindergarten, and her brother were regular patrons of the local library, making weekly trips to exchange new books for ones already read.

Her father was in the paper and twine business and her mother, a German émigré who arrived in the United States as a young girl, was a homemaker who encouraged her daughter to become a teacher. At this time, she had not fully understood the scope of her daughter's potential, but she was aware and confident that teaching would always provide Rosalyn with a steady job.

Rosalyn had read Eve Curie's book about her mother, Marie Curie, and Madame Curie became a role model for the young girl, who embraced mathematics in grammar school and then fell under the spell of the magic of chemistry while attending Walton High School. After graduating from high school at fifteen, she considered going into chemistry when she entered Hunter College. She was encouraged by physics professors Dr. Herbert Otis and Dr. Duane Roller. Her decision was crystallized after she heard Enrico Fermi, who had won the Nobel Prize in 1938, lecture at the school. Yalow earned a B.S. degree with a double major in chemistry and physics in 1941, becoming the college's first graduate in physics. She was also Phi Beta Kappa and graduated magna cum laude.

Prejudices against Jews and women nearly railroaded her pursuit of graduate studies, as rejection after rejection poured in despite support from her professors. One suggested she become a secretary at

MIT because that would enable her to take classes for a low fee or none at all. Fortunately, she did not take that route because she finally received an acceptance from the University of Illinois at Champaign-Urbana, the only woman among four hundred students, and the first woman in the College of Engineering since 1917. At Urbana, Maurice Goldhaber, Rosalyn's thesis adviser, and his wife, Gertrude Scharff, helped direct Yalow's studies and ultimately helped her master proficiencies in operating radioisotopes safely and using the first known instruments to measure them correctly.

This opportunity at Urbana not only impacted her professional life, but her personal life as well. On her first day, she met fellow student Aaron Yalow. They were married in 1943 and had two children, Benjamin, now a computer systems analyst, and Elanna, an educational psychologist. Her husband became a physics professor at Cooper Union college following his work as a medical physicist at Montefiore Hospital and other institutions.

For Rosalyn, there was never a conflict about family and career; she simply assumed she would have both, and she did. She would come home from the lab to make lunch for her children, and made dinner for the family each evening. She kept a kosher home in deference to her husband's Orthodox background, and like Bella Abzug, always acknowledged her husband's respect and support for her success.

Thanks to the modest yet important financial help provided by her teaching assistantship at Urbana, and the mentoring by the Goldhabers and others, she was able to complete her master's in 1942 and her doctorate dissertation in 1945 despite absurd comments that "an A- grade confirms that women do not do well at laboratory work."

Her first job was as the only female engineer at the Federal Telecommunications Laboratory (FTL) in New York, where she worked until it closed in 1946. Rosalyn Yalow taught physics at her alma mater, Hunter, before accepting a part-time consultant position at the Bronx Veterans Administration Hospital in December 1946. There she used her knowledge to equip and manage the hospital's Radioisotope Service.

Rosalyn was able to get this job because of her husband's assistance in contacting Bernard Roswit who was encouraging the study of radioactive substances for the diagnosis and treatment of disease.

She described the Bronx V.A. Hospital as one of the first to "recognize the importance of radioisotopes in medicine," despite the limitations of budget, laboratory space, supplies, and equipment. It was an exciting time for discovery, and she didn't let lack of tools stop her; she invented equipment as she needed it to do the research.

Medical researcher Edith Hinckley Quimby was curious about how physics could be applied to medical research, and Rosalyn volunteered to assist her at Columbia's College of Physicians and Surgeons to gain further experience with the medical applications of radioisotopes.

In 1950, she left Hunter and became a full-time researcher at the V.A. Hospital, and entered her most creative period with her longtime partner, Dr. Berson. The two used the radioisotope methodology to analyze blood for thyroid deficiencies, for the distribution of globins and serum proteins, and to study the relationship between hormones and insulin. Their work eventually led to the development of the diagnostic process, RIA, that was first used to study and analyze diabetes. They elected not to patent their methodology (which would have brought them millions), but through many papers and other educational efforts, popularized their discovery for use by the medical community. As a result, it is now one of the most commonly used ways to screen human blood and tissue—and a very cost-efficient method at that.

In 1967, Yalow became chief of the Nuclear Medicine Service (formerly the Radioisotope Section), and Berson became chairman of the Department of Medicine at the newly combined V.A. Hospital and Mt. Sinai School of Medicine. She also worked as a research professor at the medical school.

Rosalyn requested that the hospital rename its laboratory the Solomon A. Berson Research Laboratory, "so that his name will continue to be on my papers as long as I publish, and so that his contribution to our service will be memorialized," she said in *Les Prix Nobel, 1977*. The team had worked there together for twenty-two years. Her career total for research papers came to more than five hundred. Conscientious and industrious, she rarely took time off, working sixty to eighty hours a week. She viewed her lab assistants as extensions of her family, inviting them home for Passover and showing concern for their health. One anecdote reveals her approach to life: During a party honoring her selection as winner of the Lasker

Prize, she was talking to young students while helping to prepare the food for her own party.

Rosalyn Yalow was the first woman to win the Lasker Award for Basic Medical Research (1976), which is such a prestigious award in research that it commonly leads to recognition by the Nobel Prize committee. The following year, she shared the Nobel Prize in Physiology or Medicine with Andrew V. Schally and Roger Guillemin for applying radioimmunoassay to make discoveries about brain hormones.

At the ceremony, she commented, in part "... we ... [women] must believe in ourselves or no one else will believe in us; we must match our aspirations with the competence, courage, and determination to succeed, and we must feel a personal responsibility to ease the path for those who come after us."

Rosalyn Yalow was the second woman to receive the Nobel Prize in her specialty; American-born Gerty T. (Radnitz) Cori shared the prize with her husband Carl Ferdinand in 1947 for discovering the cause of the catalytic conversion of glycogen.

She met with few criticisms, except, perhaps that she did not share her part of the Nobel Prize money with the family of her research partner. She did give him credit, and acknowledged, with regret, that his death meant he could not share the honors with her.

The young girl who admired Madame Curie finally got the opportunity to show the world the importance of her role model when, in 1978, she hosted a five-part series for PBS on the French scientist whose passion for science she shared.

In 1979, she became the distinguished professor at the Albert Einstein College of Medicine at Yeshiva University, and in 1986 she was named the Solomon A. Berson Distinguished Professor at large at Mt. Sinai. During the 1980s, she also chaired the Department of Clinical Science at Montefiore Hospital and Medical Center.

She was accorded many of the honors of her field during this time including the National Medal of Science, in 1988; the Georg Charles de Henesy Nuclear Medicine Pioneer Award, 1986; and was inducted into the Women in Technology International Hall of Fame in 1997.

Rosalyn Yalow retired in 1991 to devote her time to the issues of child care and science education. "I am a scientist because I love investigation. Even after the Nobel Prize, the biggest thrill is to go to my laboratory and hope that day I will know something that nobody ever knew before. There are very few days when it happens, but the dream is still there. That's what it means to be a scientist." (As quoted in "Curiosity is the Key to Discovery: The Story of How Nobel Laureates Entered the World of Science," U.S. Department of Health and Human Services, 1992.)

Grace Paley

(1922–)

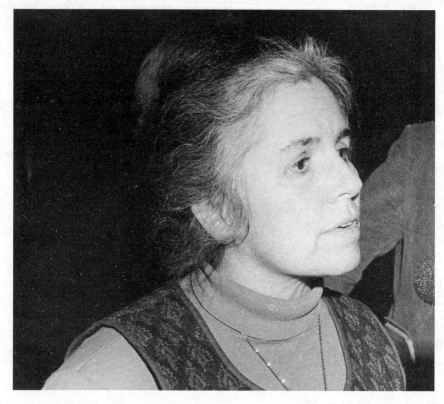

In a world where women's voices have been routinely silenced, Grace
Paley dares to create a voice that is boldly female. In her three volumes of
short stories, Paley manifests a willingness to speak the unspeakable: she is
irreverent, comic, compassionate, and wise. Critics have regularly remarked on the distinctiveness of this voice; Paley is an innovator, and her
innovations often occur in relationship to the particularly female consciousness she articulates.... Written in colloquial language, her stories
are deceptively simple; they seem at first glance to be uncomplicated and
even unadorned tales, but closer inspection reveals their careful craft.
Again and again reviewers and other authors describe her as one of a kind,
an original, unique.

— Jacqueline Taylor, *Grace Paley: Illuminating the Dark Lives*

GRACE PALEY ONCE asserted that "storytelling decants the story of life." All of her writings whether her acclaimed short stories—which are considered masterpieces of the form—her poetry, or her reflections on contemporary politics and culture, are imbued with an authenticity and conviction that ultimately affirms the human condition and uncovers the essential and universal in the particular. A first-generation Jewish American and a New Yorker, Paley derives her power as a writer from her fidelity to her past and her commitment to the present. She has given voice to those who are often assumed to have little to say and has investigated aspects of our world that, but for her, might have gone beyond our notice.

Paley's oeuvre is relatively small: three volumes of short stories, three collections of poetry, and a volume of essays, criticism, interviews, and lectures. But she is considered one of the most distinctive and important contemporary American writers. The world of her fiction centers almost exclusively on the area in Manhattan's Greenwich Village where she lived, raised her family, and began her association with the various political groups that have directed her activism ever since; yet, there is little about her work that strikes the reader as narrow or dated. Paley has distilled from the local to reveal a complex, demanding world.

Grace Goodside Paley was born in the Bronx, New York, the youngest child of Jewish immigrants. Her parents were Ukrainian socialists who immigrated to America after both had been arrested for participating in workers' demonstrations and after her father's brother had been killed by the czarist police. The family worked at menial jobs to allow Paley's father to attend medical school; after he became a physician, he set up a practice in the family's Bronx home. Paley has recalled growing up in a multilingual neighborhood in which Russian, Yiddish, and English blended together; the cadences of these languages would later inform her work.

The Goodside home became a kind of way station for recent immigrant arrivals from Russia. There, politics, not religion, dominated. Only Paley's grandmother was a practicing Jew, and Paley has recalled walking her grandmother to the synagogue when she was a child. She herself attended only a few Sunday school classes. However, as

Paley has commented, a Jew "is a person whose family is Jewish. I raised my kids to know they're Jewish, to like the idea, not to be displeased with it, not to try to hide it. To not be like in my generation, [when] there are many people who are ashamed of it." Her consciousness of her Jewish identity, together with the radical politics of her parents and friends, the suffering of her father's working-class patients, and an awareness of the sacrifices made by various female relatives for the men in their lives would have a profound influence on Paley's political beliefs and on her writing.

To the great disappointment of her family, Paley showed little academic ambition. "I was a very good student up to the age of ten," she has recalled, "then my mind began to wander." She spent a year at Hunter College, another at New York University, and studied briefly at the New School for Social Research, taking a course in poetry with W. H. Auden. After reading her poetry, Auden urged her to abandon the artificiality of language she had derived from her reading for the more authentic vernacular that she knew firsthand. It would be a lesson she would take to heart when she began to write her stories more than a decade later.

In 1942, at the age of nineteen, she dropped out of college to marry Jess Paley, a motion picture cameraman, with whom she had two children, Nora (b. 1949) and Danny (b. 1951). She devoted her time to her family and took occasional jobs as a clerical worker. On her many trips to Washington Square Park with her children, Paley listened to other mothers talking about their lives and it struck her that no one was attempting to tell their stories. She began to write while immersed in her homemaking responsibilities. As her daughter later recalled, "She should have had a door to close and be behind it—but none of that happened; it wasn't like that. I don't know when she got the time, how she did it. She must have done it sometime—maybe it was while we were in day care. . . . It's not like my father took us to the park so she could work—none of *that* was going yet." The Paleys would divorce in 1972; the same year Grace Paley married poet and playwright Robert Nichols.

Paley's first story, "Goodbye and Good Luck," was inspired by a chance remark heard from her husband's aunt on a visit to the Paleys. The aunt said, "I was popular in certain circles, and I wasn't no thinner then," and Paley used that to reveal the life of a young woman who becomes involved with a Russian actor in New York's

Yiddish theater. The story found its way into her first collection, *The Little Disturbances of Man* (1959). The stories in the collection focus on the lives of women and children and explore family life in the urban world of crowded apartments, streets, and schools. The title of the volume refers to those seemingly trivial and insignificant incidents that shape a life. The story, "An Interest in Life," from which the collection's title is drawn, concerns a husband's desertion of his wife and four children, and opens with the matter-of-fact but chilling perspective of the wife: "My husband gave me a broom one Christmas. This wasn't right. No one can tell me it was meant kindly." Another admired story in her debut collection is "The Loudest Voice," which draws on the Jewish immigrant experience in public schools by telling the story of a Jewish child who is recruited to play a prominent part in the school's Christmas pageant.

In writing about Paley's work, novelist Jamaica Kincaid has observed, "Her prose is deceptively comforting. You are wired into the most simple, everyday language, just enjoying it, and then you find yourself in the middle of enormous questions or strange territory." The British novelist A. S. Byatt has commented that "we have had a great many artists, more of them women than not, recording the tragedies of repetition, frequency, weariness, and little disturbances. What distinguishes Grace Paley from the mass of these is the interest, and even more, the inventiveness which she brings to her small world." One of the hallmarks of Paley's style is her rendering the voices of her characters in a realistic manner, capturing in their accents and gestures a rich texture of educational background and ethnic heritage.

The Little Disturbances of Man heralded the arrival of a major talent, but it would be fifteen years until her next collection appeared. A contributing reason for the delay was her increasing political activities during the 1960s and 1970s. As an active Parent-Teacher Organization member, she protested against air raid drills and organized opposition to rerouting school buses through Washington Square Park (where her children played). She also protested the Vietnam War as a founding member and later secretary of the War Resisters League, and campaigned in favor of draft resistance. In addition, she helped organize an artists' and writers' venture called Vietnamese Life, in order to share Vietnamese music, art, and culture with her Greenwich Village community. In 1969 she was part of a delegation that traveled to North Vietnam with the goal of bringing back three American pilots who had been shot down.

Other issues that claimed Paley's attention were nuclear proliferation, women's rights, and human rights. In 1973, as a member of a peace delegation to the Moscow World Peace Congress, she voiced her personal opposition to the then–Soviet Union's continual silencing of political dissidents. The Congress disassociated itself from her remarks. As one of the White House Eleven arrested in December 1978 for displaying an antinuclear banner on the White House lawn, she was fined and given a suspended sentence. In 1980 Paley was awarded the Peace Award from the War Resisters League for her activism. "I believe in the stubbornness of civil disobedience and I'm not afraid of it," she has said.

Paley's political concerns, first introduced in *The Little Disturbances of Man,* become more central in *Enormous Changes at the Last Minute,* her second collection, which was published in 1974. The collection brings back characters from *The Little Disturbances of Man,* but also employs a more open-ended experimental fictional technique and offers a darker vision of life. In "The Long-Distance Runner," a middle-aged Jewish woman returns to her old neighborhood, where the population has shifted from immigrant Jewish to African American and must face her latent racism. In the longest story of the collection, "Faith in a Tree," a woman sees her life changing before her eyes as an antiwar protest is chased from the local park. In one of her most anthologized stories, "A Conversation with My Father," Paley comments on her literary method. The ailing father requests from his daughter a simple story, "the kind de Maupassant wrote, or Chekhov, the kind you used to write." She wishes to please her father but cannot give him the straightforward, easily resolved story he desires. She reveals that she has avoided plot, "the absolute line between two points," in her writing, "not for literary reasons, but because it takes all hope away. Everyone real or invented deserves the open destiny of life."

Paley's third collection, *Later the Same Day,* published in 1985, again reintroduces characters from her earlier collections, such as Faith, who, in "Dreamer in a Dead Language," visits her parents in a nursing home only to discover that they are considering divorce. One of her strongest stories, "Zagrowsky Tells," concerns a bigoted Jewish pharmacist whose daughter gives birth to a child by an African-

American man. Zagrowsky assumes responsibility for the care of his grandson, and his love for him transforms him. It is one of the most hopeful stories in Paley's canon; its affirmation is firmly built on the actual world of mixed motives and ambiguous, complex individuals.

Paley continued her political activism and interests throughout the 1980s and 1990s, and remains active today. In 1985 she visited Nicaragua and El Salvador to better understand American diplomatic policy toward these countries. In 1987 Paley was one of the founders of the Jewish Women's Committee to End the Occupation of the Left Bank and Gaza, and has been an outspoken advocate of Palestinian rights. She was founding chair of Women's WORLD (Women's Rights, Literature, and Development), an "international free speech network of feminist writers," which posits that "nowhere on earth are women's voices given the same respect as men's." As co-founder of the organization and a member of its board, she has worked to change the minority status of women worldwide.

Paley has taught creative writing at Sarah Lawrence College since 1966; she has also taught at universities such as Columbia, Syracuse, Johns Hopkins, Stanford, and at the graduate school of the City College of New York. One of her courses is titled "Writing in Jewish." A "Jewish sound," she has said, is "some kind of questioning voice, a midrashic way of looking at the world." One example she has cited is Franz Kafka, who did not write about Jewish issues, but who had Jewish "sounds in his head."

Paley has been the recipient of numerous awards and honors for her work, including the National Institute of Arts and Letters Award (1970), a Senior Fellowship, given by the National Endowment of the Arts in 1987, "in recognition for her lifetime contribution to literature," the Rea Award for excellence in short-story writing (1993), and the National Foundation of Jewish Culture Award (1994).

Throughout her life, Grace Paley has consistently chosen to explore complex issues, whether in her politics or her writing. She has persistently insisted that both writing and action can produce the "little disturbances" and "enormous changes" she records in her stories. As she has observed, we all "have to remember, the world still has to be saved—every day." As her political activism attests, Paley has lived her life according to her conscience. She brings to her life and work the consciousness of herself as a Jew, a woman, a writer, and a citizen of the world. Nowhere is this consciousness more evident than in the voices of her characters—especially her women. They meet their challenges from playground politics to global conflicts with determination, wit, humor, and love. Paley says, ". . . people will sometimes ask, 'Why don't you write more politics?' and I have to explain to them that writing the lives of women is politics."

Diane Arbus

(1923–1971)

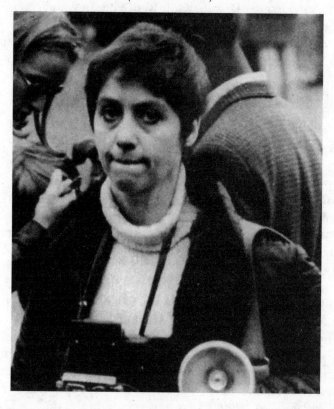

These haunting images, jarring yet magical, arrive from the past to give a lyrical poke at our collective subconscious, to wake us up—and remind us to look.

—Raul Nino, art critic, on the work of Diane Arbus

DIANE ARBUS WAS born to affluent New York parents Gertrude (Russek) and David Nemerov. She knew two families: the wealthy Russeks who had started a hugely successful furrier company in the 1890s and, only occasionally, the considerably poorer Brooklyn Nemerovs, who would host their son's family for Passover each year. The trappings of wealth did not comfort nor entertain Diane, but apparently propelled her into a lifelong search for the "reality" she believed she was forbidden in childhood.

David Nemerov championed the arts, and this played a great part in the family's pursuits: Diane's sister Renée became an accomplished impressionist painter, and her brother Howard, a Pulitzer Prize–winning poet. All three siblings attended the Ethical Culture's Fieldston School in Riverdale, a progressive school quite popular in that era.

At fourteen, Diane met Allan Arbus, a nineteen-year-old pasteup artist working in the family firm's art department, and the two conducted a clandestine affair for four years, much against the family's wishes. She was, after all, only fourteen, and Allan was then "just" a pasteup artist. Despite family reservations, the couple married, with a rabbi officiating, in 1941—shortly after Diane turned eighteen. (Television viewers know Allan best as the psychiatrist Sidney Freeman on *M*A*S*H;* however, he has had numerous acting credits and became a credentialed therapist.) The marriage lasted twenty-eight years (on paper) and produced two children, Doon and Amy.

Shortly after they were married, Allan gave Diane the gift of a camera and she learned the fundamentals of photography and development skills in a darkroom during a brief period of study with Berenice Abbott, a famed photographer of the time.

The couple formed the Allan and Diane Arbus Studio in 1946, with Russek's Furs as their first account. The duo was enormously successful in fashion photography with Diane providing the creative styling and Allan the technical expertise. In 1957, following an acute period of depression (she was to have many bouts during her life), Diane quit the studio to pursue a career in independent photography. In 1958, she happened upon her first mentor, Lisette Model, an Austrian-born documentary photographer who taught at the New School for Social Research. Diane studied with her for two years and the two remained close friends.

Allan and Diane separated after nineteen years of marriage, and Diane remained conflicted between following the program of dutiful wife proscribed by both her family and society and pursuing her visions as an artist with camera. For a while, she tried to combine the two pursuits. Allan continued to be a source of moral support and technical expertise in photography for Diane for many years, even after they separated.

To many of her first critics, the aspects of the human condition that Diane recorded were too revealing, too harsh to accept; yet her work was the beginning of a transformation, a deepening of what photography could do beyond recording pretty landscapes and portraitures of elegantly staged people.

Diane Arbus was excruciatingly shy, yet almost obsessively curious. She experienced great difficulty in approaching subjects at first, but encouraged by Model, was finally able to approach, and capture on film, the "forbidden" subjects that have come to signify her oeuvre, a kind of cultural anthropology of outsiders from drag queens to junkies, from midgets to nudists, and many other people considered freaks or odd by the most severe conventional standards.

As her shyness washed away, using an innate and sincere charm, she not only was able to get more and more people to pose for her, but also through the intimacy created by photographer and subject, she managed to elicit their most personal secrets, which those viewing the photographs can interpret in many ways. Looking at an Arbus photograph can be disconcerting, alarming, exciting, but never boring. Her photographs are stories with great subtext that she may, or may not, have intended.

Acknowledgement of her work came in the form of two Guggenheim fellowships, in 1963 and 1966, and an exhibition of her work at the Museum of Modern Art in 1967, which was one of the most popular of the time. As is the case for many artists, finances were difficult, so she took on many jobs and assignments from teaching photography to researching press photography at the Museum of Modern Art to returning to commercial photography for *Esquire* and *Harper's Bazaar.*

Diane met her second mentor, Marvin Israel, in 1959. He was to prove very influential in helping her get assignments from magazines, especially after he became art director of *Harper's Bazaar* in 1961 and used his position to publish her work. Another mentor was *Esquire* articles editor Harold Hayes, who viewed her work as "apocalyptic." The magazine's July 1960 issue published "The Vertical Journey: Six Movements of a Moment Within the Heart of the City." This was the beginning of more than 250 photographs in more than seventy magazines that would introduce her art and style to the public.

Other publications that used her work during this time were as diverse as *Sports Illustrated, Saturday Evening Post,* and the London *Sunday Times Magazine.* What was most unusual is that she did not make a distinction between her serious art photography and her magazine work, despite the commercial objectives of the latter.

Photographers are always liberated or limited by the equipment they have, and Diane was no exception. She used a Leica for many years, but then switched to a Rolleiflex in 1962. This significantly changed the mood and style of her work, because the Rolleiflex produces square framed negatives with much more clarity and less graininess than other cameras provide.

Another significance of the Rolleiflex was how it was used, literally. Diane could hold this camera at her waist, thus enabling her to make, and sustain, valuable eye contact with her subjects, creating a more intimate relationship that so obviously came across on her ensuing prints. (A 35 mm camera, on the other hand, must be held up to the photographer's eye, to ensure proper focus and framing of the subject.)

The intimacy that she achieved with a square format camera is just one of the reasons her photos are so riveting. The framing compresses space, subject matter, and viewer into an almost symbiotic relationship.

Adding a flash later on, with her Mamiya C33, contributed a feeling of vulnerability, an "exposing" so to speak, of her subjects to viewers in a gallery. Using a flash in daylight photos was a breakthough discovery, which helped her subjects avoid the squinting and posturing they would sometimes do when facing direct sunlight, the typical stance for subjects in most photography. Additional benefits were the avoidance of shadows or overbrightness, so that her photographs appear to have a flatness that is, nonetheless, painterly and, again, very intimate.

"There's a kind of power thing about the camera," she once said. "I mean, everyone knows you've got some edge. You're carrying some slight magic, which does something to them. It fixes them in a way."

In the book, *Bystander: A History of Street Photography,* Joel Meyerowitz commented that Arbus insinuated herself into someone's life with her camera. He says that the subjects ". . . are giving themselves over to her . . . they are flowing out toward her, giving up their mystery. Diane was an emissary from the world of feeling . . . cared about these people. They felt that and gave her their secret.

She wasn't expanding anybody's horizons, but narrowing down her own focus, homing in on subjects who were enthralled by her because they could feel how personal and private her interest in them was."

Diane continued to "collect" images at Hubert's Freak Museum in Times Square, Coney Island, gay nightclubs, and the tenements of Brooklyn and Manhattan, but by the late sixties, both her emotional and physical health had deteriorated. In 1966, and then again in 1968, she suffered from hepatitis. Although they had been separated for years, her marriage to Allan was not officially dissolved until 1969. This appears to have set off an acute period of depression, something she had experienced throughout her life, but which in her professional career was the continuing conflict of creation and scrambling for money. Her shyness, which she had overcome enough to approach subjects to photograph, still made her reticent about fame and exposing herself to the press or the public. The conflict of family and society pressures on how to behave and what to do were apparently always in conflict with her passion to create her own style of photography.

Still, fame came, and requests for exhibits were solicited of her. The most important of these was an invitation to show her work at the 1972 Venice Biennale, where she would be the first American and first woman to show her photographs. She accepted, although with reservations about her abilities.

The planned Vienna exhibit and the generally favorable reviews of a portfolio of her photographs in the May 1971 issue of *Artforum* seemed to be the start of positive acceptance of her work. Arbus had suffered from a recurrence of hepatitis, and the fatigue from that illness plus her unshakable feelings of inadequacy as an artist sent her into another depression she was not able to shake. Arbus committed suicide by taking an overdose of drugs and slitting her wrists on July 26; Marvin Israel discovered her body in her apartment, two days later. She was forty-eight years old.

The Museum of Modern Art presented a posthumous exhibit in 1972 that later toured throughout the United States and Europe and was viewed by more than seven million people, thus sealing her reputation as one of the most outstanding contemporary artists of the twentieth century. It was the most popular photography exhibit since *The Family of Man*, developed by Edward Steichen, and in death brought her collectors, fame, and fortune beyond her imaginings in life.

Once considered a cult photographer, Arbus's work is now considered art, having changed our culture's definitions of *odd, unusual,* or *freak*. While some people will always view her photographs that way, others have taken the time to really look, and their rewards are the revelations that within each of us is the vulnerable, fragile human condition that "pretty" can never demonstrate. Diane Arbus paved the way for experimental photographers from Robert Mapplethorpe to Andy Warhol to Katharina Bosse and so many others who have shown us different ways to view the world. Her vision, and her courage to go deeper than the superficial, is her enduring legacy.

She said of her pictures, "What I'm trying to describe is that it's impossible to get out of your skin into somebody else's. . . . That somebody else's tragedy is not the same as your own."

Cynthia Ozick

(1928–)

. . . writers are by definition impersonators. But a writer cannot be an impersonator in life, outside of the word. If you are . . . your writing will be false.

—Cynthia Ozick, on advice to writers

IN BOTH FICTION and essays, Cynthia Ozick has what A. Alvarez calls "the poet's perfectionist habit of mind and obsession with language, as though one word out of place would undo the whole fabric.

"The fabric of her storytelling is colored with what is culturally and religiously Jewish. She often writes like Chagall paints, he of the green faces, flying brides, blue cows. She can also write with such

247

specificity, such intimacy, such reality, that the reader is left shaken. The circumstances, the thoughts and feelings of her characters are so indelibly revealed that we wonder, 'How could she know?' "

For Ozick, writing fiction is not based on what you know, but on what you do not know. Otherwise, what else is the imagination for?

Her own boundless imagination was fired by a passion for reading when she was a child. Escape from the taunts of gentile classmates was found in books, dreaming was found in books, imagining herself as a writer was spurred on by the many fables and stories she read.

"Someday," she wrote, "when I am free of P.S. 71, I will write stories. Meanwhile, in winter dusk . . . in the secret bliss of the *Violet Fairy Book,* I both see and do not see how these grains of life will stay forever."

Born in Manhattan, her family moved to Pelham Bay, an area of the Bronx, where she grew up. Her parents were Celia (aka Shiphra) Regelson and William Ozick, immigrants from Lithuania. Her father knew Latin, German, and English. He made his living as a pharmacist, giving to his trade the same meticulous care he gave to his Hebrew calligraphy or Talmudic studies. Her mother helped her husband at their Park View Pharmacy, and was caring and supportive of Cynthia and her brother. For the most part, it was a gentle, sweet time, even though her parents labored long and hard at their store.

Cynthia's mother's brother was Abraham Regelson, an esteemed Hebrew language poet, and the first writer Cynthia knew personally. He became her model of what a writer could be—that one could write on both Jewish and secular topics.

At age five, Ozick was taken to Hebrew school by her grandmother who was told by the rabbi not to bring her back, because "girls don't need to study." Her grandmother, and fortunately, another rabbi believed otherwise, and she remained in school. That teacher, and her grandmother, had a second impact on the young girl's life: they introduced her to the world of another language: Yiddish. Today, Ozick is a champion for the language, calling for its preservation in essays and keeping it alive with her translations of Yiddish poetry.

Yiddish words find themselves comfortably lodged in much of Ozick's writing. In the essay, "Envy, or, Yiddish in America," she created an immigrant Yiddish poet (most probably patterned after Isaac Bashevis Singer), whom she sends on a search for a translator up to the standards of his work. It is full of delicious irony, and yet calls serious attention to the importance of keeping this language alive. The combination of serious statements coupled with humor; the drama of mysticism balanced with proverb; the melding of the Greek myth with the Yiddish fable, are all part of her wonderful story-telling tools.

Ozick attended Hunter College High School and was graduated, cum laude, from New York University with a B.A. in English. She earned her master's in English at Ohio State University at Columbus in 1950. She taught at New York University, Indiana University at Bloomington, and has been the distinguished artist-in-residence at City College, New York. Married since 1952 to lawyer Bernard Hallote, she and her husband have one daughter, Rachel, born in 1965, who holds a Ph.D. in biblical archaeology.

Ozick's Lithuanian parents were stalwart defenders of the traditions of rationalism, and critics of the Orthodox Hasidic mysticism that has, ironically, found a setting in much of her works. She claims to be a *misnaged,* one who opposes any form of mystic religion. For Ozick, the absence of idolatry is a religious tenet, and yet in her fiction, idolatry is quite often a character in and of itself to be examined and explored.

Ozick is, to be sure, both comfortable with, and learned of, Judaism. Unlike some modern Jewish writers—mostly men, who satirize or make victims of their Jewish characters—Ozick celebrates her Jewish heritage in a way that makes her work accessible to the non-Jewish reading public. She does this by creating a particular, believable world, in the vein of a Maxine Hong Kingston celebrating her Chinese heritage or a Flannery O'Connor creating her special niche of Southern Catholicism.

Critics have been lavish in their praise. Carol Horn of *The Washington Post Book World* has said of Ozick that "Her stories are elusive, mysterious, and disturbing. They shimmer with intelligence, they glory in language, and they puzzle."

In short order, three collections of short stories and novellas established her reputation as a powerful writer of the Jewish ethos: *The Pagan Rabbi and Other Stories, Bloodshed and Three Novellas,* and *Levitation: Five Fictions.* Her stories are full of comedy and drama, and generally master the art of storytelling from the Jewish textural tradition.

In one of her most disturbingly memorable stories, *The Shawl,* Ozick takes the reader into the madness of the mind of a Holocaust survivor. Elie Wiesel, himself a survivor and a prolific writer on the subject, wrote that "Ozick speaks of them [the survivors] with so much tact and delicacy that we ask ourselves with wonder and admiration what has she done to understand and penetrate Rosa's dark and devastated soul."

Her response has been that "Imagination is more than make-believe, more than the power to invent. It is also the power to penetrate evil, to take on evil, to become evil, and in that guise it is the most frightening faculty. Whoever writes a story that includes villainy enters into and becomes the villain."

Her ability to "understand and penetrate" is even more remarkable when you consider she was a happy student of literature during the first revelations of Hitler's cruelty, and was pursuing not Jewish literature but studying that most American of Americans, Henry James. Her master's thesis was *Parables in the Later Novels of Henry James.*

In 1966, Ozick published her first novel, *Trust,* an exercise in the pursuit of high art, Jamesian style. Although there is much that is good in the book, it has none of the fire and passion of her famous short stories. She has written three other novels: *The Cannibal Galaxy* (1983), *The Messiah of Stockholm* (1987), and *The Puttermesser Papers* (1997), which is considered her best. The title character's unusual surname means butter knife, as if Ozick is implying that one could cut through life to reveal its absolute meaning, perhaps even to create a true civilization. She pits a female golem, a Jewish version of Xanthippe, against the lawgiver Moses (only in this case it's the mayor of New York City), and places them in a wildly allegorical fable that ends with the golem "chanted back into a pile of mud" and life resumes its "normalcy."

So far, the Pulitzer and Nobel prizes for literature have eluded her but the honors have come. She won the first Michael Rea Prize for "career contributions to the short story" in 1986; the Harold Washington Literary Award from the city of Chicago in 1997; the John Cheever Award in 1999; and the Lannan Literary Award in 2000.

Five of her short stories have appeared in various editions of the

Best American Short Stories anthologies, and she won O'Henry first prizes for short stories in 1975, 1981, 1984, and 1992. She also has won the Edward Lewis Wallant Award for Fiction (1972); American Academy of Arts Award for Literature (1973); and the Pushcart Press Lamport Prize (1980).

She has been the recipient of several fellowships from the National Endowment for the Arts in 1968; a Guggenheim in 1982; and the Lucy Martin Donnelly fellowship from Bryn Mawr College in 1992.

The Jewish community has recognized her talent even as some have criticized her use of the mystical in her stories. Among her honors have been the B'nai Brith Jewish Heritage Award (1971); the Epstein Award of the Jewish Book Council (1972); and the Hadassah Myrtle Wreath Award (1974).

Ozick regularly writes for *The New York Times Book Review, The New York Times Magazine,* and *The New Yorker* magazine. Many of her essays and criticism have been collected into *Art and Ardor* (1983); *Metaphor and Memory* (1989); *What Henry James Knew and Other Essays on Writers* (1993); and *Fame and Folly: Essays* (1996). She also won the PEN/Spiegelman-Diamonstein Award for the Art of the Essay in 2000.

The essays in her book, *Quarrel & Quandary,* are particularly insightful, and won Ozick, much to her surprise, the National Book Critics Circle Award for criticism in 2000. The book also earned the PEN/Faulkner Award for criticism.

To date, she has made only one venture into the genre of playwriting, with an adaptation of *The Shawl.* After numerous rewrites and a few stagings, it was produced off Broadway at Playhouse 91, the American Jewish Repertory Theater, in 1996 to generally favorable reviews.

She has received honorary degrees from eleven universities and has delivered the Phi Beta Kappa oration at Harvard University.

Ozick has continuously written essays reminding both writers and readers that taking the high road not only can keep the languages of Yiddish and English vibrant, it also can elevate storytelling to its proper realm. She says: "Literature itself need make no apology for its potential as an abiding, even necessary, moral force."

Anne Frank

(1929–1945)

[One] of the many questions that continues to disturb me is why, in the past and often now as well, women of all cultures have been placed in a much more lowly position than men. . . . Soldiers and war heroes are honored and celebrated, explorers achieve immortal fame, martyrs are worshipped, but how many in the whole of humanity consider women too, as soldiers? . . . Women are much braver, much more courageous soldiers who fight and undergo pain for the continued existence of humanity, than the many freedom fighters with their big mouths!
—Anne Frank, diary entry, June 15, 1944

AMONG THE BIRTHDAY presents given to Annelies Frank on June 12, 1942, was a small, red-and-white-checked book filled with blank pages. Annelies, known as Anne, decided to begin a diary, which she would write as a series of letters to an imaginary friend she called Kitty. In her third entry Anne wrote, "It's an odd idea for someone like me to keep a diary . . . it seems to me that neither I—nor for that matter anyone else—will be interested in the unbosomings of a thirteen-year-old schoolgirl."

A few weeks after Anne began her diary she and her family, together with four other Jews, went into hiding on the top floor of an Amsterdam warehouse to avoid deportation. From 1942 until 1944, when the group was discovered by the security police and sent to concentration camps, Anne used her diary to express her innermost thoughts and feelings, to grapple with the contradictory aspects of her personality, and to chronicle life inside the *Achterhuis* (the "house behind"), as she called it. This teenage writer who perished in adolescence could not know that her epistolary autobiography would become the most influential human document of one of the most inhuman periods in history.

Annelies Marie Frank was born in Frankfurt, Germany, the younger of Otto and Edith Frank's two daughters. Both parents came from well-to-do families. Otto Frank had served as an officer in the German army during the First World War, and following the loss of the family fortune during the inflationary 1920s he was able to establish himself as a successful businessman. The rise of the Nazi Party and Adolf Hitler, and the anti-Jewish edicts that followed the Nuremberg Laws of 1935, convinced Otto Frank to move his family to Amsterdam. There, he started a business selling pectin and spices to Dutch housewives and leased a warehouse and offices on the Prinsengracht, a canal/street in the old part of the city, several miles from the Frank's suburban home.

There was little suggestion early on that Anne was interested in or capable of producing any kind of prodigious literary effort. Her older sister, Margot, was serious, well behaved, and an excellent student whose ambition was to become a nurse. Lies Goslar Pick, Anne's childhood friend, later recalled that Anne, who attended the Montessori school and later a Jewish secondary school, was "interested mainly in dates, clothes, and parties," and that she "was a mischief-maker who annoyed the neighbors with her pranks and continually was in hot water at school for her conduct." The talkative Anne was nick-named "Miss Chatterbox" and "Miss Quack-Quack," and wrote school compositions, according to Pick, that were considered by the teacher to be "just ordinary, not better than average."

In 1940, when the Germans invaded Holland, they instituted the same anti-Jewish laws that were in place in Germany. Despite her reputation for childish frivolity, an entry at the beginning of her diary shows her awareness of the desperate situation facing the Jews. Anne discusses these laws at length:

> After 1940 good times rapidly fled: first the war, then the capitula-tion, followed by the arrival of the Germans, which is when the sufferings of us Jews really began. Anti-Jewish decrees followed each other in rapid succession. Jews must wear yellow stars. Jews must hand in their bicycles. Jews are banned from trams and are forbidden to drive. Jews are only allowed to do their shopping be-tween three and five o'clock and then only in shops which bear the placard "Jewish shop." Jews must be indoors by eight o'clock and cannot even sit in their own gardens after that hour. Jews are for-bidden to visit theaters, cinemas, and other sports grounds are for-bidden to them. Jews may not visit Christians. Jews must go to Jewish schools, and many more restrictions of a similar kind.

Since Jews were also forbidden to own businesses, Otto Frank had to turn over ownership of his firm to one of his employees, Victor Kugler. At the same time, he quietly made preparations to go into hiding.

In July 1942, Margot Frank was ordered to report for deportation to a labor camp. Shortly after the Franks received the order, they made the trek on foot from their home to their hiding place, an empty attic apartment occupying three floors above Otto Frank's warehouse. Anne describes that she wore "two vests, three pairs of pants, a dress, on top of that a skirt, jacket, summer coat, two pairs of stockings, lace-up shoes, woolly cap, scarf, and still more; I was nearly stifled before we started, but no one inquired about that." In a July 1942 diary entry, Anne relates the family's journey to what she called the "Secret Annex":

> So we walked in the pouring rain . . . each with a school satchel and shopping bag filled to the brim with all kinds of things thrown together anyhow. We got sympathetic looks from people on their way to work. You could see by their faces how sorry they were they couldn't offer us a lift; the gaudy yellow star spoke for itself . . .
>
> When we arrived at the Prinsengracht, Miep took us quickly upstairs and into the "Secret Annex." She closed the door behind us and we were alone.

For the next twenty-five months the Franks shared their hideout with Mr. van Pels, a coworker of Otto Frank's, van Pels's wife, their teenage son, Peter, and an elderly dentist named Fritz Pfeffer (Anne changed their names in her diary). The group's links to the outside world were a radio, which could only be played softly at night, and Otto Frank's loyal employees, who gallantly protected them and brought them supplies obtained with forged ration cards, as well as news of the war and news of Jews they knew who had been taken to concentration camps. (The group witnessed the daily roundups of Jews from the windows in their hiding place). The company that Otto Frank had once run continued to function, and the fugitives had to be almost completely silent during business hours. They were forced to go to bed early—lights at night would arouse suspicion. In her October 1, 1942 entry, Anne wrote, "We are as quiet as mice. Who, three months ago, would ever have guessed that quicksilver Anne would have to sit still for hours—and, what's more—could?" Burglars routinely tried to rob the warehouse, adding to their fears of discovery.

It was in this paradoxical atmosphere of relative comfort and the increasing tension caused by close confinement and continual worry that Anne experienced the first years of her adolescence and where she found her refuge, her sense of quietude, and her future ambition to become a writer. With complete honesty she describes in her diary her antipathy toward the van Pelses and Pfeffer, her bodily changes and budding sexuality, the short-lived infatuation she felt for Peter van Pels, her detached feelings toward her sweet but somewhat priggish older sister, her resentment of her mother, and her faith in her beloved father, to whom she had given the pet name of "Pim." Like most adolescents she struggled to reconcile her "lighter, superficial self" with what she called "the deeper side of me"; this self-analysis, recorded with remarkable perception and detail throughout the diary, shows Anne's development from an outgoing, vivacious child to an introspective, idealistic young woman. Forced into maturity by the severity of her situation, she was, as *New Yorker* writer Judith Thurman has observed, "a strong, canny, fluent, truthful writer, who escaped the preciousness that generally mars the work of young people."

Anne's natural tendency was toward cheerfulness and optimism, but she sometimes gave in to feelings of despondency, which was not surprising, given the circumstances. In a diary entry from October 1943 she wrote, "The atmosphere is so oppressive and sleepy and as heavy as lead. You don't hear a single bird singing outside, and a deadly close silence hangs everywhere, catching hold of me as if it will drag me down deep into an underworld. . . . I wander from one room to another, downstairs and up again, feeling like a songbird whose wings have been clipped and who is hurling himself in utter darkness against the bars of his cage."

But her still youthful spirit remained undimmed. By 1944 she was beginning to envision herself as a writer and as an adult with a purpose to her life: "I know what I want, I have a goal, an opinion, I have a religion and love," she wrote in April. "I know that I'm a woman, a woman with inward strength and plenty of courage. If God lets me live . . . I shall not remain insignificant, I shall work in the world and for mankind." She had already imagined "how interesting it would be if I were to publish a romance of the 'Secret Annex' " and had begun to prepare the diary for possible publication.

Anne's last diary entry was August 1, 1944. On August 4 the security police raided the hideout and arrested the inhabitants. The group in the secret annex had been betrayed, either by warehouse clerk and petty thief, Willem van Maaren, one of the would-be burglars, Anton Ahlers, a business associate of Otto Frank, or someone as yet unknown. While searching for valuables, the police emptied Otto Frank's briefcase, with Anne's diary hidden inside, onto the floor. A week later, Miep Gies, Otto Frank's secretary and one of the group's protectors, returned to the hideout, retrieved the diary, and kept it hidden under a pile of magazines, along with Anne's other notebooks, in the hope that Anne would retrieve them one day.

The Franks, van Pelses, and Pfeffer were held in a Dutch transit camp, Westerbork, for a month and then transported by cattle car to the Auschwitz concentration camp. A Dutch woman survivor who shared the same barracks as Edith Frank and the girls later described to an interviewer Anne's courage, sensitivity, and empathy in the midst of horror: "Anne was the youngest in her group, but nevertheless she was the leader of it. . . . She, too, was the one who saw to the last what was going on all around us. We had long since stopped seeing. . . . Something protected us, kept us from seeing. But Anne had no such protection, to the last. . . . She cried. And you cannot imagine how soon most of us came to the end of our tears." In the fall of 1944, as the Russians were advancing in the direction of Auschwitz, the Germans transported a number of prisoners, including Anne and Margot Frank, to the Bergen-Belson concentration camp. The following spring, Anne and Margot, along with thousands of other prisoners, perished in a typhus epidemic that decimated the camp. One month later, on April 12, 1945, British troops liberated the camp.

When Otto Frank, the group's only survivor, returned to Amsterdam, Miep Gies gave him Anne's diary and other writings. In 1947 Frank published his daughter's diary as *Het Achterhuis,* the title Anne herself had chosen for it. In 1953 the journal was published in the United States as *The Diary of a Young Girl.* A new edition of the diary was published in 1995. A perennial bestseller, Anne's diary has been translated into more than thirty languages and in 1956 was adapted into a hugely popular play, *The Diary of Anne Frank,* by Frances Goodrich and Albert Hackett. There have been movies and a television miniseries based on her life. Anne's fables, stories, and essays have been published in collections such as *The Works of Anne Frank* (1959), *Tales From the House Behind* (1965), and *Anne Frank's Tales From the Secret Annex* (1983). In 1989 a seven-hundred page critical edition of the diary was published in the Netherlands, primarily in response to Holocaust revisionists, those who have denied that the Holocaust took place and have attacked Anne Frank's character and credibility. There also have been several critical studies of Anne's work, as well as numerous biographical studies, the most recent of which are *Anne Frank: The Biography,* by Melissa Müller (1998) and *Anne Frank: Her Life and Legacy,* by Hyman Aaron Enzer (2000).

In what is probably her most famous diary entry, from July 1944, Anne wrote: "In spite of everything I still believe that people are really good at heart. . . . I can feel the sufferings of millions and yet, if I look up into the heavens, I think that it will all come right, that this cruelty too will end, and that peace and tranquility will return again." This message of hope and expression of confidence in humanity illustrates why, sixty years after she began the diary she would not live to complete, Anne Frank continues to be a source of inspiration for so many.

Beverly Sills

(1929–)

Art is the signature of civilization.

—Beverly Sills

WHEN BEVERLY SILLS retired as Chairman of Lincoln Center for the Performing Arts in 2002, it marked the close of still another chapter in an amazing career in the arts. She stepped down, she said, because she believed it was time to rest. Certainly, leisure is well deserved, but her exceptional history, including two other "retirements," may prove that "rest" is just another word for vacation.

Sills could be the poster child for how persistence, coupled with an incredible gift, can make one a star, even if it takes decades to reach the destination.

That lifetime began in Brooklyn, when Belle Miriam was born in 1929 to Shirley (Bahn) and Morris Silverman, an insurance salesman. A bubble of spit popping out of the newborn's mouth was perceived as an omen, and to ensure their luck, her parents nicknamed her "Bubbles." It also could be said that the name was prophetic, for Beverly Sills smiles as if she's ready to burst out the most fabulous secret; her laugh is hearty and sincere, and her personality does indeed bubble over.

So, how did the winner of the "Miss Beautiful Baby of 1932" contest (of Tompkins Park, Brooklyn) end up being the grandest American opera singer of her time? It started with her mother's love for Madame Amelita Galli-Curci, whose records she played every day. By the time Bubbles was seven, she had memorized all twenty-two arias on the Italian diva's records and her mother sensed a star was in the making. Bubbles made her debut singing *The Wedding of Jack and Jill* that led to a series of appearances on *Uncle Bob's Rainbow Hour* on WOR, which were a huge hit. Bright (with an IQ of 155), fluent in French, and blessed with a phenomenal memory, Bubbles also did stints on the soap opera, *Our Gal Friday*. Despite the flush of this exposure, her mother knew that her little girl needed some professional training. A chance glimpse at *Musical Courier*, an industry magazine of the 1930s, introduced her to the woman on the cover: opera singer and voice coach Estelle Liebling.

With more chutzpah than sophistication, Mrs. Silverman called for an appointment, took her daughter by subway and bus from beyond Coney Island to Manhattan, and won the attention of the voice teacher.

For two years, Bubbles studied the rudiments. Eventually Ms. Liebling thought her student was ready for performing, and got Bubbles on the popular *Major Bowes' Amateur Hour,* where she quickly became a regular. Her show biz career was launched, and Bubbles was learning the art and craft of singing opera. It was also the beginning of a lifelong relationship: Liebling would be her sole voice teacher for thirty-four years until her death in 1970.

Bubbles was now known as Beverly Sills, thanks to a family friend who thought it would look good on a marquee. She won a scholarship in mathematics to Fairleigh Dickinson College, but turned it down to pursue work with a touring company of Gilbert and Sullivan. She was determined to be an opera star.

Sills had studied piano with Paolo Gallico, continued her vocal studies, learned Italian and German and a repertoire of fifty operas by the time she was nineteen, when she made her operatic debut as Frasquita in Bizet's *Carmen* at the Philadelphia Opera Company.

Sills took her first trip abroad to South America with a singing tour, only to come back to the news that her father had died, at age fifty-three, from lung cancer. The year was 1949, and with both her brothers away at college, she moved in with her widowed mother and looked for work. She quickly found jobs; she also auditioned for the New York City Opera Company (NYCO), but was repeatedly turned down from 1952 to 1955. On her seventh try, she was asked to join the company. She was twenty-six years old.

Sills made her NYCO debut as Rosalinda in *Die Fledermaus*, and it was the beginning of a legendary association that elevated American performances of opera to unparalleled heights.

Part of the success of her tenure at the New York City Opera was the creative input of Gigi and Tito Capobianco. Gigi designed special makeup and taught Beverly dance movements for her more demanding characters; Tito was the director with an eye for detail and a vision that made his operas dramatic, exciting, and rich. Add to that Sills's ever-growing abilities to infuse each character with nuances of meaning through her acting skill, top that off with a delicious voice, and you have an American icon. (Her videos of *Manon* and *La Traviata* are case studies of both the power of her voice and her superb acting.)

The trio helped create the four queens, which gave Sills her most resounding successes: Cleopatra in Handel's *Julius Caesar;* Elizabeth I in Donizetti's *Roberto Devereaux;* and *Anna Bolena* and *Maria Stuarda*. In all, she played in more than seventy operas from *Manon, Traviata,* and *I Puritani,* to a groundbreaking performance in *Lucia de Lammermoor*.

Sills's interpretation of the modern America opera, *The Ballad of Baby Doe,* is considered by many to be the definitive portrayal of the Douglas Moore piece. She also did avant-garde works, like *Six Characters in Search of an Author* by Hugo Weisgall, which sealed her position as the greatest coloratura soprano of the twentieth century.

She traveled constantly, bringing opera to hundreds of cities throughout the country, helping the growth of regional opera companies that did not exist when she was starting out. She recorded eighteen full-length operas and several solo recitals, which won her a Grammy, and the European equivalent, an Edison. Through the sheer force of her personality and talent, she brought a greater awareness of opera in to the homes of Americans who watched her entertain on television with Johnny Carson, Carol Burnett, and Danny Kaye, proving that opera could be fun.

She sang at La Scala, Covent Garden, La Fenice, Teatro Colo, San Carlo, and with the Berlin Opera. In 1966 she sang Donna Anna in *Don Giovanni*. But perhaps no performance was as dramatic as her official debut as Pamira in *The Siege of Corinth* in 1975 at the legendary Metropolitan Opera. She was greeted to a record eighteen-minute ovation. It was April 18, 1975.

Even the kindest critics believed the constant touring, the incredible number of performances, and, finally, her age, took the edge off her voice, and with $8 million in opera contracts left unsigned, she took on the position as director of the troubled NYCO. Twenty-five years to the day she began with the NYCO, Beverly Sills gave her farewell performance on October 28, 1980. The gala raised $1 million, a critical success for the debt-ridden company.

She became the first woman and the first singer to be the director for the NYCO and within seven years had faced such crises as labor disputes, a fire that destroyed the costume warehouse, and a debt of $5 million. She erased the debt and pushed the center into the black with a $25 million budget, sought and added new talent, launched its first summer session, and helped pioneer the use of subtitles for foreign language operas to make the stories and productions more accessible to all in the audience.

She retired yet again, only to be brought back to chair the Lincoln Center for the Performing Arts, home to a cluster of performance groups including the Metropolitan Opera, New York City Ballet, The Julliard School, the New York Philharmonic and her beloved New York City Opera.

To help promote Lincoln Center she appeared on PBS's *Live from Lincoln Center,* WNBC's *Lifestyles with Beverly Sills,* CBS's *Young People's Concerts,* and PBS's *Skyline with Beverly Sills* and *In Performance at the White House,* earning her accolades and two Emmys.

Sills traveled constantly during much of her career, introducing herself, and opera, to countless audiences. Traveling also introduced her to the man who would become her husband. In 1956, while appearing in Cleveland, Sills met Peter Greenough, part of the newspaper family that owned the *Cleveland Plain Dealer* and other top newspapers in the U.S. They married and had two children, Meredith "Muffy," born in 1959, and Peter Jr. "Bucky," born in 1961. The joy of parenting was shadowed by the realization that Muffy was profoundly deaf, an enormous blow for a woman who made a living creating beautiful sound. Bucky was mentally retarded and, eventually, institutionalized at age six. For years, Sills would carry two watches, one to track where she was, and one set to the time where Bucky was.

After taking time off to devote to her children, helping Muffy learn to speak, and caring for Bucky until it proved untenable, Sills was encouraged by her husband to return to weekly singing lessons with Liebling, prompting one of the most oft-told tales: He presented her with 52 round-trip tickets to fly to Manhattan from their Boston home. She rejoined the NYCO and enjoyed her most spectacular successes until she retired in 1980. Despite her busy schedule, she served as National Chairman of the March of Dimes raising awareness of prenatal care and research for birth defects prevention, and raised more than $80 million. She has worked for the National Victim Center, the Hebrew Home for the Aged at Riverdale, been chairman of the Multiple Sclerosis Society, served on the President's Task Force on the Arts, and as a panelist of the National Endowment for the Arts, in addition to serving on the boards of the American Express Company, Eden Institute for Autistic People in Princeton, Hospital for Special Surgery, and the board of Lincoln Center Theater.

Because of her philanthropic and cultural contributions, she has been honored with the Heinz Award for Arts and Humanities (named for the late U.S. Senator John Heinz), which carries a medallion and cash prize of $250,000; the Presidential Medal of Freedom presented by President Jimmy Carter, and the Kennedy Center Honors. Other awards include the New York City Handel Medallion for Achievement in the Arts, 1974; Pearl S. Buck Women's Award in 1979, and honorary degrees from fourteen universities.

In the fall of 2002, Sills abandoned another "retirement," which she had entered following her resignation earlier that year from her post at Lincoln Center. This time she took the reins of president of the board of directors of the Metropolitan Opera Company, proving once again that *retirement* is merely another word for "short vacation" for the indefatigable, inimitable impresario named Beverly "Bubbles" Sills.

Ruth Bader Ginsburg

(1933–)

I am a judge, born, raised, and proud of being a Jew. The demand for justice runs through the entirety of the Jewish tradition. I hope, in my years on the bench of the Supreme Court of the United States, I will have the strength and the courage to remain constant in the service of that demand.
—Ruth Bader Ginsburg, address to the
American Jewish Committee, May 1995

THE SECOND WOMAN to sit on the United States Supreme Court and the first Jewish woman justice, Ruth Bader Ginsburg's appointment added an additional luster to what was already a distinguished career. Known as the legal architect of the women's movement and credited with creating the intellectual foundations for the present law prohibiting sex discrimination, Justice Ginsburg organized and led the American Civil Liberties Union's Women's Rights Project, arguing six cases concerning gender equality before the Supreme Court and winning five of them. During the confirmation process that preceded her appointment to the Court, she won praise for her success as a groundbreaking litigator and for the scholarly precision that had marked her tenure as a jurist. She has displayed that sense of precision, and a continued sensitivity to issues of gender discrimination, during her tenure on the high court bench since 1993.

Born in Flatbush, Brooklyn, Ruth Joan Bader was the younger daughter of Nathan and Cecelia (Amster) Bader. Her father had emigrated to the United States from Russia when he was thirteen; her mother was born four months after her parents arrived in the U.S. from Poland. Nathan Bader worked as a furrier and later in a men's store, and Ruth, who grew up as a single child after her older sister, Marilyn, died at the age of eight, was raised in comfortable middle-class circumstances. Neither of her parents had been able to afford a college education, and Ruth's mother, who wished that she had been able to have gone to college, refused to teach her daughter how to cook to encourage her to choose a career over homemaking. Ginsburg has acknowledged that her mother, who died of cancer the day before her graduation from high school, had the greatest influence on her life. When Ginsburg made her speech accepting President Bill Clinton's nomination of her for the Supreme Court, she spoke of her mother as "the bravest and strongest person I have ever known, who was taken from me much too soon. I pray that I may be all that she would have been had she lived in an age when women could aspire and achieve and daughters are cherished as much as sons."

As a child Ginsburg was acutely aware of anti-Semitism. During her confirmation hearings, when Senator Edward Kennedy brought up the subject of her sensitivity to discrimination in the context of her pioneering work on behalf of gender equality, she told the committee, "I am alert to discrimination. I grew up during World War II in a Jewish family. I have memories as a child, even before the war, of being in a car with my parents and passing . . . a resort with a sign out front that read: 'No dogs or Jews allowed.' Signs of that kind existed in this country during my childhood. One couldn't help but be sensitive to discrimination living as a Jew in America at the time of World War II."

At James Madison High School in Brooklyn, Ruth edited the school newspaper and wrote articles for it on subjects such as the Magna Carta and the Bill of Rights. After graduating from high school she went to Cornell University, where she financed her college education through a scholarship and financial assistance from the school. To earn extra money, she also took on part-time clerical jobs. At college during the height of the McCarthy era, she majored in government and became interested in pursuing a career in law while working as a research assistant for one of her professors, who, she has recalled, defended "our deep-seated national values—freedom of thought, speech, and press. . . . That a lawyer could do something that was personally satisfying and at the same time work to preserve the values that have made this country great was an exciting prospect for me."

In 1954 Bader graduated from Cornell with high honors and was elected to Phi Beta Kappa. In June she married Martin Ginsburg, who had been a year ahead of her at Cornell and who had just completed his first year at Harvard Law School. Ruth Ginsburg was accepted to Harvard Law School as well, but when her husband was drafted into the army, she went with him to Fort Sill, Oklahoma. She took a job with the Social Security Administration in Lawton, Oklahoma, but when she became pregnant and her superior decided she could not travel to a training session that was necessary for her position, she was relegated to a lower position with less pay. The Ginsburgs' daughter, Jane, was born in 1955.

In 1956 Ginsburg entered Harvard Law School, where prejudice against professional women in American society was reflected in a variety of ways. During a dinner given for the female law students, each student was asked by the Dean to explain how she could justify taking the place in the class of a qualified male student. A room in the Lamont Library was closed to women, making it impossible for Ginsburg to obtain a periodical she needed for the Harvard Law Review. In class, the professors sometimes treated women students in a derisive manner out of the assumption that they were incapable of mastering the material. Despite the professors' nonsensical behavior, Ginsburg distinguished herself academically, while at the same time caring for a small child, gathering notes for her husband's classes when he became seriously ill for a time, and serving on the law review. In 1958, after Martin Ginsburg graduated from Harvard and accepted a position with a prestigious New York law firm, Ruth Ginsburg transferred to Columbia University. There, she joined the Columbia Law Review and tied for first place in her class. She received her law degree from Columbia in 1959.

In 1960 one of Ginsburg's former professors at Harvard recommended her as a law clerk to Supreme Court Justice Felix Frankfurter. Although Frankfurter was impressed with Ginsburg's impeccable academic credentials, he confessed that he was not ready to hire a woman. Similarly, none of the top law firms in New York offered her a position. As Ginsburg later recalled in a 1993 interview, "In the fifties, the traditional law firms were just beginning to turn around on hiring Jews. . . . But to be a Jew, a woman, and a mother to boot, that combination was a bit much." After working as a law clerk for a New York district court judge, Ginsburg joined the Columbia Project on International Civil Procedure, researching foreign systems of civil procedure and studying and proposing improvements to United States rules on transnational litigation.

In 1963 Ginsburg accepted a teaching position at the Rutgers University Law School, one of the few schools willing to hire women professors. She was only the second female faculty member at Rutgers, and among the first twenty women law professors in the nation. While at Rutgers, Ginsburg became pregnant for the second time. Worried that she might lose her position because of university employment policies regarding pregnant women, Ginsburg wore loose-fitting clothes borrowed from her mother-in-law to conceal her condition. The Ginsburgs' son, James, was born in September 1965, shortly before the fall semester began.

The year of Ginsburg's appointment at Rutgers coincided with the publication of Betty Friedan's landmark treatise, *The Feminine Mystique,* the book popularly considered to have set in motion the women's movement of the 1960s and 1970s. Ginsburg soon would have her own part to play in the newfound quest for women's rights. In the late 1960s, when the New Jersey affiliate of the American Civil Liberties Union (ACLU) began to receive sex discrimination complaints, the organization referred the complaints to Ginsburg. In 1971 she was the principal author of the brief in the case of *Reed* v. *Reed,* which resulted in a unanimous decision by the U.S. Supreme

Court to overturn a state law giving men preference for appointments as administrators of estates. The following year, Ginsburg taught a course on women and the law at Harvard, and when the school denied her tenure, she accepted a position at Columbia University, where she became the first tenured woman on the law school faculty.

Between 1972 and 1980 Ginsburg directed the ACLU's Women's Rights Project and taught courses and seminars at Columbia in civil procedure, conflict of laws, constitutional law, and sex discrimination. She also wrote several articles and prepared the first casebook on gender discrimination. She gained a reputation as a legal scholar, but made her greatest impact as a successful litigator. Ginsburg displayed political acumen together with an awareness of complete gender equality by taking on cases in which men and families, as well as women, were victims of government policies that discriminated on the basis of gender.

In a 1973 case before the then all-male Supreme Court, Ginsburg successfully argued against a federal statute that provided greater medical and housing benefits to male members of the armed services than to servicewomen. In another case, she convinced the high court that a provision of the Social Security Act discriminated against men and families by awarding benefits to widows but not to widowers. More than any other lawyer, Ginsburg demonstrated that the equal protection amendment provision of the Fourteenth Amendment applies to gender as well as to race.

In 1980, as one of the last acts of his administration, President Jimmy Carter appointed Ginsburg to the Court of Appeals for the District of Columbia. In her judicial capacity, Ginsburg did not pursue a liberal activist agenda; instead, she brought a measured and cautious temperament to the court, voting at times with arch conservative Robert Bork and at times with staunch liberal Patricia Wald. She continued to find favor with liberals, however, with her votes supporting freedom of speech and broadcasting access.

In 1993 Ruth Bader Ginsburg joined the first woman Justice, Sandra Day O'Connor, on the Supreme Court. But Ginsburg had not been President Bill Clinton's first choice to fill the seat left vacant by a retiring Justice Byron White. Seeking a replacement with the intellect to counter the high court's chief conservative, Justice Antonin Scalia, Clinton first chose former New York governor, Mario Cuomo.

When Cuomo declined the nomination, Clinton tried, without success, to nominate Interior Secretary Bruce Babbitt. After the president rejected the third candidate, Boston Judge Stephen Breyer, he turned to Ginsburg, who had been on his short list. She proved to be a popular choice. Liberals felt that she would balance Scalia's conservatism, as Clinton had desired, while conservatives were pleased that the president's nominee was not a liberal ideologue.

Some women's groups opposed Ginsburg's appointment because, although she was pro-choice, she had criticized the high court's decision in *Roe* v. *Wade* giving women the right to have abortions under a privacy provision not explicitly mentioned in the Constitution. However, she also responded to this tinder-box issue by asserting that the right of a woman to have an abortion was based on the equal protection clause of the Fourteenth Amendment to the Constitution. Most women's groups, as well as legal scholars and academics strongly supported Ginsburg's nomination, and she was praised for her incisiveness, commitment to the details of the law, and her talent for reaching consensus with dispassionate and well-reasoned argument. On August 3, 1993, after an uncomplicated confirmation process, Ginsburg became the second female Supreme Court Justice and the first Jewish justice to sit on the high court in twenty-four years.

During Ginsburg's first term she showed an assertiveness that belied her status as a junior justice, but some high court observers criticized her lack of activism on behalf of women, minorities, and liberal causes in the tradition of former justices Thurgood Marshall and William Brennan. It was also felt that her prose lacked power and compassion. Still, more than most of her colleagues, Ginsburg ruled in support of gender equality and the separation of church and state, and opposed police harassment of citizens.

In 2000, Ginsburg ruled on the minority side during the arguments that resulted in the decision to award the presidency to George W. Bush. The following year she wrote the majority opinion ruling that freelance writers had the right to receive royalties for work displayed online. A consensus-building moderate, Ginsburg has praised conservative Chief Justice William Rehnquist for deciding on facts and law despite unpopular opinions, and she has remained true to her belief, stated during her confirmation hearings, that the courts had a role to play on social issues when the political process failed.

During the course of her career, Ginsburg has shown her determination to serve justice and to overcome prejudice and restrictions based on gender and culture. As a Jewish woman on the Supreme Court of the United States, Ruth Bader Ginsburg represents a concept of diversity that finally has become a reality.

Susan Sontag

(1933–)

. . . The real life of the mind is always at the frontier of 'what is already known'. . . great books don't only need custodians and transmitters. To stay alive, they also need adversaries. The most interesting ideas are heresies.
—Susan Sontag, from an interview in *Salmagundi*, April 1975

WHEN SUSAN SONTAG glided into the 1960s world of the New York intelligentsia, she committed the ultimate heresy: She proved that a woman of striking attractiveness, youth, and assured style could also write and speak with a commanding intelligence—and be heard.

She was not, of course, the first woman to discuss ideas in a philosophical manner, nor was she the first one to be heard and read. She was, however, the best example of how to effectively use the media and their sister, public relations, to elevate her writing to center stage in mainstream America in a way that made her art of philosophy chic—if not necessarily understood.

And, her timing was fabulous. She was exactly the kind of voice that the rebellious ones of the sixties wanted to hear.

With the article, "Notes on Camp" in the *Partisan Review* in 1964, Sontag wrote about how "one can be serious about the frivolous, frivolous about the serious," such as in the works of Aubrey Beardsley, Busby Berkeley, and Oscar Wilde. She coined this culture "camp," yet she could not have known how this word and its concept would become part of the cultural lexicon. *Time* magazine, the quintessential mainstream publication aimed at the mainstream public, picked up on it and brought the words "camp" and *"Partisan Review"* into popular usage.

Since then, Sontag has written widely, often contradicting herself, and has touched on subjects such as the politics of Cuba, Sarajevo, and North Vietnam in a dispassionate way that, nonetheless, has generated totally passionate opinions. She also forever changed our way of thinking about photography, illness, and how interpretation can be a stumbling block to the real appreciation of art. For some admirers, she is more appreciated for the reaction she has received from critics than for what she has written; yet it cannot be denied that she has raised important, and often exciting, questions.

Sontag has demonstrated irrevocably that encouraging dialogue and stimulating thought about the world's events can be almost glamorous. One needn't be a waspish trust-fund baby writing from a cubbyhole of a rarely read journal or a cranky senior professor reciting the same lectures for decades, to keep philosophical dialogue alive and, frequently, in *The New York Times*.

For almost forty years she has positioned herself in the spotlight of commentary on her ideas, yet she remains fiercely private about her own life. Some facts have surfaced nonetheless, and she has alluded to others in writings in *Pilgrimage* and *Project for a Trip to China*.

Susan Rosenblatt was born January 16, 1933, to Jack "Jasky" and Mildred (Jacobson) Rosenblatt in New York City. Her parents, descendants of Polish Jews, were frequently traveling in China overseeing his fur trading business (Kung Chen Fur Corporation), and

Susan and her younger sister Judith remained behind with her grandparents. It is not hard to imagine a little girl experiencing her life as she described it, as a "psychologically abandoned child." When her father died in 1938, Susan was just five years old. Shortly thereafter, she developed asthma; and her mother, searching for a hospitable climate for Susan, traveled to Miami, and then settled in Tucson where she, Susan, and Judith lived in a very modest house. Susan spent her first week in school being promoted from first to third grade because "I could do the work."

The travel writer Richard Halliburton opened her eyes to what the life of a writer could be, and the biography of Marie Curie was an intriguing example of an accomplished, independent woman. As a young girl, Susan wrote poems and stories that she stenciled into a journal of sorts, selling copies for five cents apiece—her first literary and publishing effort.

When Susan was twelve, her mother married decorated Army Air Corps Captain Nathan Sontag, who was shot down five days after D-Day. The family adopted his name, and moved to Los Angeles, where neither Susan nor Judith experienced any Jewish traditions or any religious education.

After her graduation from North Hollywood High School at age fifteen, Susan Sontag enrolled in the University of California but left after one year to attend the University of Chicago. Here, her examination scores were so high, she was allowed to take graduate courses. Among her teachers were Leo Strauss, Kenneth Burke, and a sociology instructor, Philip Rieff, whom she married ten days after they met. She was nineteen and he was twenty-eight.

Two years later Rieff took a post teaching at Brandeis University and Sontag attended Harvard University, earning an M.A. in English in 1954 and one in philosophy in 1955. Her scholarship attracted several mentors, including theologian Paul Tillich. She also contributed to her husband's seminal book, *Freud: The Mind of the Moralist*. Rieff has become a preeminent Freud scholar.

In 1952, the couple had a son, David, who is now a journalist. "The most meaningful relationship I've had in my life was with my child," she has said. In the fifties, however, the pursuit of her career was important enough that Sontag left David with his paternal grandparents to attend St. Anne's College at Oxford and work on a doctoral thesis, "Metaphysical Presuppositions of Ethics," which she never finished. She soon left Oxford for Paris and, through writer Alfred Chester, met many of the New York and French literati of the time.

Sontag returned to America at age twenty-six and got a divorce. In an article in *The Guardian* by Gary Younge, Sontag said that the end of her marriage marked the beginning of her adolescence . . . "I had a very enjoyable adolescence from twenty-seven to about thirty-five, which coincided with the sixties—I enjoyed them in a way people much younger experienced them. I was practically thirty and I learned to dance. I became a dancing fool." The "adolescence" did not preclude renewing her responsibility with David, who was then six. She has remained close to him. "Parenting is an upgrading experience," she said.

Living in Manhattan, she lectured in philosophy at the City College of New York and Sarah Lawrence. She later lectured on religion at Columbia University and spent a year as writer-in-residence at Rutgers University in New Jersey.

Sontag worked as an editorial assistant at *Commentary* magazine, and began writing her first novel, *The Benefactor*. It was sold to Robert Giroux of Farrar, Straus & Giroux, who would become her literary mentor. FSG has been Sontag's publisher for more than four decades, keeping all her books in print—no small accomplishment for any publisher/writer relationship over such a length of time. Giroux's management of her career is an essential link to her enduring success in American letters.

Sontag continued to write, contributing primarily to the *New York Review of Books, Atlantic Monthly, Harper's,* and *The Nation.*

Her first really big splash came with the publication of *Against Interpretation and Other Essays* in 1968, in which she posited the idea that intuitive response, not interpretation or analysis, was the key to understanding art. One should, she wrote, "experience the luminousness of the thing in itself, of things being what they are." Among her other acclaimed works are *Styles of Radical Will* (1966), an examination of contemporary culture, and her seminal work, *On Photography* (1976), an exigesis of photography as an act that inserts itself between reality and the experience of viewing it. A viewer could look at a photograph, she implied, without any expectations of figuring out what it meant. She later reexamined photography in

Italy: One Hundred Years of Photography (1988, with Cesare Colombo).

The criticism of and the making of films has long held her interest. She has written and directed *Duet for Cannibals* (1969), on "emotional cannibalism"; *Brother Carl* (1974), a film about the agnostic Carl Theodor Dreyer; *Promised Lands* (1974), about the October 1973 Yom Kippur War; and *Unguided Tour* (1983), based on her own short story. Her films, *New Yorker* film critic Pauline Kael observed, were all lacking "dramatic sense."

Sontag also has directed several plays, most notably Milan Kundra's *Jacques and His Mother* in 1985, and Pirandello's *As You Desire Me* in Italy in 1979–1980. Her play *Alice in Bed* (1992) is both a humorous and tender retelling of the invalid sister of writers Henry and William James; it has been frequently produced, generally to good reviews.

Sontag has had her share of critics, primarily those who argue against her lack of inclusion for the human elements in the subjects of world affairs. She appears to position herself as cloaked commentator, criticizing governments, ideas, and how the world should "think" in a way that makes her appear to be uninvolved and uncaring. This rather screened-off persona was opened up, in part, when she went to Sarajevo in 1993 for a two-week fact finding trip. She returned to Sarajevo that June to live and work for three years.

Among the many activities she pursued in Sarajevo was directing Samuel Beckett's *Waiting for Godot* in 1993, managing a nursery school for children, working in a hospital, teaching theater and doing radio commentary, all while the city was under siege with little or no running water, electricity, or telephones. It was a totally voluntary experience that left her personally sensitized, yet aware that theater and education were real tools for the spiritual recovery of a people left devastated by the ravages of war.

In 1999, she published her viewpoints on modern ethnic cleansing and civil conflict in "Why Are We in Kosovo?," which is included in her collection of essays in *Where the Stress Falls* (2001). In it, she wrote, "The principal instances of mass violence in the world today are those committed by governments within their own legally recognized borders. Can we really say there is no response to this? Is it acceptable that such slaughters be dismissed as civil wars, also known

as 'age-old ethnic hatreds.' (After all, anti-Semitism was an old tradition in Europe; indeed a good deal older than ancient Balkan hatreds. Would this have justified letting Hitler kill all the Jews on
German territory? Is it true that war never solved anything? Ask a
black American if he or she thinks our Civil War didn't solve anything.)"

She has often championed style over content. This was most notable in her essays about the films of Leni Riefenstahl, who staged
the documentary of the Nuremberg rallies at the beginning of Hitler's
rise to power in Germany. In "Fascinating Fascism" (1974) Sontag
argued that Riefenstahl was an "artistic and political collaborator"
whose work made "theater of history" which is "precisely in the
continuity of its political and aesthetic ideas."

Sontag's experience with breast cancer in 1976 led her to challenge the obfuscation that the vocabulary of disease can generate,
writing with great eloquence in *Illness as Metaphor* (1978). She asserted that the most truthful way to view illness is to resist thinking
of it as a punishment metaphorically or otherwise. Sontag did not
have medical insurance to cover her hospitalization and treatments,
and American PEN and many friends contributed to her $150,000
of medical bills. It was observed by many of her contemporaries that
the intellectual Sontag did not take the intelligent route of quitting
her cigarette smoking, and she developed a rare form of uterine cancer in 1998 and sought alternative treatment. She is apparently making a good recovery.

Among her other nonfiction works are *Literature* (1966); *Trip to
Hanoi* (1969); and *The Story of the Eye* (1979); in addition to intro-
ductions to the writings of Danilo Kris, Roland Barthes, and
Antonin Artaud.

When the AIDS epidemic surfaced, she expanded her treatise and
retitled it *AIDS and Its Metaphors* (1988).

Sontag's novels have been roundly criticized for being plot heavy,
character thin, and crowded with ideas that leave the reader ex-
hausted instead of exhilarated. Her other fiction, *The Death Kit*
(1967) and short stories of *I Etcetera* (1977), were modest sellers but
The Volcano Lover (1992) was a surprise hit with the reading public. In the case of *In America* (1999) she was accused of including
material vaguely familiar from other sources. It nonetheless won the
National Book Award in 2000.

Sontag is the recipient of the Jerusalem International Book Fair Prize for her body of work (2001); a five-year fellowship from the MacArthur Foundation (1990–1995); and has been presented with the American Academy Ingram Merrill Foundation Award (1976); the Academy of Sciences and Literature Award (Germany, 1979); the National Book Critics Circle Award (1977) for *On Photography:* and the Malaparte Prize in Italy (1992).

She is a Commandeur de l'ordre des Arts et des Lettres from the French government and served as an officer in 1984. She has been an activist for imprisoned writers as part of her work with the American Center of PEN, the international writers' organization, and served as its president from 1987 to 1989.

She has been awarded two Guggenheim fellowships (1966 and 1975), two grants from the Rockefeller Foundation (1964 and 1974), plus a fellowship from the American Association of University Women, which helped finance her studies in France in 1957.

She also was given the Brandeis University Creative Arts Award in 1975, and the George Polk Memorial Award for criticism that advanced the fields of theater, film, and literature, in 1966.

Susan Sontag, in her constant effort to reinvent herself, has defied labels, except to say she is a modernist in the tradition of twentieth-century French intellectuals, yet she has been accused by some pundits of "writing brilliantly and with conviction about topics she knows very little about."

While Sontag seems to have largely dismissed feminism and ignored her own Jewish identity, she did address the conflicts in the Middle East in her film, *Promised Lands.* It also could be said that Jewish academics, critics, and the feminist culture have largely ignored her.

It is hard to deny that Susan Sontag has stretched her considerable intellectual reach far and wide, writing cultural criticism that has always been, as she asserts, what being an intellectual is all about. And, what does she think her work says? "Be serious, be passionate, wake up."

Judy Chicago

(1939–)

*One reason for my staunch and abiding commitment to feminism is that I
believe its principles provide valuable tools for empowerment—and not
only for women . . . feminist values are rooted in an alternative to the pre-
vailing paradigm of power, which is power over others. By contrast, feminism promotes personal empowerment, something that, when connected
to education, becomes a potent tool for change.*

—Judy Chicago, from *Beyond the Flower:
The Autobiography of a Feminist Artist*

Judy Chicago is the mother of feminist art. Her seminal work, *The Dinner Party*, has been seen by more than one million people in fifteen venues since it premiered at the San Francisco Museum of Modern Art in 1979. *The Dinner Party* has sparked controversy, conjured embarrassment and even anger among viewers, and, most important, it has changed lives. Women seeing this aggressive installation have, often for the first time, recognized the inequities of being a woman in this world.

Judy was born in Chicago to Arthur and May (Levenson) Cohen, who were active liberals. Despite a twenty-three-generation lineage of rabbis, including the Gaon of Vilna, a noted eighteenth-century Lithuanian rabbi, her father became a Marxist and labor organizer. During the McCarthyism of the early 1950s, he was investigated, sparking a spiraling decline in his ability to work, and eventually in his health. He died of complications from childhood peritonitis, which compromised his stomach. Judy was thirteen and her brother Ben seven. Their mother did not discuss their father's death with them, and did not allow them to attend the funeral. It was not until adulthood that they were able to speak of this difficult time. In the early sixties Judy found herself in the hospital for nearly a month from a bleeding ulcer, which she attributed to unresolved grief, and pursued counseling to great effect.

Judy's mother, a medical secretary, was a former dancer who transferred her love of the arts to both her children. (Ben became a potter.) Judy began to draw at three years of age. Her mother made sure Judy experienced as much art education as possible from the Art Institute of Chicago and the Junior School. Judy attended UCLA on a scholarship and earned a B.A. in art in 1962, was Phi Beta Kappa, and earned an M.A. in art in 1964. Judy had married Jerry Gerowitz in 1961, but was widowed when he died in a car crash in 1963. This stirred up a brewing identity crisis: She was no longer Judy Cohen, daughter of . . . nor Judith Gerowitz, wife of. . . . Her father was dead. Her husband was dead. Sorting out these losses, she reaffirmed her need for a separate identity that was female, and not attached to any man.

Gallery owner Rolf Nelson had nicknamed her "Judy Chicago"

for her strong Chicago accent and personality. She decided to change her name legally, and was appalled that she needed her new husband's signature to do so. (She had married sculptor Lloyd Hamrol in 1965. They were married until 1979). At her one-woman show in 1970 at California State University at Fullerton, Judy posted a banner across the gallery that read "Judy Gerowitz hereby divests herself of all names imposed upon her through male social dominance and freely chooses her own name, Judy Chicago."

Judy studied "macho" arts, like auto body work, to learn the spray painting techniques that later provided her the ability to fuse color and surface in many media, a hallmark of her work in later years. She also learned boat building to create sculpture and pyrotechnics to understand how to develop fireworks. As a result, she became expert at an incredibly diverse range of skills that were incorporated into her metal and fiberglass sculptures and fireworks installations. (She would later take up an apprenticeship with Mim Silinsky to learn china painting for her project, *The Dinner Party*, and learned to work with stained glass for *The Holocaust Project*.)

Chicago took on a teaching position at the California Institute for the Arts and was a leader of the Feminist Art Program, which in 1972 produced, with Miriam Schapiro, "Womanhouse," the first installation demonstrating an openly female point of view in art.

Perhaps no other experience was as groundbreaking as the establishment of the first feminist art program under Chicago's direction (and again with Schapiro) at the risk-taking Fresno State College in 1970. This benchmark program gave birth to all the hundreds of women-centered art programs that followed.

Judy Chicago's personal artwork was evolving, too, from the large spray-painted canvases, some with geometric forms, to works that were centered on celebrating the spirit, power, and importance of the feminine.

Chicago was deeply affected by historian Gerda Lerner's writings, which revealed that women who are unaware, ignorant of their own history, will continue to struggle. Chicago set out to break this chain of repetition with her seminal work, *The Dinner Party*, which took more than five years to complete. Working alone at first in her Santa Monica studio, she conceived the monumental project that resulted in a huge triangle (measuring forty-eight-feet by forty-three-feet by thirty-six-feet) of thirty-nine place settings, each commemorating a female image: goddess, pharaoh, artist, or political figure. More than four hundred people, nearly all women, volunteered anywhere from a month to a year's worth of labor, doing needlework, creating the structures, and other parts of Chicago's designs that ended up in the project. They donated their time, they said, "to honor women's achievements."

Her next large work, *Birth Project,* took five years (1980 to 1985). This piece celebrated women's role as the giver of life, with images of labor—something Chicago soon realized was rarely seen in any art form. The work would reinterpret Genesis and its idea that a male god created a male human being without any commentary of women's involvement in the process.

The work involved the participation of 150 needleworkers from New Zealand, Canada, and the United States, who worked on the one hundred panels of the project using quilting, petit point embroidery, macramé, and almost a dozen other techniques. The project was another example of the breadth of Chicago's work, once again accenting not only her vision but also her ability to collaborate with others on a grand scale. Because of the number of panels, it is not shown in its entirety, although the core collection resides at the Albuquerque Museum.

In the mid-1980s, Chicago met photographer Donald Woodman, who was to become her third husband. They married New Year's Eve in 1985. Although her two previous husbands were also Jewish, it was not until she met Woodman that Chicago would thoroughly explore her Jewish roots, and for the first time. This renewal made her receptive to her next project in ways she would not have been earlier.

The *Holocaust Project* began when Chicago met poet Harvey Mudd, who had done an epic poem on the subject. After much research, Judy believed that illustrating his poem would not be feasible; she wanted to make it totally her own vision, using her own words and visuals.

The three-thousand-square-foot exhibition, complete with audio tour, videotape of the process, and documentation panels of background information, took eight years to complete. She worked alongside her husband on the project, and she shares credit with him. *Holocaust Project: From Darkness into Light, An Exhibit by Judy Chicago with Donald Woodman* premiered at the Spertus

Museum in her hometown, Chicago, in October 1993, and continues to travel to museums throughout the country.

The project, which records the loss of so many people at the hands of the Nazis, was done during a particularly sad period in Chicago's life. Her brother Ben died after several years of degeneration from Lou Gehrig's disease, and her mother died from a long bout with cancer.

In addition to its philosophical treatise, the project is an incredible amalgamation of media. It has sixteen large-scale works, which combine painting, photography, tapestry, stained glass, wood, and metal work, and includes the stitchery of Audrey Cowan among others.

Another aspect of her monumental projects is Chicago's amazing skill as a conduit to coordinate and attract skilled artisans, craftsmen, needleworkers, and other workers to come together, often volunteering their time to complete the project. Each worker had different reasons to participate, but many believe that the message of her work is life changing.

To develop the project, Chicago and Woodman had viewed the epic documentary *Shoah*, visited concentration camps and exhibits in Poland and Germany, and read extensively. Some of the criticisms of the work center around her use of other issues—Vietnam, pollution, and other terrors—but for Chicago, all these issues are interwoven because they remind us that looking the other way makes us all culpable. To her, the Holocaust remains a moral dilemma, one that she attempts to touch into the viewer's consciousness. It is, she says, her contribution to *tikkun olam* ("repairing the world").

The work takes viewers into the darkness of the worst period of humanity and ends with a prayerful piece for hope in which people of all types are seated around a Sabbath table as a woman blesses candles at one end of the table, and her husband offers a prayer over wine at the other end.

The *Holocaust Project* has toured seven venues, including New Mexico, where she now makes her home. When a retrospective exhibit was installed at New Mexico State University Art Gallery, it prompted great interest among New Mexico's small but vital Jewish community. Rabbi Gerald Kane, of Las Cruces's Temple Beth El said that using her work produced a number of significant discussions among congregants on such issues as the value of life *(Birth Project,*

Holocaust Project), the meaning of love *(Psalms, Dinner Party),* and the role of faith *(Holocaust Project)* from a Jewish perspective. Like many provocative works of art, he said it continues to have a "cumulative effect that is significant and beneficial."

After more than twenty-five years, Chicago began teaching again, first as a presidential appointment in art and gender studies for a semester at Indiana University in Bloomington in 1999, then as inter-institutional artist in residence at Duke University and University of North Carolina, Chapel Hill, in 2000. To celebrate the thirtieth anniversary of *Womanhouse* in 2001, she worked with students at Western Kentucky University on the project *At Home,* which analyzed the subject of the house from the perspective of Kentuckians.

Resolutions: A Stitch in Time combined needlework and painting in what is certainly a softer, more playful installation. Working with adages and proverbs that conjure up memories of women, the project encourages the viewer to look at female elders for their wisdom and to connect themselves once again with the memories of these women. Among the adages used are Home Sweet Home, The Hands That Rock the Cradle Shape the World, Paddle Your Own Canoe, and Bury the Hatchet.

Although the adages and proverbs highlight the feminine, they are not without the power to demonstrate that the struggle for equality, humanity, and cooperation are still goals to be achieved. Begun in 1994, it was first exhibited in June 2000 at the American Craft Museum in New York and then toured various venues through the country.

Probably the finest book about her work is *Judy Chicago, An American Vision* by art critic and historian Edward Lucie-Smith, which not only tracks the development of her major installations, but also gives valuable insight into her more personal drawings and paintings and other projects from *Powerplay* to *Song of Songs.* Lucie-Smith also collaborated on Chicago's eighth book, *Women and Art: Contested Territory.*

Chicago gives voice to her struggles and triumphs as an artist in two autobiographies: *Through the Flower: My Struggle as a Woman Artist,* 1975, and *Beyond the Flower: The Autobiography of a Feminist Artist,* 1996. She has also compiled books for her various installations: *The Dinner Party: A Symbol of Our Heritage,* 1979; *Embroidering Our Heritage: The Dinner Party Needlework,* 1980;

The Birth Project, 1985; *Holocaust Project: From Darkness into Light,* 1993; and *The Dinner Party Judy Chicago,* 1996.

Films about her work are *Right Out of History, The Making of Judy Chicago's Dinner Party* by Johanna Demetrakas; *The Birth Project* by Vivian Kleinman; *Under Wraps* and *The Other Side of the Picture* from the Canadian Broadcast Corporation; and a video of *Holocaust Project,* edited by Kate Amend. Chicago's work has been exhibited in Canada, Europe, Asia, Australia, New Zealand, and throughout the United States. She has lectured in Japan, Taiwan, and participated in the Robb Lecture Series in New Zealand.

Her art is in numerous private collections and in the permanent collections of the Los Angeles County Museum of Art, the Brooklyn Museum, San Francisco Museum of Modern Art, Oakland Museum of Art, and the Pennsylvania Academy of Fine Arts. She has had more than fifteen one-woman shows, both here and abroad, in addition to retrospectives.

For all her projects Chicago has done enormous research. She is the first living artist to be included in a major archive, the Arthur and Elizabeth Schlesinger Library on the History of Women in America at Radcliffe College, to which a significant collection of her papers has been donated.

Chicago's extensive collection of books by and about women have been donated to the University of New Mexico, and much of the *Holocaust Project* materials now reside with the Holocaust Center of Pittsburgh.

She was given the UCLA Alumni Professional Achievement Award in 1999, and has received several honorary degrees—from Russell Sage College, Smith College, and Lehigh University.

Chicago was the subject of the National Museum of Women in the Arts (NMWA) exhibit from October 2002 to January 2003, which featured more than ninety of her works, dating from her earliest in the 1960s. Her intimate and monumental works on paper became part of the first comprehensive retrospective of her work in an exhibit opened in 1999 at the Florida State University Art Museum in Tallahassee, which was curated by Dr. Viki Thompson Wylder, a recognized scholar of Chicago's work. The exhibit traveled the country until 2002.

Throughout her career, Chicago has had dedicated sponsors, particularly Elizabeth Sackler, plus early supporters like Holly Harp and

Stanley and Elyse Grinstein, who recognized the strengths of her artistic vision and political viewpoints. *The Dinner Party* was purchased by The Elizabeth A. Sackler Foundation from the Judy Chicago Charitable Remainder Trust, and presented to the Brooklyn Museum of Art, where it will take up permanent residency in 2004. It was part of the retrospective of more than one hundred pieces of Chicago's art shown at The National Museum of Women in the Arts in Washington, D.C., in 2002–2003.

Although she says she no longer clings to the possibility that her work will be "understood," her art is both a commitment to her beliefs and a personal expression.

Barbra Streisand

(1942–)

The beauty of art is that it can show humanity to itself.
—Barbra Streisand, from her acceptance speech for the
Cecil B. DeMille Award, 2000

FOR MORE THAN forty years, Barbra Steisand has demonstrated that honoring who you are and what you are is more important and, ultimately, more satisfying than changing yourself to suit the opinions of others.

She has accomplished the apex of achievement in each medium she has attempted: Broadway, television, film, recording, and the concert stage. She has offered contribution to *tikkun olam* (repairing the world) by standing up for civil and human rights, fighting against homophobia and anti-Semitism, encouraging Americans to vote, and supporting other issues she feels strongly about.

She is an icon to her fans, a marvel to the entertainment industry, and no small thorn in its side for daring to do so many things—and doing them well.

The road to success has not been without stumbling blocks, but like most accomplished people, she dealt with her obstacles with creativity, tenacity, and an ambition that has led to singular success.

The first obstacle was never really knowing her father, who died of a cerebral hemorrhage when she was fifteen months old, which brought Sheldon and Barbara Joan Streisand and their mother Diana (Rosen) Streisand close to poverty. When her mother remarried, it became obvious that her stepfather, Louis Kind, was "allergic to children." The union produced one child, Roslyn Kind, and eventually ended in divorce.

Working as a bookkeeper, Diana was unable to give enough attention to her children, setting the stage for them to be gangsters or geniuses. Fortunately, Barbara Joan understood early that her own genius was entertaining others.

At Erasmus High School in Brooklyn, she was an A student, and was graduated in 1959. She immediately left home for Manhattan to pursue her dream of becoming an actress. She applied to the Actors Studio. They rejected her. She auditioned everywhere and was turned down. Fortunately, her friend Alan Miller, an actor, spotted her talent and became her first teacher outside of high school.

She shortened her name to Barbra but kept the Streisand, the first in a series of professional statements that said, "I'm Jewish and I'm proud of it."

It was another friend, Barry Dennen, who suggested that singing at a theatrical event could lead to a part on Broadway. She tried out her act at the Lion Club talent show and garnered terrific applause and a one-week gig at the popular gay club. With no other promotion than word-of-mouth, Barbra packed the room nightly and her engagement was extended. The audiences loved her singing, her humor, and, the declaration that yes, it was okay to be and look different, especially if you have a talent to share.

Next up was the Bon Soir Club, where she continued to wow audiences, and her initial three-week engagement, at double the Lion

Club salary (a reportedly whopping $108), was extended to thirteen weeks. She was on her way . . . with stops in Cleveland, Detroit, St. Louis, wherever people wanted her. Back in New York, television talk show host Jack Paar invited her onto his show in 1961 and the buzz intensified.

Finally, someone on Broadway took notice. Barbra appeared in Harold Rome's *I Can Get It for You Wholesale* in the role of Miss Marmelstein, bringing down the house each night with her eponymous song. Her appearance won her a Tony nomination and the New York Drama Critics Award. The production was notable for two other reasons: her leading man, Elliott Gould, would become her first husband and the father of her son Jason Emmanuel, and her performance caused Columbia Records to consider signing her to a recording contract. The executives at Columbia hesitated, however, because they thought her too "Brooklyn," too Jewish, too eccentric, even her songs were criticized as being too obscure. Streisand persevered and in 1964 she debuted *The Barbra Streisand Album,* which remained on the charts for eighteen months and won two Grammy Awards, one for Album of the Year. At twenty-two, she became the youngest person at that time to have received a Grammy.

Barbra Streisand the popular singer was born. Martin Erlichman became her manager/agent, and she has remained his sole client ever since.

Back to Broadway she went, this time playing the popular comic actress Fanny Brice in the Jules Styne–Bob Merrill musical, *Funny Girl,* which opened on March 26, 1964 and played 1,348 performances. She won her second Tony nomination, and took the show to London where she was voted best female lead in a musical for that season. *Funny Girl* also would become her first film.

Before that, however, she conquered television with a series of five shows beginning with *My Name Is Barbra,* in 1965, which earned five Emmy Awards and the Peabody Award. She was given complete artistic control, still a rare concession for performers. This demand for control is part of Barbra's perfectionist persona, one that many coworkers find exhausting, but the usual result is a performance that is a perfect match to her vision, and one her legions of fans adore.

In *Funny Girl,* Streisand (as Brice) looks into the mirror and says the now-famous line, "Hello, Gorgeous!" Call it chutzpah, call it charm, call it anything you like, from that moment on the door swung open to a more positive attitude toward ethnic appearance, proving both to Hollywood and to the people on the street that beautiful takes on many hues, shapes, and styles. In this singular gesture, Barbra invited those on the periphery to "come into the center."

In 1968, for her first film effort, she shared an Academy Award with another independent spirit, actress Katharine Hepburn. She also won the Golden Globe Award and was named Star of the Year by the National Association of Theater Owners.

To date, Barbra has appeared in sixteen films, many of which cast her in a decidedly, sometimes defiantly, Jewish role. She was a Jewish political activist in *The Way We Were* (which earned her a Best Actress Oscar nomination), the matchmaker Dolly Levi in *Hello, Dolly!*, the yeshiva boy who is really a girl yearning to study Talmud in *Yentl,* a Jewish psychiatrist in *The Prince of Tides,* and Jewish comedienne Fanny Brice in two films, *Funny Girl* and *Funny Lady.*

As the producer, she turned her part in *A Star Is Born* into a Jewish character and did the same for Rose in *The Mirror Has Two Faces,* which was adapted from a French farce and directed by Streisand.

Prince of Tides was the first film directed by a woman who was to receive a nomination as Best Director from the Directors Guild of America. It also earned seven Academy Award nominations.

Barbra made her directorial debut in *Yentl,* the story of a nineteenth-century young Polish girl who pretends to be a boy to pursue her academic studies. It was the first time a woman would write, direct, produce, and star in a major motion picture. The film was controversial, first because Isaac Bashevis Singer disliked her interpretation of his short story, "Yentl, the Yeshiva Boy," although there is no record that he ever returned the compensation he received. Second, Streisand was not nominated for her work as director or producer, a patent snub by the Academy, which gave the film five nominations (it won for music). The Hollywood Foreign Press Association certainly thought otherwise; it gave Streisand its Golden Globe Award for Best Director and producer of the Best Picture. (Barbra has won a total of ten Golden Globe Awards, the most awarded to any single entertainer, and in 2000, she received the Cecil B. DeMille Award for lifetime achievement.)

Not every Streisand film has been a success, but each has been unique. They include *On a Clear Day You Can See Forever, For Pete's Sake, The Owl and the Pussycat, What's Up, Doc?, The Main Event, Up the Sandbox*—one of the first films in the U.S. to address the women's movement and the first made by her own production company, Barwood Films—and *Nuts,* in which she gave a remarkably complex dramatic performance as a person charged with murder who refuses to cop an insanity plea.

The American Film Institute awarded Streisand its Life Achievement Award in 2001 for her work as composer, actress, director, writer, and producer.

Streisand's singing career has been so overwhelmingly successful, it's impossible to think of a recording honor that is not hers. She has sold more records and CDs than any artist, living or dead, except Elvis Presley. Of the fifty recordings she has made, twenty-eight turned platinum. She is the only female to win thirteen multiplatinum albums. Her recording peers have recognized her talent, too, and have presented her with eight Grammy Awards, the Legend Award, and the Grammy Lifetime Achievement Award. Other accomplishments include forty-seven gold albums, eight gold singles, five gold videos, five platinum singles, two platinum videos, and one multiplatinum video.

In 1976, she was the first female composer ever to win an Academy Award, for "Evergreen," which was cowritten with Paul Williams as the theme song for *A Star Is Born.* The soundtrack for the film is a quadruple-platinum winner.

The National Foundation for Jewish Culture awarded Barbra Streisand the first annual Jewish Image Award for her efforts as coexecutive producer of the Showtime presentation, *Varian's War,* which aired in April 2001. The award recognizes "outstanding work reflecting the Jewish heritage through film and television."

Streisand has been an ardent fundraiser for the Hollywood Women's Political Caucus to support liberal political candidates, which helped elect five democratic senators, raised over $5 million for the Gore/Lieberman presidential campaign, and supported the campaigns of thirty-five candidates in the general election (twenty-seven won). She has endorsed one hundred ninety-four candidates on her Web site, of which one hundred and fifty-five were elected.

Both personally and professionally, Streisand has never shied away from standing up for what she believes in, and she will support her personal beliefs in her work when she can. Barwood Films earned three Emmy Awards for *Serving In Silence: The Margarethe Cammermeyer Story*, which revealed the results of sexual harassment and prejudice against gays in the military. It also produced a series of six two-part dramas for Showtime in 1997 and 1998 called *Rescuers: Stories of Courage* to acknowledge non-Jews whose efforts saved the lives of Jews who might otherwise have perished in the Holocaust. *The Long Island Incident* (1998) told the true story of Carolyn McCarthy who staged a crusade for gun control, and *Two Hands That Shook The World* (2002) related the life stories of Yitzhak Rabin and Yasser Arafat and their peace efforts for the Middle East.

In 1985, she established the Streisand Foundation for human rights, civil rights and liberties, women's equality, and environmental preservation. It directly funded the U.S. Environmental Defense Fund's research for and participation in the Global Warming World Summit conference in Kyoto. She also donated her five-home, twenty-four acre Malibu estate to the Santa Monica Mountains Conservancy to be a center for ecological studies. The foundation has channeled more than $10 million to various charities including The Salk Institute, John Wayne Cancer Institute, and AmFAR, an agency that fights against AIDS.

Her hugely popular concerts, like *Timeless* and *Barbra Streisand: The Concert,* have won every major television award, from the Peabody to the Emmy, but more important, they have raised more than $10.25 million for charities, AIDS organizations, and issues such as children and women in jeopardy, Jewish/Arab relations, and agencies working to establish better relations between African Americans and Jews.

She was awarded the Commitment to Life Award from the AIDS Project Los Angeles in 1992, and the ACLU Bill of Rights Award for her defense of Constitutional rights.

Streisand is the recipient of an honorary doctorate in the arts and humanities from Brandeis University (1995), the National Endowment for the Arts' National Medal of Arts, and the French Commander of the Order of Arts and Letters.

Barbra Streisand has achieved much more than the dream to be an actress that she fostered as a young girl in Brooklyn. She has been an

acknowledged success in acting, singing, directing, writing, and producing in the entertainment field. She has demonstrated that taking
control is a form of responsibility to create the best one has to offer.
Throughout her career, she has been true to her heritage, and is using
her position and wealth to lend her voice to support ideas and issues
that matter to her.

Sally Jane Priesand

(1946–)

*I'm not here to be Jewish for anyone else, I'm here to help other Jews be-
come responsible for their own Judaism.*

—Sally J. Priesand

ON A VISIT to Spokane, Sabbath School Principal Ray Frank realized
there was no rabbi to officiate for High Holidays. So, she conducted
services herself and more than one thousand people came to hear her.
The year was 1890. The "girl rabbi of the west" did not officially become a rabbi and even gave up public speaking after she married, but
for a decade or more it was her voice, a woman's voice, on the pulpit
in many American synagogues.

Martha Neumark challenged Hebrew Union College to a two-year debate about admitting women, beginning in 1921. The first "ordained" woman rabbi was a German Jew, Regina Jonas, who never attended a seminary but was privately tutored. She did not live long enough to pursue her rabbinic calling. She perished from the terrors of the Holocaust in 1935.

During the 1930s, Americans Irma Levy Lindheim, Dora Askowith, and Helen (Levinthal) Lyons challenged the then-conventional position of the male-dominated rabbinate. Lyons actually completed the entire rabbinical curriculum but was awarded a Master's in Hebrew literature—not the ordination she had worked so hard for, and was able to preside over High Holiday services only once, in Brooklyn, in 1939.

It would not be until 1972 that Sally Jane Priesand would become the first female ordained rabbi to actively pursue her calling.

Born in 1946 to Irving Theodore and Rose Elizabeth (Welch) Priesand in Cleveland, Ohio, Priesand didn't like Hebrew school as a child. However she was inspired by the Jewish youth groups and camps she attended during the 1960s. They provided her with a spiritual vision of Reform Judaism that she welcomed, and which has sustained her all these years. The experience also gave her a purpose. "I just wanted to be a rabbi," she said, not fully understanding then how radical a goal that was.

"I was very lucky," she said. "When I told my parents I wanted to be a rabbi, they didn't dismiss the idea, they said if that's what I wanted, I should do it."

Priesand began studies in 1964 at the University of Cincinnati, which had a joint undergraduate program with the Hebrew Union College–Jewish Institute of Religion (HUC–JIR). Fortunately for her, she won the support of then college president, Rabbi Nelson Glueck, who paved the way for her to pursue studies at the rabbinical school.

Simply enrolling in the rabbinical program, however, was big news. She found herself—a shy, very private person—inundated by the press, secular and religious. By this "quirk of history" as she calls it, she became the media darling of that era.

Pushing the distractions aside, she applied herself to the program, earning bachelor's and master's degrees of arts in Hebrew letters (like Helen Lyons) plus a B.A. in English from the University of Cincinnati. Priesand was admitted to the rabbinical school in 1968 with full support and approval of Glueck, but not, at first, her fellow students or even some of her teachers.

In June of 1972, new HUC-JIR president Alfred Gottschalk greeted Priesand, who walked up to the bima of the Plum Street Temple in Cincinnati to receive her ordination. She lifted the Torah into her arms to face the congregation and saw her thirty-five colleagues—all male—rise to give her a standing ovation. Sally Jane Priesand had become the first publicly ordained woman rabbi in the history of Judaism. Today, her daily commitment remains the empowerment of her congregation; her rabbinical position is still a work in progress.

That progress started off slowly. Despite the publicity (or notoriety, perhaps), the young Rabbi Priesand had to struggle against the curious, the indignant, the skeptical, and the angry to find a job.

But, the persistence that got her into rabbinical school, and the tenacity that enabled her to complete her studies, were now a natural part of her, and eventually she found a position. Her first appointment was at the historic Stephen Wise Free Synagogue in New York, where she became an assistant rabbi. After several years, she became an associate rabbi. The logical next step would be that when the senior rabbi retired, she would be promoted to senior rabbi. But, the synagogue board was not ready. And, it was no small irony that Stephen Wise, for whom this synagogue was named, thought otherwise. In 1915, he said, "Woman ought to be as free as is man to determine the content of life for herself. Woman must not have life marked out for her by custom or convention or expediency . . ."

Priesand again put the mantle of tenacity around her shoulders and sought a position, but even after seven years, there was still resistance. That was until she found the dual posts of part-time rabbi of Temple Beth El in Elizabeth, New Jersey, and chaplain of Lenox Hill Hospital in Manhattan, from 1979 to 1981.

In an ideal world, the publicity spin should have propelled her into the welcoming arms of temples eager to hire the first woman rabbi; but this was real life, not the movies, and even today, prejudice against women rabbis can be found. The path for Rabbi Priesand, and those who followed, was strewn with the proverbial resistance to change by both congregants and the rabbinate.

It was particularly hurtful that women congregants were often the most vocal opponents. Many of these same women supported bat mitzvah ceremonies for their daughters, but did not embrace the idea of women being spiritual leaders.

More than 350 women are now rabbis in this country; however, none represent the Orthodox branch, although female interns, meeting the needs of female congregants is a welcomed new trend. The greatest number of women rabbis, 255, have been ordained by Reform Judaism's Hebrew Union College–Jewish Institute of Religion; seventy-three in the Reconstructionist Rabbinical College beginning with Sandy Sasso in 1974; and fifty-one from Conservatism's Jewish Theological Seminary beginning with Amy Eilberg in 1985.

In 1981, Priesand found a permanent pulpit when she became rabbi of the now 285-family Monmouth Reform Temple in Tinton Falls, New Jersey. On her twentieth anniversary as a rabbi, Priesand remarked, "The women's movement has served as a catalyst in encouraging a rethinking of previous models of leadership . . . to move away from hierarchy and power toward new opportunities for networking and partnership. Today, the rabbinate has been empowered to help Jews become more responsible for their Judaism, to foster education, to promote observance, to encourage participation, to inspire commitment, to create a feeling of family."

In honor of Priesand's twenty-fifth anniversary as a rabbi, The Women's Rabbinic Network and the College-Institute established the Rabbi Sally J. Priesand Visiting Professorship of Jewish Women's Studies at her alma mater, which had fourteen women rabbinical students. Nearly half of the school's enrollment is now women, pursuing cantorial, educational, communal service, or other graduate programs in Judaism.

In 1993, Rabbi Priesand was presented the Woman Who Dares Award from the National Council of Jewish Women in celebration of its centennial, and the University of Cincinnati and its Friends of Women's Studies gave her the Distinguished Alumnae Award.

She believes the Reform movement remains the most vital and vibrant part of Judaism today. She continues to work with the Central Conference of American Rabbis Task Force on Women in the Rabbinate to pave the way for more women to pursue their spiritual calling, the Union of American Hebrew Congregations, and is a member of the board of governors of the Hebrew Union College–Jewish Institute of Religion (HUC–JIR).

Her seminal work, and thesis, *Judaism and the New Woman* (1975) remains a fascinating source for women in all branches of Judaism who want to pursue rabbinical studies. Although the optimism she expressed in her thesis has not been totally realized, her own personal dedication cannot be doubted. She has demonstrated intelligence, persistence, and a spiritual commitment to Judaism, coupled with a dynamic leadership that has made being a Jew a welcomed responsibility to her congregants. "My congregants can study Torah, observe mitzvoth, and do Judaism for themselves. The Jew-by-choice concept is very alive and well here," she has said.

Her mentors are remembered with fondness and gratitude: Alfred Gottschalk for his commitment to the cause of equality; Nelson Glueck, who laid the foundation that made the ordination of women possible; and Edward E. Klein, successor to Stephen Wise, who Priesand believes "taught me how to be a rabbi." She adds, "My rabbinate reflects his spirit and the legacy he left behind."

In 2002, thirty years after her ordination, Rabbi Priesand said, "This anniversary is not just mine, it's also the thirtieth anniversary of the Reform movement's support of bringing women into the rabbinate. I wanted to do something unexpected, a little different, so the HUC-JIR Museum arranged for my first solo exhibit of abstract watercolors in the summer of 2002, 'Rabbi Sally J. Priesand: Private Thoughts of a Public Person.'"

All twenty-two paintings sold; "people seem to find them spiritual and moving," she added. Rabbi Priesand began teaching herself how to paint while confined to her home during an illness. "Abstract watercolors are particularly exciting. The paint has a mind of its own, so I must match wits with it. Painting is particularly important for me in dealing with the stress of my work. Because I'm frequently called upon to go from funeral to wedding, from happy to sad occasions, I have learned that one has to be present in the moment, no matter how stressful that may be."

She plans to retire in 2006 marking twenty-five years with the Monmouth Reform Temple, but she has no plans to move away. "This is my home, this is my family," she said. When her brother died of cancer, they mourned with her. When she sustained not one but two bouts of breast cancer, they gave her strength. And, when she survived a car accident, they were there to support her while she recuperated. Through these personal crises, she has had to give up her innate sense of privacy to allow the support and grace she has given others to come back to her.

"I'll continue to be involved in some capacity. But, I think it's important for younger congregants to have a rabbi to grow with, just as the older congregants grew with me." The congregation says they have received much more than they have given. Rabbi Priesand is their spiritual leader and conscience. She never recycles a sermon, so congregants can look forward to fresh insights each week. While she does not perform intermarriage ceremonies, she does everything she can to welcome non-Jewish spouses and children into the temple's programs and services. She is there to counsel, to fight, to champion, to share in the joys. She comforts, even cheers, the sick, counsels the bereaved, teaches, challenges, inspires, leads.

Her volunteer activities include supporting the National Breast Cancer Coalition; being president of Interfaith Neighbors, which provides rental assistance and support for the homeless in her community; working with the National Organization for Women, and being on the Board of Advocates of Planned Parenthood. She was a founding member of the Association of Reform Zionists of America (ARZA), president of the Rabbinic Alumni Association, is active with Jewish Women International, Hadassah, and the UAHC-CCAR Commission on Synagogue Affiliations, a member of the Board of Governors of HUC-JIR, and on the Executive Board of the Central Conference of American Rabbis and the Union of American Hebrew Congregations.

She is a contributor to *Women Rabbis: Exploration and Celebration* and *A Treasury of Favorite Sermons by Leading American Rabbis.*

A rabbi has many obligations—to conduct services, counsel congregants, and, perhaps most important, to teach. "One benefit [of female rabbis]" Rabbi Priesand says, "is we have made male rabbis more nurturing, and helped them move away from the authoritarian rabbinate to a genuine partnership with their congregations."

For the members of Monmouth Reform Temple, and to Jews throughout the country, Rabbi Sally J. Priesand has indeed taught well, and in many ways. She has embraced the idea of *tikkun olam,* our obligation to continue the work of God's creation, and to repair the wrongs in the world. At Monmouth, she said, "I found a place to start . . ."

Shulamit Ran

(1949–)

[Composing to] Biblical text is important; it is my personal way as a Jew, as an Israeli, as a human being, of saying "Do not forget."

—Shulamit Ran

As A LITTLE girl growing up in Israel, Shulamit Ran found music in the words of children's books read to her by her mother. "I thought everyone heard music in the words, I did not know others didn't have the same reaction to words. It was a very intuitive thing."

Music and books were a given in her home, and growing up in the 1950s in Tel Aviv, Shulamit was exposed to the finest music and poetry and theater available on radio and in concert halls.

Fascinated by the piano, she suggested that her mother save the money she spent on babysitters to buy one. Her parents struggled financially, but soon little Shulamit had her piano. She soon began studying with a teacher who lived across the street. "He was a good pedagogue and helped me write down the tunes I wrote, setting my music to poems of several Israeli poets." Many of her childhood compositions were subsequently performed by the Children's Corner Choir on Israeli radio. "Hearing songs of mine performed was so exciting, but in some way, they were no longer mine," she said.

Her parents, Berta and Zvi Ran, met in Israel after emigrating from Russia and Germany, respectively. In the tradition of Israel, Zvi changed his surname from the German Rand to the Hebrew name, Ran, which means "to sing joyfully." Perhaps that was a prophetic beginning for their young daughter. She said, "In Israel, there is a thriving society of music, literature, and art, so playing music or composing is seen as a perfectly natural thing to do, so no one made a big deal of my playing and composing my little songs."

Eventually Ran's piano instructor came to an impasse, believing he had taught her all that he could. Ran studied with several other teachers before performing in concerts professionally throughout Israel. Those initial concerts led to her receiving a scholarship cosponsored by the America-Israel Cultural Foundation. This scholarship enabled her to pursue her piano studies at the Mannes College of Music in New York; she also studied piano with Nadia Reisenberg and Dorothy Taubman.

Ran was soon playing, and often her own compositions, at the best halls throughout the United States, Canada, Europe, and in Israel. At fourteen, she performed her original, *Capriccio,* with the New York Philharmonic as part of the popular television series, Young People's Concerts with Leonard Bernstein.

Despite the excitement of performing, it was composing that most absorbed Ran. She gave up performing to pursue studies with Israelis A. U. Boskovich and Paul Ben-Haim, and Americans Norman Dello Joio and Ralph Shapey, an original and influential American composer of the avant-garde who would have the most significant role in her career.

Shapey was given a recording of Ran's *O the Chimneys* and thought she had the intelligence and sensibility it would take to become a composition teacher in his department of music at the University of Chicago, a world-renowned institution that attracts the finest students from China and Korea, Europe and Russia, and throughout the world. She took up Shapey's offer to teach in 1973, and, for a year, also studied composition with him. She has held the William H. Colvin Professorship and today teaches graduate students part-time to free her to continue composing. "These students are so thoughtful, they come to a place of serious inquiry, to redefine the basics and ask important questions. I love working with people who know how to ask the important questions." Teaching, even part-time, stimulates her. "I learn a lot from my students; they are so dedicated and determined."

Ran was composer-in-residence with the Chicago Symphony Orchestra, as part of its Meet the Composer Orchestra Residencies Program for seven seasons, beginning in 1990. She was also the fifth Brena and Lee Freeman, Sr., composer-in-residence with the Lyric Opera of Chicago in 1997 and her relationship with the Lyric has enabled her to premiere several works, most important, her opera.

Composing for various instruments is all part of her coloristic compositional palette, and Ran has written works for cello, percussion, clarinet, flute, and her favorite, voice. "I love to compose for the voice, the most exciting, most deeply expressive of all instruments," she said.

Nothing has been as much of a challenge as writing an opera, which she says "was an ecstatic experience, a full collaboration which I would love to repeat." The opera, based on the Shloime Ansky play, *The Dybbuk* or *Between Two Worlds,* enlarges upon the dramatic 1916 Yiddish classic in which an evil spirit wanders the world. The libretto by Charles Kondek, critics said, was a perfect match to Ran's powerful music, leaving audiences mesmerized by a performance that was both mysterious and passionate.

The work took three years, but it was, she says, an invigorating experience of pure collaboration. It is an ingenious work written with the assurance of a composer at her peak. The interplay of the almost "ghostly" voices balanced with music that is clearly evocative of Jewish heritage (Klezmer, Hassidic chants) is a complex feast for the audience to savor and a demanding workout for the musicians to perform.

Setting music to a folk tale for an opera was a major undertaking for her; however, poems, sometimes just a line or two, can be totally inspiring. "I don't require many words;" says Ran. "I like to search for the concise, the expressive, the intense phrase on which to elaborate with my music. The work of Israeli poet Yehuda Amichai [a favorite of hers], was the basis for *Amichai Songs,* a chamber work created in 1985. Other poets, Shakespeare and, of course, biblical text, are all-important in my work. Still, the most important quality is something 'I can learn from,' to compose against; something meaningful that has to do with who I am, to make a statement."

Reviewers of Ran's work describe it as filled with power and grace, lean and lush, emotional and intelligent, and some have likened her music to both Mahler and Mozart. It requires attention, and serious listening to discover the full depth and complexity of what she says with music. On recordings and in concert halls throughout the world, her compositions have been played under the batons of Zubin Mehta, Daniel Barenboim, Pierre Boulez, and others in Europe, America, and Israel.

"My music selects its performers because it is difficult to perform. My music is demanding technically. Intellectually, my music needs excellent performers, and I love hearing my music played by others, hearing their individual approaches," she has said. Does she miss performing? "No," she says, "the day is so full, but sometimes when I sit down and play, I must admit to myself, 'this feels good.' "

Her awards have been many, highlighted by the Pulitzer Prize in 1991 for her *Symphony,* originally commissioned and performed by the Philadelphia Orchestra. The Pulitzer Prize was awarded for "distinguished musical composition of significant dimension," and won over ninety-nine other nominees. *Symphony* also won a first place Kennedy Center Friedheim Award in 1992, and her work, *Hyperbolae,* won the Second Artur Rubinstein International Piano Competition in 1977.

As an influence in contemporary classical music, she was visiting professor at Princeton University (1987), has been elected a Fellow of the American Academy of Arts and Sciences (1992), and has been awarded numerous honorary doctorates. She has received awards and commissions from the Guggenheim Foundation, Illinois Arts Council, Fromm Foundation, the Da Capo Chamber Players, and the National Endowment for the Arts. Among the works created are *Vessels of Courage and Hope,* an orchestral piece created in 1998, commemorating the fiftieth anniversary of the State of Israel and the voyage of the SS *President Warfield,* *"Exodus 1947."*

She is married to Dr. Abraham Lotan, an otolaryngologist, and they have two sons. The boys play trumpet and flute and the younger is composing. "It's like looking at myself in the mirror when I hear him," she said.

Holding up a "mirror" to the works of Shulamit Ran, one can sense a reflection of both the poetry and the music of her heritage. It is even a part of her name: Shulamit, who was the comely princess of "The Song of Songs," is often regarded as a "mirror of the Jewish people."

HONORABLE MENTIONS

Dina Abramowicz (1909–2000). Lithuanian-born American author; chief reference librarian, YIVO Institute for Jewish Research.

Stella Adler (1901–1992). Celebrated American actress and influential acting teacher.

Gertrude Berg (1899–1966). American actress, writer, producer of radio, film, and television; star of *The Goldbergs,* one of the first and most popular television situation comedies.

Chana Bloch (1940–). American poet, scholar; translator, the biblical *Song of Songs.*

Anita Block (1882–1967). American writer and editor; founder of the influential socialist newspaper, the *New York Call.*

Judy Blume (1938–). Influential American author of children's and young adult books: *Are You There, God? It's Me, Margaret; Forever.*

Barbara Boxer (1940–). American politician, U.S. senator (D. California, 1992–).

Fanny Brice (1891–1961). American singer and comedic actress.

Dr. Joyce Brothers (1929–). American psychologist; popular media personality.

Hortense Calisher (1911–). American novelist, short-story writer, memoirist: *In the Absence of Angels; False Entry.*

Hattie Carnegie (1886–1956). Viennese-born American fashion magnate and design trendsetter.

Phyllis Chesler (1940–). American feminist activist, psychologist, author: *Women, Money and Power; Women and Madness.*

Betty Comden (1917–). American librettist, lyricist, screenwriter: *On the Town; Singing in the Rain; The Band Wagon.*

Lucy Davidowicz (1915–1990). American author and historian: *The War Against the Jews.*

Helene Deutsch (1884–1982). Polish-born American psychiatrist: *The Psychology of Women.*

Dorothy Dinnerstein (1923–1992). American psychologist, feminist, author: *The Mermaid and the Minotaur: Sexual Arrangements and Human Malaise.*

Gertrude Elion (1918–2000). American biochemist, Nobel Laureate for research resulting in the development of chemotherapies and drugs for a wide variety of diseases.

Esther (dates unknown). Biblical heroine who saved the Jews of Persia.

Helen Frankenthaler (1928–). American abstract expressionist painter.

Rosalind Franklin (1920–1958). British biologist, researcher of DNA.

Carol Gilligan (1936–). American feminist psychologist, sociologist, author: *In a Different Voice: Psychological Theory and Women's Development.*

Alma Gluck (1884–1938). Celebrated Rumanian-born American soprano.

Jennie Grossinger (1892–1972). Legendary American hotelier.

Ruth Handler (1916–2002). American "mother" of the Barbie doll and breast cancer awareness campaigner.

Louise Hay (1935–1989). French-born American mathematician recognized for her research in mathematical logic, recursive function theory, and theoretical computer science; founder, Association of Women in Mathematics.

Lillian Hellman (1905–1984). American social critic, playwright: *The Little Foxes; Scoundrel Time.*

Gertrude Himmelfarb (1922–). American historian, conservative essayist: *The De-Moralization of Society.*

Bertha Kalich (1874–1939). Celebrated Austrian-born American actress of the Yiddish theater.

Lee Krasner (1908–1984). American abstract expressionist painter, wife of painter Jackson Pollock, whose career she encouraged and managed.

Mathilde Krim (1926–). Italian-born American biologist, AIDS researcher; founder, AmFAR (American Foundation for AIDS Research).

Ann Landers (Esther Friedman Lederer) (1918–2002). American advice columnist.

Annie Leibovitz (1949–). American photographer of politicians, actors, rock stars, and literary figures.

Sophie Maslow (1916–). American modern dance pioneer, choreographer.

Hephzibah Menuhin (1920–1980). American virtuoso pianist, social activist.

Belle Moskowitz (1877–1933). American settlement worker, social and civic reformer; labor mediator; political adviser and strategist.

Rose Pesotta (1896–1965). Ukranian-born American labor union activist and official.

Letty Cottin Pogrebin (1939–). American editor, women's rights' activist, author: *Getting Over Getting Older; Deborah, Golda, and Me.*

Leah Rabin (1928–2000). Israeli first lady; peace activist.

Adrienne Rich (1929–). American poet, nonfiction writer: *The Diamond Cutters; Of Woman Born: Motherhood as Experience and Institution.*

Anna Rosenberg (1899–1983). Hungarian-born American business leader; government official; first woman assistant secretary of defense.

Helena Rubinstein (1870–1965). Polish-born American manufacturer of beauty products.

Muriel Rukeyser (1913–1980). American poet; peace activist.

Rosika Schwimmer (1877–1948). Hungarian-born labor organizer, suffragist, pacifist.

Irene Selznick (1907–1990). American theater and film producer.

Hanna Senesh (1921–1944). Israeli pioneer and paratrooper captured and executed by the Nazis while attempting to save Jews in her native Hungary.

Abigail Van Buren (Pauline Friedman Philips) (1918–). American advice columnist, a.k.a. "Dear Abby."

Wendy Wasserstein (1950–). Pulitzer Prize–winning American playwright: *The Heidi Chronicles.*

Ruth Westheimer (1928–). German-born American sexologist, author: *Dr. Ruth's Guide to Good Sex.*

Louise Wise (1874–1947). American philanthropist; Zionist.

Anzia Yezierska (1885–1970). Polish-born American novelist, chronicler of Jewish immigrant life: *Children of Loneliness; Bread Givers.*

BIBLIOGRAPHY

Arcana, Judith. *Grace Paley's Life Stories: A Literary Biography*. Urbana and Chicago: University of Illinios Press, 1993.

Brooks, Andreé Aelion. *The Woman Who Defied Kings: The Life and Times of Doña Gracia Nasi—A Jewish Leader During the Renaissance*. St. Paul, Minn.: Paragon House, 2002.

Buck, Harry M. *People of the Lord: The History, Scriptures, and Faith of Ancient Israel*. New York: Macmillan Co., 1966.

Chicago, Judy. *Through the Flower: My Struggle as a Woman Artist*. New York: Doubleday, 1975.

—————. *Beyond the Flower: The Autobiography of a Feminist Artist*. New York: Viking Press, 1996.

Davis, Kenneth C. *Don't Know Much About the Bible*. New York: William Morrow, 1998.

Dresner, Samuel H. *Rachel*. Minneapolis: Fortress Press, 1994.

Ettinger, Elzbieta. *Rosa Luxemburg: A Life*. Boston: Beacon Press, 1986.

Ferber, Edna. *A Peculiar Treasure*. New York: Doubleday, 1938.

—————. *A Kind of Magic*. New York: Doubleday, 1963.

Frank, Anne. *The Diary of a Young Girl: A Definitive Edition*. Eds., Otto H. Frank and Mirjam Pressler. New York: Doubleday, 1995.

Friedan, Betty. *The Feminine Mystique*. New York: W.W. Norton, 1963.

—————. *It Changed My Life: Writings on the Women's Movement*. New York: Random House, 1976.

—————. *Life So Far: A Memoir*. New York: Simon & Schuster, 2000.

Gold, Arthur, and Robert Fizdale. *The Divine Sarah: A Life of Sarah Bernhardt*. New York: Alfred A. Knopf, 1991.

Goldman, Emma. *Living My Life*. New York: Dover Publications, 1931.

Grosskurth, Phyllis. *Melanie Klein: Her World and Her Work*. New York: Alfred A. Knopf, 1986.

Horowitz, Daniel. *Betty Friedan and the Making of the Feminine Mystique.* Amherst: University of Massachusetts Press, 1998.

Hyman, Paula E., and Deborah Dash Moore, eds. *Jewish Women in America: An Historical Encyclopedia.* New York: Routledge, 1997.

Kates, Judith A., and Gail Twersky Reimer, eds. *Reading Ruth: Contemporary Women Reclaim a Sacred Story.* New York: Ballantine Books, 1994.

Keller, Werner. *The Bible as History.* New York: William Morrow, Inc., 1981.

Kristeva, Julia. *Hannah Arendt.* New York: Columbia University Press, 2001.

Lauder, Estée. *Estée: A Success Story.* New York: Ballantine Books, 1986.

Lerner, Gerda. *Fireweed.* Philadelphia: Temple University Press, 2002.
——————. *Why History Matters: Life and Thought.* New York: Oxford University Press, 1997.

Lisle, Laurie. *Louise Nevelson: A Passionate Life.* New York: Summit Books, 1990.

Lucie-Smith, Edward. *Judy Chicago, An American Vision.* New York: Watson-Guptill, 2000.

Martin, Ralph G. *Golda: Golda Meir, the Romantic Years.* New York: Scribner's, 1988.

Meir, Golda. *My Life.* New York: G. P. Putnam's Sons, 1975.

Metzger, Bruce M., and Roland E. Murphy, eds. *The New Oxford Annotated Bible.* New York: Oxford University Press, 1994.

Nettl, J. P. *Rosa Luxemburg.* New York: Schocken Books, 1989.

Picon, Molly. *Molly!* New York: Simon & Schuster, 1980.

Rubenstein, Charlotte Streifer. *American Women Artists: From Early Indian Times to the Present.* New York: Avon Books, 1982.

Schneiderman, Rose, and Lucy Goldthwaite. *All For One.* New York: Paul S. Eriksson, Inc., 1967.

Taylor, Jacqueline. *Grace Paley: Illuminating the Dark Lives.* Austin: University of Texas Press, 1990.

Wexler, Alice. *Emma Goldman: An Intimate Life.* New York: Pantheon Books, 1984.

Wagenknecht, Edward. *Daughters of the Covenant: Portraits of Six Jewish Women.* Amherst: University of Massachusetts Press, 1983.

Young, Bette Roth. *Emma Lazarus in Her World: Life and Letters.* Philadelphia: Jewish Publication Society, 1995.

Young-Breuhl, Elisabeth. *Hannah Arendt: For Love of the World.* New Haven: Yale University Press, 1982.

Photo Credits

Bella Abzug—Library of Congress
Diane Arbus—Time, Inc.
Hannah Arendt—American Jewish Historical Society, Newton Centre, Massachusetts and New York, New York
Sarah Bernhardt—Fisher Collection
Judy Chicago—©Through the Flower/Donald Woodman
Deborah—Fisher Collection
Edna Ferber—Library of Congress
Anne Frank—Anne Frank Foundation
Betty Friedan—*Modern Maturity*
Anna Freud—Library of Congress
Ruth Bader Ginsburg—Richard Strauss/Collection of the Supreme Court of the United States
Emma Goldman—National Archives
Doña Gracia Nasi—Olin Library
Rebecca Gratz—Library of Congress
Peggy Guggenheim—Library of Congress
Melanie Klein—Wellcome Library, London
Estée Lauder—Library of Congress
Emma Lazarus—Library of Congress
Gerda Lerner—Courtesy of Gerda Lerner
Rosa Luxemburg—Library of Congress
Mary—Fisher Collection
Golda Meir—*New York Times*
Louise Nevelson—American Jewish Archives
Emmy Noether—Olin Library
Cynthia Ozick—American Jewish Archives
Grace Paley—Bettye Lane
Dorothy Parker—Corbis
Molly Picon—Library of Congress
Sally Priesand—Courtesy of Erte Studio, Maspeth, New York
Shulamit Ran—Theodore Presser Co.

Ayn Rand—Library of Congress
Ruth and Naomi—Fisher Collection
Sarah, Rebekah, Rachel, Leah (*Rachel at the Well*)—Fisher Collection
Dorothy Schiff—Corbis
Rose Schneiderman—Olin Library
Beverly Sills—Courtesy of Beverly Sills
Anna Sokolow—AP/Wide World
Hannah Greenebaum Solomon—American Jewish Archives
Susan Sontag—Library of Congress
Gertrude Stein—Library of Congress
Barbra Streisand—Corbis
Henrietta Szold—Library of Congress
Barbara Tuchman—American Jewish Historical Society, Newton
    Centre, Massachusetts and New York, New York
Pauline Trigère—Corbis
Lillian Wald—Library of Congress
Rosalyn Yalow—Nobel Foundation

Index